DOUGLAS WIGHT is the *Sunday Times* bestselling author or ghostwriter of sixteen non-fiction books, most recently *India Uniform Nine* (Icon, 2022), *Son of Escobar* (Ad Lib, 2020) and *The Bad Room* (Harper Element, 2020). His books have sold over 100,000 copies, and previously include *The Laundry Man* (Penguin, 2012), the memoir of Ken Rijock, a Miami-based money launderer for Colombian drug smugglers; the autobiography of Olympic gold-medal-winning hockey player Sam Quek (White Owl, 2018), which was long-listed for the *Telegraph* Sports Autobiography of the Year 2019; *Unforgivable* (Penguin, 2014), the *Sunday Times* bestselling memoir of a woman who won a landmark legal case against a local authority who failed to protect her from an abusive mother; and *Wish I Was There* (John Blake, 2013), the autobiography of actress Emily Lloyd, whose glittering Hollywood career was blighted by mental illness.

BITE
Club

**Real-life attacks
by sharks and other
killer predators**

Douglas Wight

AD LIB

First published in the UK in 2023 by
Ad Lib Publishers Ltd
15 Church Road
London SW13 9HE
www.adlibpublishers.com

Text © 2023 Douglas Wight

Paperback ISBN 978-1-802470-90-1
eBook ISBN 978-1-802471-51-9

A CIP catalogue record for this book is available from the British Library.

Every reasonable effort has been made to trace copyright-holders of material reproduced in this book, but if any have been inadvertently overlooked the publishers would be glad to hear from them.

Printed in the UK
10 9 8 7 6 5 4 3 2 1

This book is dedicated to anyone who has suffered the trauma of an animal attack and to the families and loved ones of those unable to share their stories. You are not alone.

CONTENTS

FOREWORD

When the proposal for this book was first mooted, the idea was to curate a collection of first-hand accounts from shark attack survivors in the hope that by sharing their stories, they would provide deeper insight into incidents that often attract global media attention.

As my inquiries progressed, however, I realised how the impact of such attacks goes way beyond the bite. And little did I know how profound an experience it would be to listen to such moving stories of courage, which often involved heroic acts of bravery, life or death decision-making and heartbreaking personal trauma. For several contributors – even those whose attacks happened many years ago – recounting their ordeal awakened emotions long since buried. Their unexpected reactions surprised even themselves.

After speaking to Dave Pearson, an Australian surfer who founded his own Bite Club – a support group for shark attack survivors that grew to take in people who'd suffered bites from all sorts of animals – the scope of the book changed significantly. Like Dave's Bite Club, the book looked beyond shark bites to examine the psychological impact of animal attacks, regardless of species. In doing so, I discovered that from unique ordeals emerged common experiences, traumas and remarkable positivity.

Researching this book took me on a journey – figuratively at least – from the remotest reaches of the Southern Ocean to the Sierra Nevada mountains of California and dramatic deep underwater dives in the Caribbean, via Queensland, Australia, where tropical rainforest meets the Great Barrier Reef.

Sharing our personal stories can be healing, as it can help us negotiate the impact of trauma by connecting us with ourselves and each other. Revealing our deepest traumas, both physical and psychological, can be transformational, as it can encourage us all to look beyond labels, break down stigma and learn from each other. Story sharing can also encourage us to reframe problems and help us face our challenges as we explore different perspectives. Stories can be empowering and we all have things to say.

Every story matters.

And the goal of this collection of stories is to inspire understanding and healing. As the American professor and author Brené Brown said, 'When we own our stories, we get to write a brave new ending.'

Douglas Wight, December 2022

INTRODUCTION

It is the club no one wants to join – because being a member means life is unlikely to be the same again.

Welcome to Bite Club – where everyone is united by one unenviable factor: they have all experienced the unique trauma of a violent animal attack. Unlike other life-threatening scenarios, surviving a terrifying encounter with a shark, lion, bear, wolf – or any other apex predator at the top of its food chain – creates its own set of challenges.

While, by the nature of their ordeal, everyone who experiences such an encounter is part of an unspoken global club, in Australia, one survivor sought to change the outcomes for people like himself. Dave Pearson was bitten by a bull shark and nearly lost his arm while surfing near his home in New South Wales in 2012. There was no support network for animal attack survivors, no specialist advice forum and nowhere to share stories with the people who would know what he was going through. He created a Facebook support group – and Bite Club was born. Ten years on, Bite Club has over 440 members from all over the world, a safe space for people who have suffered trauma from any animal attack.

Practising clinical psychologist Della Commons, who has been offering assistance to Bite Club members since

September 2020, says, 'In some ways, trauma resulting from animal attack is similar to trauma resulting from other causes. That is, all trauma involves a serious threat to one's – or another's – life, is experienced as beyond personal control, creates intense distress, overwhelms normal coping and often results in life-changing consequences.

'So, theoretically, animal attack survivors should find some degree of comfort in talking to other traumatised individuals, regardless of cause, as they would have more in common than not. However, there are differences. The key one is that serious animal attacks, especially shark attacks, tend to attract a lot of media attention, both mainstream and social, which the affected person then has to deal with. This can be very stressful and, some say, a re-traumatising experience. Also, the nature of the incident that involves another animal seeing you as a potential food source or threat, an animal that can't be reasoned with, would lead most to view this as quite unique compared to other traumas. Furthermore, animal attacks might involve injuries that are unique compared to injuries sustained by other causes of trauma. It's not surprising, then, that people would find connecting with others traumatised by a highly similar event, who can relate to specific aspects of the experience, especially helpful; and indeed, comments made by Bite Club members on the forum confirm this to be the case.'

Della had been interested in sharks, particularly conservation and risk mitigation issues, for many years. She came across a podcast by Dave Pearson in 2020 about shark attacks, their impact and how Bite Club supports victims, and asked if she could volunteer. 'I contacted Dave, we had some long chats over video, and he accepted. Since then, I have been offering assistance to members in the form of chats and input on the forum.'

When Dave – or another Bite Club member – learns of a new animal attack, they will reach out to the family of the victim to tell them about the club and invite them to join. 'There is never any pressure to join, and not all take up the offer, or some take it up later down the track,' Della explains. 'When new members come into the group, they are encouraged – but never pressured – to share their story of survival on the forum. They are warmly greeted with supportive messages, helpful suggestions and offers of assistance, which they say they find really comforting. At that point, I might introduce myself publicly or in private and offer to chat if they need it. Sometimes people will already know about me from conversations they have had with Dave before joining the group. Really, the whole setup is pretty informal, and from what I can tell, the members appreciate this kind of format. I should note that when I make contact, I am careful not to push in any way or assume they need to talk, since doing this might come across as intrusive. Respecting people's privacy is paramount.'

Some people join the group soon after their experience while the trauma is still raw, while others arrive many years on from their ordeal. Della has been struck by the high level of resilience many members have demonstrated. 'Psychological resilience refers to an individual's ability to adapt to difficult or challenging circumstances; in essence, to bounce back from adversity,' she says. 'Some people seem to have an extraordinary ability to accept what has happened, even if their attack was particularly gruesome or their injuries horrific, and adapt to their circumstances in a positive and constructive way. They have their down times, but they seem to be able to recover more quickly and are highly active in navigating the challenges, solving problems and moving forward. They tend to get back on the horse, resuming the activity they love, or, if they are unable to do this, they find something similar or a new passion. They find meaning in their suffering and use their trauma to grow and develop in new and positive ways.

'Don't get me wrong; everyone is resilient to some degree and everyone I have met has demonstrated enormous courage in coping with their trauma, it's just that some people, for whatever reason – be it their genes, their upbringing or other life experiences – have higher levels of resilience than the average person who might struggle more. Having said this, resilience is also something that can be nurtured and developed, and in my conversations with people, I try to tap into and build on that resilience.'

During the course of her work, Della has found that the language people use to describe their traumatic experience varies depending on factors such as their personal background or history, their specific trauma experience and, in particular, the way they interpret aspects of that experience. People's knowledge, experience and view of the species involved can also influence the language they use.

Therefore, while some will readily describe their trauma with words like 'stalked', 'attacked', 'hunted' or 'prey', others prefer to say simply that they were 'bitten' or that they experienced an 'encounter'. These individuals prefer to believe that the animal simply mistook them for its natural prey or that it acted out of curiosity, fear or surprise.

Della emphasises that the language used is neither right nor wrong. What counts is what fits for the person using it. And it's crucial to appreciate the power of language to validate or dismiss an individual's experience.

'For instance,' she says, 'in the case of sharks, some members indicate feeling dismissed, hurt, angry – incensed, even – when they see their ordeal being described in the media using neutral terms like "encounter", or when they read about efforts by scientists and conservationists to remove the word "attack" from shark literature. Scientists' use of the term "provoked" to describe some shark events can also offend as it implies blame on the part of the victim. Hence, when I am speaking to affected individuals, I try to mirror some of the language they use. For example, if someone refers to their experience as an "attack" then this is the term I will use to respectfully acknowledge their interpretation, which also helps to facilitate communication and build rapport.'

Whatever language is used, one thing is clear: the fear of being attacked by a large predator is ingrained in the human psyche. 'From an evolutionary point of view, humans are geared to be afraid of anything that might pose a risk to physical survival,' Della explains. 'This includes animals, especially larger animals like bears, lions or sharks that have visible weapons such as big teeth or claws that could obviously injure or maim. It's hardwired – an inbuilt, biological mechanism which kicks in even if you've never experienced these situations yourself or learnt about these threats from others.' This natural fear is amplified through what we learn from others – shocking tales of terrifying animal encounters, sensational newspaper headlines, movies like *Jaws*, and twenty-four-seven media coverage brimming with grisly detail to fuel fear even further.

Despite the need for a group like Bite Club, it should be worth noting, however, that animal attacks are still relatively rare. Although reported shark attacks appear to be on the rise, with an increase of ten in 2021 from 2020, it remains the case that a total of around a hundred people are attacked by sharks every year. Tragically, however, nine people lost their lives in such attacks up to September in 2022. In terms of bear attacks, according to the journal *Scientific Reports*, on average there are forty-eight brown bear attacks each year, resulting in eight deaths. The study looked at brown bear attacks in North America, Europe, Russia, Iran, Japan and Nepal. Five people have been killed by black bears in North America since 2020. Eleven people were killed in the previous decade. Two people have been killed by polar bears since 2000. On average, twenty-two people are killed each year by lions. A greater number – around fifty – lose their lives to tiger attacks, while crocodiles account for around a thousand fatalities each year.

Although not predatory animals, elephants and hippopotamuses account for a higher number of deaths each year. In India, between 150–200 people on average lose their lives due to attacks by elephants each year; while in Sri Lanka and Kenya, two other countries with sizeable elephant populations, around fifty people are killed annually. Hippos are responsible for an estimated five hundred deaths annually, mainly due to their territorial behaviour and habit of targeting and capsizing boats.

Domesticated dogs account for far more attacks than wild animals. The World Health Organisation estimates that, globally, tens of millions of people are bitten by dogs each year. In the US alone, around 4.5 million people are bitten by dogs every year, with between 6,000–13,000 resulting in hospital treatment. Up to fifty people a year lose their lives in dog attacks in the US. Since 2018, nineteen people in the UK have been killed by dogs, with over 8,500 people treated for injuries in 2021. Over the same period, ten people were killed in Australia.

The nature of animal attacks and people's stories of survival, telling how they overcame the many challenges that resulted from their ordeal, can help us understand, debunk some myths and hopefully make sense of the world we live in. Through the courage – not only their own, but of the many people who responded, often making split-second, life-saving decisions – we can learn something of the human condition, and ask ourselves, how would we react in a similar situation?

Each of the stories in this book is personal and unique but they all share a common theme: they allow us a glimpse of a world that is different to ours. By sharing these stories, we can learn through the eyes of others, which can help us develop empathy and understanding.

CHAPTER 1
DAVE PEARSON

*'I swam back to the surface and climbed onto my board.
Only then did I look at my arm.'*

It was a day much like any other – but for one exception.
Dave Pearson had just bought a new, cream-coloured,
6-foot-4-inch Firewire Tri Fin surfboard and, after
finishing work, was keen to head to his local beach to
try it out. Picking up his neighbour Scott Faulkner on
the way, Dave, who was forty-eight, grabbed his new
board and headed to Crowdy Head, a vast expanse of
unspoilt beach a twenty-minute drive from his home at
Coopernook in New South Wales, Australia.

Although it was approaching 5.30 p.m., it would still
be light for another two hours. The temperature was a
balmy 25C, the waves in the Tasman Sea, while nothing
special, were a reasonable enough size to test out the new
board. Another mate arrived at the same time and Dave
could see Aaron 'Noddy' Wallis out on the water. He was
the last of a number of people who had flocked to the
shores that day to catch some waves after the recent spell
of rain and stormy weather.

1

Dave, Scott and another mate, Sean, walked out to a rock known locally as Iron Peg and began paddling out. Dave caught two waves before his other friends got going. Being on the inside, closer to where the waves were breaking, Dave called to Noddy, asking if he wanted to catch the next one.

'You go, you're in a better spot,' Noddy called back.

Dave didn't need a second invitation. He paddled out to the wave, was on his feet in a flash and caught the wave – his best of the day so far – nearly all the way to the beach. Starting to feel good about the new board, Dave paddled out again through the deeper channel where the water was about five metres deep. He was in the rip, checking out the next set of waves, when he glanced over to his left where his mates were. Then it happened …

'From just over to my right side, something came up from underneath. Whatever it was must have been moving fast, and it came at me, hitting the surfboard on the way up. It continued out of the water with my surfboard in its mouth, then flipped over the top and went back into the water, trapping my left arm between its top jaw and the surfboard. Its nose hit my right temple, nearly knocking me out.

My next memory is being deep under water. There were lots of bubbles and something browny-grey was in front of me, thrashing around. I had no idea what was going on. When we hit the bottom, after thrashing for a bit, it let me go. Getting back to my senses, I swam back to the surface and climbed onto my board. Only then did I look at my arm: a massive amount of flesh was hanging off. My forearm muscles were hanging to one side with all the skin that holds it together. Blood was squirting

2

out quite a distance. The water around me was turning red.

Shit, I thought, that's not good.

As I sat on my board, I tried to stop the bleeding myself and realised Noddy was shouting at me.'

Noddy watched it all happen. He heard the loud smacking noise – which was Dave's surfboard being hit – and, looking over, saw what he thought was a dolphin jump out of the water and plunge back in. He then thought, Wasn't Dave paddling there a minute ago? Confused and with no sign of his friend, Noddy then saw his mate's surfboard pop back up to the surface. A few seconds later, Dave emerged and scrambled back onto it.

Immediately, Noddy shouted, 'What happened? Was that a fuckin' shark?'

For quite a while Dave was unresponsive as he was coming to terms with what had happened.

'I was looking at the wound in my arm, thinking, Wow, it must have been a shark. I've just been attacked by a shark. I looked in the water and saw beneath me it was a big shark – probably three metres, so nearly ten feet. Bull sharks are wide, like a forty-four-gallon drum under water. I saw how big it was and I thought, Wow, that's a big shark.

I shouted back to Noddy, "Yeah, and it's still here. I'll get out and I'll see you on the beach. I'll be all right, I'll get out."

I tucked all the skin back together and lay on it and put as much pressure as I could on my arm, so I could paddle in using my other arm. A set of bigger waves came through and I thought, Beauty, if I catch one of those, I'm going to be out of here. I wasn't in the right spot though, and as the wave pitched up and I paddled on, it pitched me over the falls and drove me back down under the water again.

My board and I separated. Under the water, I could feel all the skin and muscle from my arm flapping again. I remember thinking, Don't fall off …

I was trying to hold my muscles together under the water. As I came back to the surface, I got hit again by another wave and it felt like one of those scenes in a movie when someone is in trouble in the surf and the minute they come back up they are hit by another wave. For four waves in a row that's what happened to me. I couldn't catch a breath between any of them and I was back under the water at the bottom again.

I started to see stars, which told me I'd run out of air and wasn't far off from drowning. You know what? I thought. I'm going to die today. Then I started to think, It's not a bad day for dying. I've had a pretty good life. I have a wonderful partner and wonderful children. But then I felt the sand under my feet and I thought, Not today, Dave.

I pushed as hard as I could and popped back up to the surface again. I knew I had to get out, so I tucked my arm back together and jumped back on my surfboard. That's when I heard Noddy right behind me. He and the other guys had witnessed what was going on. Even though I told them to get out and even though Noddy thought he was heading towards the beach, instinctively, he'd been paddling towards me. If it wasn't for those two guys I wouldn't be here. I was pretty buggered by then.'

Noddy had grabbed one of the other guys, Sean, to come with him and between them they helped get Dave out of the water. It took them nearly ten minutes to get

Dave to safety on the sand. By then, he'd lost a significant amount of blood.

'When you have a pretty traumatic event, you get that adrenalin surge that gets you through the first couple of minutes of it, but after that you run out of strength, and the near drowning didn't help me at all. I was absolutely knackered. I was fortunate though. When the shark attacked me from below, its teeth had gone into the surfboard and stuck there. It meant the bottom teeth were not in the equation when it came to biting me.'

Dave's mates went into first-aid mode. The priority was to stop the bleeding. Dave was wearing a leg rope, the strap that Velcroed from around his ankle to the surfboard. They took it off and wrapped it around Dave's left arm as tightly as they could. Dave's dog, which had been waiting patiently by his car while he went surfing, then came running down the beach with a stick in his mouth. The guys grabbed the stick and used it to tighten up the makeshift tourniquet.

Noddy and Sean – and some other friends who'd rushed to their aid – half-carried their stricken mate the fifty metres or so up the beach to the carpark, holding his arm as high as they could to try to prevent the blood going to his arm in an attempt to slow the bleeding. At the carpark, Dave's neighbour Scotty, who'd helped carry him, produced some towels but gave a grim assessment of the injury.

'It's not looking good,' he said.

'It's not, Scotty,' Dave said, 'but we'll be all right.'

The guys lifted Dave onto a picnic table, wrapped him in towels and whatever else was handy to keep him warm and tried to tighten the tourniquet.

Then they had a dilemma.

'The question was, do they wait for help or throw me in a car and take me to hospital? It was a tough one. We've all heard of people who were on their way to hospital but didn't make it because the ambulance passed them on their way and missed them. We were forty minutes' drive from the nearest hospital so they made the decision to wait. We were all trained in first aid but I don't think we were aware of the seriousness of the situation.

That was when the waiting game started.

As I lay on the table, I started taking my own heart rate and looking at my own vital signs. My resting heart rate is normally about 56–60 b.p.m., but it was running well over two hundred.

Wow, that is fast, I thought. I have lost a lot of blood.

I was also losing the feeling in my arms and legs. That wasn't good, because your body shuts down what it doesn't need and tries to keep the blood going to the places where it does.

Adam Eady, the caretaker of the surf club, which is on the next beach over, arrived with some oxygen. "This'll help with the shock," he said, fitting the mask on while they threw more blankets over me to keep me warm.

When we'd got out of the surf, I'd asked Sean to ring my partner, Deb, to let her know what had happened and break it to her that it might not be a good afternoon. When he told her I'd been attacked by a shark, she thought he was messing around.

Apparently, the call went something like, Deb answering, "Hey you."

Sean saying, "Hi Deb, it's Sean."

Deb saying, "What's he done now?" thinking that I had hurt myself in some way.

Sean: "He's been attacked by a shark. You need to get down here."

Deb: "You're shitting me. Stop messing around, Sean."

Sean: "I am serious, Deb."

She's a nursing assistant, and, driving fast, made it to the beach quite quickly, around the same time the sister of a mate from the surf club, who was also a nurse, turned up. My mates had done a really great job but it was good for them to be able to hand me over to people who were a little more professional.

I thanked them for getting me that far, and apologised for ruining the afternoon. They were all in a bit of shock.

"Look guys," I said, "if I don't make it tonight, it's through no fault of you. It's my responsibility. I'm the one surfing. Whatever happens, please don't forget how much effort you've put in to get me this far."

While we waited for the ambulance, I watched the sun slowly set, wondering if it might be for the last time. I said to Deb, "Not a bad night to die."'

It took nearly fifty-five minutes for the first ambulance to arrive. A bad car accident in the local area had required both local ambulances that were then on duty. By then, about four police cars had shown up, and fifteen minutes later, a helicopter arrived. Paramedics worked on Dave for an hour and a half before his heart stabilised enough for them to put him in the helicopter to take him to the John Hunter Hospital. This was in Newcastle – the nearest major city and the only trauma centre in New South Wales outside Sydney.

'They let Deb come in the helicopter in case I didn't make it through, which was a nice thing for them to do. The pilot said to me later, though, that it just makes it so much easier when it comes to identifying the body and getting the paperwork done. Typical Aussies! We joked afterwards, but everything is done for a reason.

Although the hospital was only a forty-minute flight away, I didn't get there until nearly 9.30 p.m. due to the delays and treatment. By then, though, I knew I wasn't going to die. I was loaded on morphine and wasn't feeling too bad. Plus, they had pumped so much fluid into me at the beach that I started to get more feeling back into my feet.

When we made our approach, I saw what I thought were landing lights below. It was the media. There must have been around twenty news crews there. I couldn't understand why. I wasn't that important. Then it hit me. A week earlier there had been another shark attack not far down the coast. Whenever there are a couple close together, the media get frantic.'

Once in the hospital, X-rays were taken. As well as the avulsion of his arm muscles and tendons – the process of them being pulled away from the bone – Dave had suffered bruises and lacerations to his face, cracked and bruised ribs, damage to his lower back, and whiplash. His mates initially suspected he had broken his wrist because his hand was floppy. However, this was due to his forearm muscle being completely severed and the tendons in his wrist cut through. The shark's teeth had done so much damage they even scored the very bone.

The duty surgeon told Dave that when it comes to shark attacks – as with any animal bite – infection is one of the biggest enemies of all. They would need to take drastic action to avoid it taking hold. By the time the X-rays had been analysed, it was near 2 a.m. The surgeon said, 'I don't want to be the bearer of bad news but that arm is probably going to come off in surgery tonight.'

Dave was shocked. 'But I can still wiggle my fingers.'

'I know, but once you get infection in the bone, it's paramount we get rid of all of that, otherwise it's going to kill you.'

'Suddenly, I became aware this was even more serious than I thought. A couple of minutes after being told that I was probably going to lose an arm, a nurse asked me if I thought I'd surf again.

"It's going to be a bit tougher with one arm," I said. "But why not? I've surfed my whole life and my love of the ocean is greater than my fear of sharks so I will surf again. I'll figure out how to do it."

Then the surgeon came back. After discussing it with someone else, he said they had a guy coming in later that morning, a specialist trauma surgeon who might have a different opinion than this, so would I like to wait?

"I'll wait a few hours if there's a chance he can he save my arm," I said.'

After five hours of surgery, Dave awoke to the news that that his arm had been saved. The surgeon said he'd been lucky. Not only that but in time it should heal to a useful strength.

'In the years afterwards, I had a number of visits with him to see if there was anything he could do to give me more movement, more flexibility, more strength. It wasn't until during one of the visits, when he was telling me how good my arm was going, that he said, "Dave, we've done all of these ultrasounds. There's not much muscle connected but it is connected. You can now work that arm as hard as you can. If you try to pick up too much, your arm is going to drop it. But it isn't going to damage it."

Then, taking me by the shoulders, he said, "I just want to tell you one thing. You've got to remember something here, you were attacked by a fucking shark and I saved your arm. Be grateful."

I said, genuinely, "Yeah, thanks for that."

It was something I did need to hear and understand. Be happy, work on it, give it as much as you can because you aren't going to make it worse, you're only going to give it more strength.'

While Dave was still in hospital, his partner, Deb, brought him a laptop so he could view emails between his friends. The thread on his injuries had been going for two days and began with his mates sharing their concern. Some news reports had said he'd lost an arm and a leg – which naturally prompted a lot of worried messages about what quality of life he might have in the future. As time had gone on, however, he noticed the tone change:

'One of the last posts from one of the guys said that Deb had told him I'd come out of surgery, that they'd saved my arm, and it was all this good stuff. Then one of the comments was, "So, is it too early to start making jokes?"

These are the guys I've mucked around and joked with for years. I replied, "Hi guys, it's Dave here, out of surgery, things are looking good for the future, we don't know what the results are going to be with my arm but it's still going to be attached. By the way, let them rip. It's not too early to make jokes. I've got a big grin on my face reading this."

What resonated with me straight away was that when you turn things around and make it a bit funnier, it makes it easier for everybody to deal with. From then on, when I ran into people, if I could see the stress on their faces, I'd make a joke out of it. And it helped them come to terms with it too. Deb would say it was my turn to cook dinner that night and I'd do anything to get out of it! She actually said that to me when she arrived at the beach the afternoon of the attack; which was true, it was my turn to cook!

It became a good coping mechanism, and a great lesson for me when I saw my mates straight away breaking into humour to come to terms with, I guess, nearly losing a mate.'

Dave also started reading some of the news stories about the attack. In their desperation to acquire any information at all, journalists had harvested photos of him from Facebook and tracked down all manner of his acquaintances, however slight, to glean any kind of insight into his character. Although he was amused by some of the content of the stories, at the bottom of each news report was the comments section.

'There were comments along the lines of, "Who does this guy think he is surfing at night? I guess he expects us to feel sorry for him."

I responded, "Hey guys, this is Dave from the hospital here. I'm doing all right, thanks. Just thought I'd clear a few things up here. I wasn't surfing at night. It was in the afternoon. We were on the beach for more than three hours afterwards, so yes, any footage was taken of me coming to hospital was well and truly at night."

I thought that might put a stop to it but they came right back.

"Nah, you were surfing in the dark."

They were telling me stuff about myself.

"You're going to go out and kill all the sharks now. That's what you want, isn't it?"

I said, "I don't really care about sharks. I'm pretty indifferent to them. If they want to leave me alone, I'll leave them alone, but if I have to fight one off to save my life, I will do that as well."

I couldn't believe the horrible picture they were painting of me. It was disgusting the anger towards me, just because a shark had attacked me. After three or four hours, I saw a comment from one guy who said, "You know what, mate, I wish you'd just have fucking died."

My last comment was, "Woah. Yesterday I was a pretty good bloke but today, because of this, I am everybody's worst enemy and you want me to die. You're welcome to make up your stories about me, because you obviously don't care ... you can all go and get fucked."'

As soon as Dave was able to get back on his feet in the hospital, he paid a visit to the young woman, Lisa Mondy, who had been attacked by a shark while wakeboarding just seven days before. Lisa, twenty-four, had come off her board and was waiting for her boat to pick her up at Jimmys Beach, Port Stephens, around two hundred kilometres south of Crowdy Head, near Newcastle, when the shark – believed to be a great white – struck. The shark's teeth caught her face and arm before it went back under the water. It released her but not before it had bitten her upper arm. Thanks to her life jacket she managed to stay afloat, but suffered a severed artery in her arm, losing nearly half her total blood, as well as suffering severe injuries to her head, neck and shoulder. She required fifteen hours of surgery.

When Dave and Lisa started talking, they compared scars and he was struck by how similar their experiences were and how easily they could relate to each other's ordeal.

'I remember walking away from that conversation thinking, Wow, there's something in this. I was working in Newcastle the day of her attack and watched the rescue helicopter fly over. When I heard on the radio there had been a shark attack I realised that's who was in the helicopter. I followed her story on the news but who was to know that the next week I'd be in the same hospital? The instant connection was intriguing to me.'

After a week in hospital, Dave was able to return home and begin an intense period of rehabilitation. His job, as operations manager for a fabrication company, involved a two-hundred-kilometre round trip every day but, with his left arm out of action, he couldn't drive. He negotiated with his boss to conduct 90 per cent of his work from home, which alleviated any initial financial worries. Within three weeks, he was back at work full time with the help of some considerable pain management. Dave was also fortunate that his family – his parents, partner Debbie Minett, son Kyle and daughter Marnie – lived close by to support him in his recovery.

'The financial side is something that is really tough for people who have been attacked by a shark, because the recovery can take weeks, months or years – and some people will never work again. There's no insurance to cover this sort of thing so I'm really aware of how lucky I am. I never lost a day's pay. My work looked after me better than I could ever have asked for. The money worry for me wasn't part of my recovery. I stopped counting the money I was spending on rehab treatment, physio, chiropractic and massage therapy when it hit thirty thousand dollars as I found worrying about spending the money was not good for my mental health.'

There were other worries, however, as Dave tried to come to terms with what had happened. Although having his family close was a source of great comfort, there were things they couldn't help him with:

'It was dreams and things going through my mind. Initially, there's a lot of your mind playing that "What if?" game. What if I'd gone for a motorbike ride in the afternoon instead of going to the beach? You second-question everything that you've done. What did I do in the ocean to get bitten? It was when I surprised myself waking up with a scream that Deb mentioned I was doing it a lot and maybe I should see someone professionally.'

'Is the ocean out to get me?'

Dave's other big challenge would be whether he could go back into the water. As someone for whom surfing was a big thing, it seemed inconceivable he would give it up. Not only was he facing the reality that his arm might never regain its full strength, he also had a huge mental hurdle to overcome.

'The Saturday after I got out of hospital was the first chance I had to get to the beach. It was a beautiful morning, the sun was out, the water was crystal clear, and I put some boardies [shorts] on and walked out into the ocean.
It was the most horrific experience of my life.

Every little bit of seaweed was a shark. I got out of the water with tears running down my face. I was thinking, What is going on here? I went back in up to my ankles and one of my mates pulled up on the beach and he said, "You're out of hospital, Dave? How's it going?"

"I really don't know," I said.

"When someone said it was a forty-eight-year-old, I knew it was you," he said. "You're the only silly old bloke who'd be out there that time of day."

"Yeah," I said, "everyone's saying they knew it would have been me. I wish someone told me that the day before and I wouldn't have been down the beach."

We had a chat and I went back in. I got up to my knees again. "This is not that dangerous," I said to myself. "You have done this millions of times."

As I was doing this, my partner grabbed her surfboard, ran straight past me and paddled straight out the back. There was no one else out on the water, but it was as if to say, "Look, there is nothing out here, you are going to be fine, life is going to be fine." I walked out up to my chest, which was as deep as I could go because my arm was in a cast, holding my arm above my head. I got that deep – but it felt like a moment.'

For the next few weeks, while his arm was still in a cast, Dave went to the beach but had to be content with watching his mates surf. Until he felt strong enough to put some weight on his arm, surfing was out of the question. Or so he thought.

Then in June, three months after the attack, his brother in Sydney rang up, asked how he was doing and whether he was surfing yet. Dave explained that his arm was still frozen and even when he pulled the cast off, he had no movement in his hand or fingers. His brother said, "Well, suck it up, princess. Bethany Hamilton does it with one arm; I'm sure you can do it with one and a half." Bethany, an American surfer, had survived a tiger shark attack in 2003 when her left arm was bitten off. Against the odds, though, she returned to professional surfing. His brother's comment struck a chord with Dave.

'"You bastard!" I said.

The next morning, I went down to the beach and attempted some one-arm push-ups, thinking if I could do those, I could get up to my feet on the surfboard. I was failing miserably but I was determined that today was going to be the day I surfed again – and nothing was going to stop me. I had a fibreglass cast on my arm but any weight I put on my hand produced intense pain. I pulled out a couple of ankle straps I had in the car and strapped them around my wrist, then found a couple of sticks on the beach and made a splint around my wrist. I got a roll of gaffer tape and bound my whole wrist up.

I still couldn't put any weight on it but I wasn't worried about hurting it any worse, so I paddled out on an old foam surfboard. It took me a lot of time to figure out how to push up with one elbow and one hand and get to my feet. There were a lot of wipeouts, but stubborn I am, if nothing else. Finally, I caught a wave and got to my feet, the best wave of my life.

One of my mates was walking up the beach with his wife. They came to me as I ran up the beach and I gave them a big hug.

"I caught a wave; I can surf again. I'm back. This is so good, to feel the surf!"

"You're going to be fine, Dave, aren't you?" he said.

I needed that focus from my brother. I wanted to show him when he next came up that I was surfing properly again.'

It had been ten weeks since the attack when Dave got back in the water.

From then, his focus when paddling out was how he was going to get to his feet. He became so distracted, he didn't worry what fish were in the water. It was all about figuring out how to surf again. Four weeks later, he got a reminder he wasn't alone in the surf.

'I had another close encounter. That's when everything really started to really change for me and the ocean. I was pretty fine up until then, but then I saw another shark. And it wasn't much longer after that – a couple of weeks – when one swam straight past me fast, obviously chasing something. It was quite funny because the guy paddling beside me screamed. I held up my arm, still in a cast, and said, "They hurt a bit."

Within the next twelve months, I had six encounters where a shark either came that close to me that I could see its eyes or actually rubbed me or bumped me on the way through. I thought, Is the ocean out to get me? It was tough. Numerous times I questioned whether I could still surf.

On one occasion, I watched a bull shark stalk me. It was coming at me as a wave was coming. I changed direction; so did the shark. As the wave got close, I turned and paddled straight onto the wave, jumped up to my feet and rode it right through to the sand. I got out, threw my board in a bush and just sat on the beach and cried. I just thought, I can't do this any more. It seemed everywhere I went there were sharks.

My son had moved home by then. He said, "What's up?"

"You didn't see that shark? It was huge."

"Come on, Dad," he said. "We'll just go up the beach a bit more and catch a few more waves."

We went for a walk up the beach – fifty metres, because obviously a shark is not going to swim fifty metres for me! We paddled out and caught a few more waves. It wasn't very comfortable but I could see Kyle was putting in the effort to be with me so I put in the effort to catch some waves.

It was something I needed to do – get back on the pushbike again.'

With ongoing treatment, Dave was slowly able to improve the movement, flexibility and strength in his arm. After he was discharged by his surgeon, Dave began work building a two-storey house with his son – and it turned into the best form of physiotherapy.

'It was tough work with one and a half arms, but it was great work. I could see the improvement week on week. I helped him after work and on weekends and my arm got better and better. It's got to the stage now that I pretty much don't notice that I have anything wrong with my arm. It's just become part of who I am. I only lost fifteen per cent usage in my arm, which is a reasonable amount. I can't lift heavy things with my left arm. I can't grip things very well, which for someone who rides motorbikes is a challenge. After I nearly crashed at the race track, I have learned to ride them differently – not go quite as hard, slow down earlier.

I've been really lucky and pretty fortunate from day one. Everything fell into place when it came to my survival and surgery and my recovery.'

Although his arm healed well, Dave was left with a permanent reminder of his attack – the scar on his arm where the shark's teeth had bitten through. As much as he tried to play down the impact of his ordeal, particularly in the early days, Dave discovered that taking ownership of his experience helped others deal with it. Remembering how his friends' eagerness to crack jokes helped lighten the mood, he bought T-shirts that not only were ice-breakers, but also helped show people he was at ease talking about his attack:

'There was one with a shark swimming underneath a guy on a surfboard, which said: "Surfers: the other red meat." I had another that said, "I don't have to outswim the shark, I just have to outswim you." If I were to see the T-shirts on someone I didn't know, I might have found it in bad taste, but people were reading them and realising that I was OK talking about it and making fun of it. It put them at ease and my friends could deal with me quite easily that way.'

It's funny because when I meet someone I don't go, "I'm Dave, I've been attacked by a shark." I try not to make that who I am. It is a definite part of who I am but it doesn't define me, it defines part of my life. I'll start a new job somewhere and it's usually months before someone figures out or someone sees the tattoo on my arm.

"What's that about?"

"Oh, I got attacked by a shark."

"You're kidding me!"

Or I'll be doing something at work and someone will say, "Why are you trying to hold that like that, you idiot?"

"It's because my arm doesn't work."

"Why's that?"

"A shark bit it."

"You're kidding."

The tattoo was my partner Deb's suggestion. We were expecting the scar to be quite ugly because I did lose some of the meat out of my arm. She said, "You could always get a tattoo over it."

I went to six or seven tattooists but every shark they wanted to put on my arm was a big, vicious-looking thing. It wasn't what I was looking for.

A couple of years later I met a guy in hospital, Glen Folkard, who had also been attacked and was a tattooist. He asked me what I was after and we came up with a design and he whacked it on my arm. It's really good. It's a bull shark and basically a badge of honour. It's got a banner at the top and the bottom. The banner at the top says "Survivor". Back then it was a word that I needed to remind myself that no matter what was going to happen, I was going to survive. It's got the date, because obviously that's an important time in my life. It's not something I want to forget – not that I ever will.'

What Dave didn't appreciate at first was how his group of surfing mates was also affected by what happened.

'Some of my mates didn't go surfing for nearly six months. I was back surfing before they were. That was a surprise to me. Guys who I surfed with on the weekend before my attack – but weren't at the beach on the day – couldn't go back in the ocean.

I remember running into a mate at the beach in June, three months after my attack. He told me he was still trying to get back in the water. "I can't go out in the ocean," he said. "I keep thinking about what happened to you."

We'd surfed together for I don't know how many years. I said to him, "In all that time, you know of one shark attack here, so the risk is not that high." He was about to head home but I said, "There's a few waves, how about we go for a surf?"

"I can't surf," he said.

"I'm going surfing," I told him, "and I need you to come out with me. I don't want to be out on my own."

So, from that moment on, he started surfing again. He just needed that bit of help to get him back in the water.'

'We have become each other's answers.'

Dave's physical scars might have healed – and he might have overcome the psychological hurdle of getting back into the water – but he still suffered the mental trauma of his attack. He continued to have nightmares, often waking up screaming, or he spent sleepless nights replaying the events in his mind.

Recalling the shared experiences he'd had with Lisa Mondy in hospital, he started searching the internet to see if there was a group of shark attack survivors who helped others navigate through the trauma. In 2012, when he failed to find any such group, he decided to set up his own, which later became Bite Club. Dave acted after he heard about another shark incident in Australia. He rang the hospital, explained his situation and offered his phone number so the victim could get in touch if they wanted. His idea was for somewhere safe for survivors and families of victims who lost their lives to shark attacks to communicate with each other. A year on, following similar approaches and thanks to the detective skills of Glen Folkard, who was a major force in the formation of the group, Bite Club had twelve members. Dave kept the Facebook group inaccessible to the general public.

In 2013, he was keen to help two members in Western Australia who were struggling but, faced with having to fund the travel costs themselves, turned to TV producers who were keen to highlight the group on their current affairs programme.

'We were still very small then.

It took me months to negotiate with the producer how the show was going to go so that it was along the lines of what we wanted – which was to show a bunch of people who had been through a similar traumatic experience helping each other cope with what's ahead. And that's what we got. That's when we learned we were something … not special, but a bit unique.

What we were trying to do was get two of our members back in the water who hadn't been in the ocean since their shark attacks. We went surfing, then swimming in an aquarium with grey nurse sharks and it was great. The show was very successful. The reporter who narrated the show rang me up after and said they were getting great feedback from people wanting to reach out and say, "What a great thing you guys are doing." That was really heartening to hear. We were already seeing what a great thing it was and the benefit people were getting from it.

From that first TV show, I received a number of inquiries from other people who had been attacked many years ago asking whether they could talk to me and join what we were doing. I started having conversations with people who were attacked in the 1970s, and others involved in more recent attacks. Two years ago, I met a man who was attacked in 1955. He was suffering from life-ending dementia and going through night terrors about his shark attack. We sat down and talked about it, and he took me through the day like it was yesterday. It was awesome, such a nice thing to meet him and talk about his shark attack, which brought many other more important things out.

After I visited him, he stopped having night terrors. It was just having someone understand what he had been through. Unfortunately, he passed away soon after that and I only got a couple of visits with him. He was a great man and it was phenomenal that he made it out of his attack. His son got in touch through the staff to thank me for going to see his dad. It was really nice.

That's when it dawned on me that when you look back at the older days, there were many things people never got to deal with. I grew up in that time. You'd hurt yourself and big brother would dust you off and say, "Suck it up and get on with it, we have got work to do." That was how you dealt with shit. You didn't tell anyone you were struggling. It was a case of keep it inside, don't tell anyone and get on with your life.'

Bite Club has grown much bigger than Dave ever expected. As it has developed, he has been contacted by people who have suffered all kinds of animal attacks. Over ten years on, by late 2022, Bite Club had over 440 members from all over the world.

'A girl who was attacked by a crocodile asked to join, saying, "I know I'm not a shark attack survivor but I've never had anyone to talk to."

"Why not?" I said. "Come and join our group."

Any brutal animal attack is as bad as any other one. And from having that attitude that we have all been through an animal attack of some kind, it's very similar. One girl was attacked by a dog. She really needed to talk, she was struggling so bad. Some of the worst stories I've gone through with survivors have been because of dogs.

One guy got attacked by two big pig dogs, which people breed here to bring down wild pigs. This guy was a mechanic, and his neighbours had the two dogs. He was big – 6 foot 4 inches, 110 kilos – and he was working on his car when these two dogs came up. The next thing, one got him by the arm, pulling him down. One of the dogs held him by the throat as the other one chewed his arm off. His attack went on for about an hour and a half.

I had a conversation with him while I was driving home from work, and when he told what happened, I had to pull up, I was shaking and physically sick beside the road. It was horrible. It was the same with another dog attack we had. So, if someone says, "Look, I know I've only been attacked by a dog but I'm really going through some mental issues with it," I say, "Not a problem. Come and sit down and join the group and come and talk with people; you'll be amazed at the similarities."

We have three lion survivors in our group, including a girl from Canada who got attacked by a lion while she was working in a reserve in South Africa. We have three girls who were attacked by a hippopotamus. We have a girl who was attacked by two wolves. One lady was torn apart by a brown bear. We're getting all these people from all over the world.

One girl said to me she'd looked all over to find an animal survivor group and we were the only guys she could find anywhere in the world that were just here to support people who have been attacked. I said, "That's why we exist, because when I was looking I couldn't find anyone. Out of need, we just started something."'

The more people Dave has spoken to, the more he's been amazed at the striking similarities between each story. The road to recovery can be long and there are common hurdles to be overcome along the way:

'We will all have bad dreams. We will all have the questions we torment ourselves with. They're the questions that don't have an answer, but we all search for that answer.

About five years ago, I met a guy in hospital. He lived not far up the coast, and I reached out to him and was up at his place, having dinner with him and his family. He said to me, afterwards, "When I was lying in hospital looking for answers, you came in." And he said, "Because there are no answers; we've all become each other's answers."

And that's right, we have become each other's answers. We've all been through that experience. The funny thing is, among our group, we hardly talk about our attacks much at all. We will talk about our shark attack once, usually and there's really not a lot to add because we've all got that story. I know what I went through and I know what they're going through as they're telling me their story. I want to help them get through that stuff. There are lots of things that seem to be so common among all of us. There are certain timelines that play out.

Whenever I meet someone in hospital, I tell them the truth up front. It's not going to be good. You're going to go through the next month or so and you're going to be so happy you're alive and everybody's going to give you more attention than you want. But you'll get sick of that – and then nobody's going to give you any attention …

and that's even harder because, all of a sudden, the feeling is that you'll become a burden on everyone else.

I remember saying it to myself. After a few months, I'd run into someone. They'd say, "Ah you're all better now." Once your arm's out of a cast, everything is "fixed". I got to the stage where, rather than explain what was still in the future for me, I would just say, "Yeah, my arm's doing OK now and I'm all better."

That's a defence mechanism we all take on. People who suffer from mental health do exactly the same thing. Nearly all of us end up suffering post-traumatic stress at one stage or another. It's pretty much as regular as clockwork that somewhere between six and twelve months you develop a bout of post-traumatic stress that is going to bring your life down worse than what you thought it would.

When you tell that to someone in hospital, it's a shock; but the good news is that, usually, twelve months after that, you start to come to terms with everything, you come to terms with your new life. This is now your new normal. You can accept that this is your new life, that you're now going to struggle at certain things. Once you can accept that, you can turn things around. You can come to terms with it and deal with it better.

You won't get rid of the post-traumatic stress. I see it coming all the time with people, but you can learn to live with it. I still have what we call stress attacks – some people call them panic attacks; it all depends on what the trigger is and what's causing it.

I see it all the time in our group. I always try and teach people ways of dealing with that. In one way, I've become an unofficial counsellor to the group. And now I've managed to bring on official counsellors to the group, which is really good. I have a specialised trauma counsellor and a psychologist who will help us out. So, if some people are not improving, we can offer them a professional service if they need it to help them through.

I'm usually the first one who reaches out to people and connects with them. If I am speaking to someone overseas who is really struggling, we'll talk about what they're dealing with and how I can help them deal with what they're going through. If that's not going to work, I can also help them with more trauma skills to help them deal with the future that's going to come. If they think life is bad now, it's not going to get better unless they start to learn how to cope with what's happening and learn how to move forward from what's happening. We've had lots of success within our group because of that.'

And Bite Club offers people a safe space away from other social media, where the reaction to an animal attack can be especially cruel.

'We cop it a lot on social media for some reason. Unfortunately, because I know they are out there, I watch them. After every shark attack, especially a fatal one, it is traumatic for me to read the stories on social media and the horrible things people say. One that comes to mind was a grandmother whose grandson was a spearfisherman. He died six times on the way to hospital and they'd managed to keep bringing him back. He was still in intensive care in an induced coma. Yet there were all these horrible comments and the grandma was trying to defend her grandson.

I saw the comments and reached out to her. I commented on one of her posts, "Please get off your computer, get off your phone, you don't need this. These people don't know you, they don't know your family, they don't know your grandson. They are not healthy for you. They are certainly not going to do you any favours." I then got in touch and said, "Please, this is very forward of me, but I have been there; I've been through this and it's not been healthy for me, and it's going to be unhealthy for you."'

After Dave reached out, the grandmother responded, grateful for the offer of support. Her grandson fought back from his near-death experience and joined Bite Club. After an initial bleak outlook, speaking to other survivors helped the spearfisherman turn his life around, as Dave recalls:

'He is a very inspirational guy. We've done some great things with him after his attack and we helped turn his life into something totally different from what he expected it to be. I'm glad to be able to help do that. I've managed to train a lot of social media people that it's just not acceptable to be like that to someone who is basically dying or has died – their family is going to read these comments – just to let them know they are not acceptable in their dealings with other human beings. That's some of the reasons why we have Bite Club.

I reach out to every hospital as soon as someone is attacked and leave messages. Basically, all we are is a bunch of people who want to help other people through a traumatic event. That's probably the easiest way to sum up what Bite Club is.'

Bite Club has attracted worldwide attention since its formation. As a result, Dave has been inundated with requests from people to join:

'I get thousands of requests. Some people say, "I am fascinated by sharks, I just want to hear people's stories who have been attacked." I politely try and get back to everyone but sometimes I have to say, "We are not about sharing our stories, we are about helping each other."

Do you want to go to a breast cancer survivor group and start hearing about their stories? It's basically the same thing – we've got a bunch of people who have shared a similar traumatic experience and have made it through it. Or, in the case of others in our group, the families of people who haven't made it through, who still need to understand lots of things that happened to us and support us through our lives too. It's a double-edged sword for them because they are chasing answers and they're getting answers from people who have been through the same thing as their loved one and survived.

I often feel a little bit of survivor's guilt after hearing some of the stories because I know full well they don't have that loved one to whinge to them about the nerve pain in their arm or whinge about not being able to ride a motorbike like they used to. Some don't have anyone at all.

And I'm very conscious about how I deal with my own social media as well, to some extent. I am as bad as anyone; we are all bad, we're all opinionated, but I try to always be considerate to those I know are in our group. They are reading my comments as well.'

Not everyone gets accepted, however:

'Believe it or not, we've had people who have fabricated shark attacks so they could get into our group. People never fail to amaze me. I have to say to people, "I'm sorry but I am still trying to verify who you are." Unfortunately, we've had all sorts trying to get into our group. If you accidentally let someone in, they can do all sorts of damage to people.

I got caught out early on thinking that everyone had our best interests at heart when they wanted to join, when in fact they didn't.'

> *'An hour and a half counselling session
> with a few waves thrown in.'*

As Bite Club has evolved, the group has morphed into a multifaceted forum that deals not just with the incidents and their effects but also with wider issues in the shark world, such as the frequency of shark attacks and the measures in place to try and mitigate them. New products are continually being developed to protect surfers and other water users, including electronic or magnetic devices that repel sharks and rays and revolutionary wetsuits that are bite-resistant or can make the wearer invisible to big fish:

'We run our own shark discussion page where we discuss sharks and shark attacks and shark mitigation and anything that's happening in the shark world. We don't discuss that on our normal page because many of our members do not want to see anything about sharks – it can be very triggering to them and bring back too many bad experiences – but many of our members also want to know as much as they can. Most of us spent the first twelve months after the attack doing nothing but researching and trying to understand things like the number one question, which is, "What did I do to get myself attacked?" We all want to learn how not to get attacked again.

We've become a go-to place for people who are bringing out shark mitigation inventions. Who better to endorse your product than someone who has been there? We've got electronic or magnetic devices and bite-resistant wetsuits, where the shark's teeth won't cut the material, so even if you are attacked the chances of you bleeding to death are hopefully reduced somewhat.

The mortality rate of shark attacks has improved over the years for two or three reasons. One is the number of people who know first aid and have the right equipment in their vehicles is better than before. We've got more people in the water now, so the number of people who can come to your aid has also increased.

I was lucky. There were four of us surfing at the beach on the afternoon I was attacked. My neighbour spent nearly an hour and half with his hands around my upper arm acting as a tourniquet.'

Now when Dave goes surfing, he carries out a series of checks to see if there is an increased chance of shark activity at his local beach:

'The minute I'm out of the car, I'm looking, and if a fin pops up anywhere within my eyesight, even peripheral vision, I will see it. Whether that's because of how observant I am now or because I'm just lucky, I don't know, but I will see if there is fish activity.

I have my own drone so I fly it over and try to spot anything in the water. If there's a school of fish, is there anything among them that is bigger?

I look for bird activity. If a lot of big fish are biting little fish, lots of bits and pieces float to the surface. When you see a lot of birds circling and diving down into the water, you know there's some fish activity happening below. Even if you're not seeing fish activity, that's a good indicator that that it's there.

The power of observation is the most important tool we have because things can change within fifteen minutes in the ocean. You can be surfing and the wind can suddenly change, the tide turns or the swell can suddenly pick up, so if you're keeping an eye on everything that's happening, the chances are you can hopefully see the nasty things that are out there as well.

I've tried deterrents – like the magnet you strap on your ankle – for a while, and I tried to find more research into whether there was a scientific study into the effectiveness of such equipment. I also tried an electronic device where a couple of electrodes on the bottom of your surfboard run a current between them, similar to an electric fence, to repel the sharks. That one did have some scientific research behind it. They tested a surfboard with a lump of tuna on it to attract sharks, and 58 per cent of the approaches turned away when they got too close. That's the best thing we have at the moment.

It's tough to surf with, however, because you can get a lot of electric shocks with it. They just brought out a different version that has electrodes in slightly different positions. I actually got one for one of the guys involved in a recent shark attack. He hadn't been surfing for about a year. I got him one of these devices and he went out with it and he says he's not getting zapped by it at all. This is a great improvement. He's really happy with it. He now thinks he's got some protection as well.

Here in Australia, two guys are working on wetsuit material that is bite-proof. One has released his, which has been good for people diving. It's like having a bullet-proof vest on, which is going to be uncomfortable if you're surfing but diving is slightly different. This is another promising development.

One of the guys went for Kevlar-type [the material used in bullet-proof vests] panels, while the other guy has developed a whole new material which is promising. I am putting a lot of my faith in that because nothing is going to stop us getting attacked a hundred per cent of the time; but if something does bite you, even if it crushes a bone, if it doesn't cut a femoral artery or a major vein, you've got a greater chance of surviving.

Another thing that has been trialled in the last ten years or so is the camouflaged wetsuit. Some have stripes to make them look like a sea snake, and there's a material that makes you blend into the environment. If you're swimming on the surface, the shark can't see you.

There are lots of things out there and I try to help these guys get the studies they require so people will believe in their product.'

One controversial method used to reduce the number of attacks is shark nets. Deployed in New South Wales and Queensland, they are submerged at hotspots and are designed to limit attacks by catching sharks of a certain size. Critics insist, though, that they only catch ten per cent of the intended species and the risk of harm to the sharks is high. It has also been shown that if they're not properly maintained, they can lose their effectiveness.

Another tactic to reduce shark activity at popular beaches is the use of drum lines – baited traps used to lure and capture large sharks. Drum lines, particularly when used with nets, can kill sharks, but they have been proven to be effective. They were introduced in Ballina, in New South Wales, after a spate of six attacks in twenty-one months led to beach closures. However, Dave prefers SMART (Shark Management Alert in Real Time) drum lines, which use technology, and have been shown to move sharks on rather than trap them, as he explains:

'The exclusion nets are about 150 metres long, and the idea behind them is they disrupt the shark's normal movement. They have pingers on them that emit a high frequency pulse that's registerable to dolphins and other animals. As well as sharks, they do catch the occasional dolphin, ray and turtle sometimes, but not that many. And the idea is that they interrupt the shark's pattern so it doesn't want to hang around in that area. As a result, there haven't been many attacks in Sydney.

SMART drum lines have become a huge thing here in Australia. They were introduced in the Ballina area in 2016 after a spate of shark attacks. There was a lot of controversy when they were going to do it. Environmentalists said you're going to start catching sharks and dolphins and turtles, you're going to kill everything in the ocean. But the way it works is that as soon as anything gets caught on there, it sends an SMS message to the contractor running the lines and to the government Department of Primary Industries [Australian governmental agricultural agency]. The contractor has thirty minutes to get whatever animal is caught off the line. I think the average is twelve minutes from the time the shark is caught.

They are only targeting white sharks. Since 2016, drum lines have been used on and off, depending on funding, where they're put and how many are out there, and they've caught around seven hundred white sharks, two hundred tigers and a hundred bulls. In that time, they only lost two sharks and, I think, one dolphin. In the Ballina area, they introduced drum lines and nets and were catching lots of sharks but they pulled the nets back out very quickly. The shark attacks stopped. They were towing the shark out to sea, tagging it and letting it go.

The shark gets freaked out by the whole experience and keeps going east into the deeper water and doesn't come back for quite a while. Usually when they do see it again, it's much further up the coast. It's been a win for everyone. It's not killing anything and it appears to be stopping the attacks. Now they're talking about maybe removing more of the nets in Sydney and replacing them with full-time SMART drum lines.'

Whenever there is an attack in New South Wales, the shark team at the Department of Primary Industries alerts Dave. Not only do Bite Club members counsel other individuals but often they hold events in communities that collectively can be reeling from a devastating incident. And Dave says if he hears it's a location he knows well, his first thought is for his buddies who surf there:

'We've had, in the past year, two fatal attacks, one just down the coast from me. The shark team gives me as much information as they legally can at the time. I never get names or injuries or anything like that. They'll just say where someone has been attacked and whether they passed away. I immediately make a few calls, and the sense of relief when someone I know answers the phone is unbelievable.

They might go, "Oh, Dave, I thought you might be ringing. There's been an attack, and I wasn't there," or, "I was there and it wasn't me, luckily."

I recently met with a guy who was out during a fatal shark attack. The shark actually went for him first. He used his surfboard as a shield to fight it off and then it turned and went for someone else. It was a horrific attack. The poor guy, he helped get the other guy, who didn't survive, out of the water. He's got young kids, and he said, "I can't get through this."

"Yes, you can," I said. We went surfing together not long ago. I said to him, "Let's go back into the ocean together."

We sat there – and a lot of people will describe when I surf with them as being an hour and a half counselling session with a few waves thrown in. That's the comment I get. I enjoy it. I enjoy helping someone get back the enjoyment of something they love doing. Plus, it's a win for me. I get to feel good about what we do when that happens.

Last year, we started to run community events after fatal attacks. We've got a team of people together now, which includes the Department of Primary Industries, a professional mental health provider and myself. We meet up with communities and offer them the opportunity to come and talk about their experience. I tell them about my experience and the communities I have been to and what I've witnessed from spending time with community members after shark attacks. The community itself needs healing as well. It's not just a personal thing; it spreads far and wide. I get to talk about that to the community, and if people want to talk to me about what my experience was like, they can.

After one fatal shark attack up the coast, I sat down with the victim's pregnant widow. She asked me what her husband's last moments would have been like.

I said, "I can't tell you that, but I can tell you what mine would have been like."

It helps people come to terms with it as well. She's in our group and has since had a beautiful baby. She is doing really well and the local surf community are looking after her as well. Being in the group is like getting a big hug from everyone. It's rewarding in one way and traumatic in another.

I remember coming back from that event, where I had met with forty surfers who had witnessed what had happened – and it was a horrific attack. My mates and my son were at the local motorbike track. I didn't have to say anything to those guys – what the week had been like. I just needed to hang out with my mates again and have a fast ride on a motorbike and not think about anything else but that. When I finished, it was like the best recovery I could have had from the few days I'd had away.

It is tough and my partner has to deal with the fallout from all these things. She's awesome and if it wasn't for her, I don't know where I would be. But it's really nice to be invited into someone's life and make a small difference in their life and help them come to terms with the future and help them get better. That's why I still do this as much as I do.

I once spoke with a mother in the USA. I spent three hours on the phone after work, having a discussion with her about her son and some of the struggles he's going through. Afterwards, I didn't sleep at all that night. It was quite concerning what the family were struggling with. But she rang me up the next day and said, "We all had the best night's sleep for nearly a year. I'm so glad you called and we had a chat."

"Wow," I said, "that is so good. I'm so glad."

I might have had a couple of bad nights' sleep, but they had a lot of answers and they are doing really well now, so if it's a little bit of discomfort for me but a lot of comfort for someone else, then I'm willing to do that.'

Although Dave is in touch with people all over the globe, he lives with the reality that another serious shark attack could happen at any time on his own patch. The safeguards – those controversial and otherwise – currently in Queensland and near Sydney are not in place near him. And while sharks like great whites and bulls pose the greatest threat to human life, there are other dangers lurking beneath the surface.

'Two guys were attacked within thirty minutes of each other at our beach. One was bitten by a wobbegong shark [a species that spends much of its time resting on the sea floor and is not considered as dangerous to humans], so fortunately the injuries weren't too bad. When you've got a fish that's two hundred kilos with you in its mouth and you're getting dragged away under water, your first instinct is to think shark, and the wobbegong shark has done a lot of damage to a lot of people mentally, if not so physically. They have horribly sharp teeth, and it's a tough one to deal with because all your mates want to make light of the situation, but mentally, you can really get some trauma from the attack itself.

The other guy left hospital prior to our shark researchers getting there, but I am going to meet up with him to have a chat. It's something I never push, but if he wants me to, I'll help him identify his fish because we have had quite a number of attacks since mine on the NSW coast in my area.

When there was a fatal attack, I've gotten to know their families and I've met with people who were in the water at the time. I try to help them all come to terms with what happened. I still remember those first few months after my attack, not knowing what my future was going to be like. When I had my first post-traumatic stress attack, it was just the worst –

like my whole life was about to end. When people have that now, they have someone else to reach out to.'

Bite Club receives no regular government money but has benefitted from state funds in the past and runs its own charity. The rest of the time the members cover any expenses. It's worth it, however, as the reward is seeing the improvement in people through talking about their ordeal.

'It's just great to be able to bring these people together, and it's not all me. I don't do all the work. I've instigated the group and I do a lot of the work involved in it to make sure the group stays healthy and happy, but so much other stuff goes on that I only become aware of later. I might introduce someone to someone else because they live close together, and they've helped each other through the trauma. It's so good to be part of this – where people are willing to help out someone they have never met before.

There's never going to be any reward out of it for any of us. The reward of helping someone else is that you get better for it. I often say I wish everybody could nearly die so they could understand how important life is and how we help each other get through it. The world would be a much better place.

Getting attacked by a shark can be financially ruinous. Your earning capacity can take a massive dive. When we go somewhere, it's all about the help, not the money involved. We figure that out ourselves. We run a charity, so we got some funding for that to kick it off. I have been financially bankrupt at one stage, so I know how much of a financial struggle it can be. Every year we try to do one special thing that will benefit one person immensely, and everybody else gets a big lift as well just by seeing the results. We have a little bit of money saved up but anything I do, I fund myself. I never want anyone to say that I do this to make money.

We also have a few people in the group who are willing to pay for dinner or beers when we meet up. The mighty Dale Carr [an early Bite Club member] will always be the first to shout, but everyone contributes in their own way.

Funding is something I've been spending a lot of time talking with people about because a lot of people ask me, "Why do you keep funding this yourself?" I say because it's important to do, and if there's no other funding there, then I'll use mine. I don't care. If I see something that's important to do, I'll do it; and if it's going to cost me a couple of hundred, a couple of thousand or whatever it doesn't matter.'

'I've got a whole family of animal attack survivors that I get to see their lives getting better.'

In 2023, Dave turned sixty, and the year marked twelve years since his attack. Although he knows he is not as physically fit as he was before his ordeal, he still surfs a lot and recently started hydrofoiling – a different type of surfing on a hydroplane where he can take off on the swell and go for greater distances. That takes him out into deeper water, where he's likely to be on his own, as fewer people participate. Mentally, it's challenging; and although he overcame his fear enough to get back in the water, he will never get complacent.

He will never get over his shark attack – but thanks to Bite Club, it has changed his life for the better:

'When I walk down the beach and strap my leg wrap on, I say to myself, "Are you ready for a surf today? Because today you could die."

That's not to be dramatic or anything, it's just to accept the fact that when I go into the ocean, the risk is on me. I have to be careful when I'm out there because it could be the last thing I ever do.

Why do I do it? Because I love it. Surfing gives you a buzz that nothing else does. But it's not our ocean. I cannot go near a body of water without understanding the dangers that are there. It's a place of enjoyment – and it's my place of mental health recovery. As much as it has been bad for me, it's also been good for me.

I miss the blissful ignorant days before I was attacked – because I never realised what a shark could do to my life until it actually happened. It's not just the bite and it's not just the near death and it's not just the injury and the recovery, it's just my whole life has been affected. That, every time I go surfing, is in the back of my mind now.

Unfortunately, my whole life is about shark attacks. But it's life-affirming.

That's why I keep doing it. Some people ask me, "It's been eleven years since your shark attack, aren't you over it yet?"

You just don't get over it. But I have something better than my shark attack. I've got a whole family of animal attack survivors that I get to see their lives getting better. There are a few whose lives aren't getting better, unfortunately, and I get to try and help them as well. It's tough when I see people struggle.

It's funny, we often get people turning up here, in the small town where we live. We'll go to our local pub where everyone knows everyone. I'll go in with a stranger with me, and when I'm buying a beer at the bar, the locals ask, "What's their shark attack story?" They know if I bring a stranger to town, it's usually someone who's been attacked.

My kids and grandkids live in the same town and they're so used to seeing people from different walks of life. They see city kids coming around here, people with missing limbs, people who are much older than I am, some much younger, all hanging out at grandad's place. It's good for them because they are learning about life in a different way as well. They're getting to see people who are coming to terms with life and who are loving life. The positive attitude within most people in our group is awesome.'

CHAPTER 2
MICK BEDFORD

CONSPICUOUS CLIFFS, WALPOLE, WESTERN AUSTRALIA, SUNDAY 6 JUNE 2010

'If I was going to reach my board, I was going to have to climb over the shark.'

For keen surfer Mick Bedford, fifty-three, the presence of sharks near his hometown of Walpole, on Western Australia's south coast, is nothing unusual. When iron ore operator Mick, then forty-one, went to catch some waves with his friend Lee Cummuskey on a clear winter's day at one of his regular spots, Conspicuous Cliffs – a rugged and isolated stretch of the Southern Ocean – he might well have expected to encounter wildlife of some sort …

'We see a lot of sharks there, also whales and seals. Being on the south coast, it's that kind of environment, and dealing with nature is a common occurrence. I've had numerous encounters with sharks over the years. I've had sharks approach me, circle me, swim underneath me, brush against and flick their tails at me. On three or four of those occasions, it was a great white shark.

Where we were surfing was one of my regular spots. It's a beautiful beach, one of the most iconic down there, but, although it's one of the easiest ones to access, it's still isolated.'

It was approaching midday and Mick and Lee were the only people out surfing, taking advantage of the beautiful, still conditions. They were surfing on a beach break, on top of a sandy ocean floor, which meant the water was clear. Where Mick was surfing was reasonably shallow, but a deep channel from the sandbank created several rip currents – and it was in those deeper gutters where sharks sometimes lurked.

'Lee caught a wave but came off his board and was wiped out. His board was washed in, and as he swam in after it, a shark appeared in the channel out of the deep water. I watched it go past me about ten to twelve metres away. It was acting very aggressively. Its fins were out and it looked agitated. It looked at me, went around me and then went into the channel.

"That's good," I thought. Then it disappeared. I was sitting out there on my board, which is larger than standard – a 9-foot-2-inch-long board. Within a minute, the shark was back. It looked about four and a half metres long, and it semi-circled me, staying on the deeper side. Then it went down and curved away from me. Just then, it turned and shot straight up, directly underneath me. Its fins were out, teeth were out, it was like a giant projectile coming straight at me.

It came up directly underneath my board. I moved my right leg out of the way just in time before it hit me, knocking me straight out of the water. I went into a kind of time-lapse situation because I could see every droplet of water as I was in the air. Time just seemed to stop. I then felt enormous pressure on my right leg. The board must have given me some protection, but the shark hit my right leg and the board while I was still in the air.

It let go but then had another bite while I was still in the air. It still had hold of my leg when I came down on top of it. From the impact, it let go and we both ended up together in the water.'

It was only then that Mick started to come to and realise how perilous the situation was. Remarkably, the shark lay still in the water beside him. It was as though it had used up all its energy in the initial strike and now was spent, most likely waiting for its injured prey to give up the fight ...

'It was just sitting there looking at me with its black eyes, pretty much waiting for me to bleed out. I saw my surfboard was on the other side of it. If I was going to reach my board, I was going to have to climb over the shark.

By now, panic set it. I somehow managed to clamber over the shark onto my board but it was upside down and I was now facing the wrong way from the shore. I didn't care though, I just started paddling. I was heading further out to sea but I just wanted to get away from the shark.

I was in shock and screaming. I was so scared.'

From the beach, Lee had seen his friend propelled out of the water and knew immediately what it meant. He was powerless to help as Mick paddled furiously away from where the shark had been. After a few moments, however, Mick turned to see if he could still see it.

'It sank down and disappeared again. I realised then that I was going the wrong way and on the wrong side of my board, which made it very slippery. A wave came through and, because I was facing the wrong way, I came straight off my board and was completely wiped out.

I was back in the zone, in among the white water and bubbles again.

Then I saw the board. It was about ten metres away and I frantically scrambled towards it, managed to grab it and just hung on for dear life as waves smashed over me. I was being taken into the beach, where my friend and some fishermen who happened to be there grabbed me by the shoulders and hauled me ashore. It was then I put my hand down and realised I had a massive hole in my right leg. That's when the pain set in.'

Mick had suffered a cut from the side of his right thigh down to the middle of his leg. He was bleeding profusely, as the shark's jaws had sliced the femoral artery, the main blood vessel from the upper thigh to the back of the knee that supplies blood to the lower body. It hadn't completely severed it.

'I lost about two litres of blood, but if the artery was severed, I might have bled out and died. Down on the beach there was no mobile phone reception, so one of the fishermen's wives ran up the two hundred stairs to the cliff top where she had one bar on her phone. Thankfully, she managed to call the emergency services but it was going to be a while before they reached me.

Up until that moment, I hadn't felt anything, probably due to the adrenalin. Some people say that shark teeth have some sort of anaesthetic when they bite but I don't know about that. The leash to my board had been attached to my leg wrap but that had been ripped off in the attack. It was still attached to my board, though, so I used that as a makeshift tourniquet. The guys found some shirts and other material to pack the wound and try to stop the bleeding,

Everyone wanted to get me off the beach, so they used my board as a stretcher and paddled me up a creek to where they could access the stairs to get me to the car park. That was probably the worst time, waiting for the ambulance to arrive. I wasn't bleeding as much now but I was in shock and cold. It was scary.'

Lee and the fishermen used a tackle box as a pillow and elevated Mick's leg on an esky (cool box). Two hours after the bite, at 2 p.m., the ambulance arrived. To prepare for the 66 km trip west to Denmark and the nearest hospital, paramedics gave Mick a 'green whistle' to suck on. This is the pain relief methoxyflurane – commonly known by its brand name Penthrox and given its nickname due to its shape and colour:

'Unfortunately, it did nothing for the pain, which by then was excruciating. The funny thing was, when we reached the hospital, the doctor had been playing golf and, apparently, wasn't too happy at being called away from the course. She had been told a guy had been bitten by a shark but was pretty relaxed about it. The nurses told her I'd need surgery. She cut away my wetsuit, but when she took off the tourniquet, blood started shooting across the surgery. She told them to send me to the regional hospital in Albany.'

When Mick arrived at Albany, 54 km further west, doctors gave him the grim prognosis that there was a risk he might lose his leg and he had to sign his consent for surgeons to amputate if it was necessary to save his life.

'They cut off the rest of my wetsuit and I was lying there naked, cold and embarrassed. I was then heavily sedated for surgery.

When I woke, however, and saw that my leg was still there, I was stoked. They had managed to save it. I had suffered muscle damage and knee damage though – as well as the sliced femoral artery. Some nerves were severed and I didn't really have any feeling in my leg. For three months I couldn't walk, and it took a further six months before I could really use my leg.'

In addition to the physical challenges, Mick also had to deal with terrifying flashbacks in which he relived his trauma.

'I had nightmares – in particular, a recurring one in which I was in an upturned dinghy with an aluminium hull, and I kept slipping and was trying desperately to get my legs out of the water. I could see the shark coming towards me and I used to wake up in cold sweats all the time.'

As if that wasn't bad enough, Mick had to deal with unwanted attention from the media as word of his ordeal spread.

'I was hounded by the media. They harassed my family, camped in my driveway. They were trying to glorify the attack, sensationalise it and were making up the parts they didn't have. They wanted my opinion on whether sharks should be culled. I decided to give one story to ABC and they sent it all around.'

Mick's incident came during a spate of shark attacks in Western Australia. In the four-year period before and after June 2010, there were seventeen shark attacks and, tragically, seven fatalities. Feeling frustration at not being able to tell his story the way he wanted, he began writing down his experiences, which became a form of therapy.

'I did go through a stage thinking if there were rogue sharks attacking people – like the old *Jaws* thing – and I did wonder if maybe that same shark could be responsible for a lot of attacks at the same time. There was a whole spate of attacks in Western Australia at the same time. But I just don't know if it's that or if it's environmental or climatic or whatever else is causing them. We've had conservation measures for sea lions that have increased the seal population, so that's a food source for great whites. Then there's the issue of overfishing.

It doesn't really gel with me to voice my opinion, though, because when I do, someone will always say something to challenge it. I stopped talking to the media because all they wanted to know was about the killer shark. I never spoke to any psychologist at the time but wrote some of these experiences [with the media] down, together with what had happened to me, as a form of therapy. I never felt I had a chance to tell my story properly before now.

As far as I am concerned, I was in the shark's natural environment. I've been surfing for forty years, seen lots of sharks, and this was the largest one I've ever had to deal with. The aggression was more than I'd handled before. This was a four-and-a-half-metre adult adult shark – not a juvenile or old shark. These sharks are looking for food.

Australia is classic, everywhere you go there is someone in the water. They do eat us, people do get attacked. It's not like I look like a seal or look like its food, but it was waiting for me. It didn't attack me again.

I've since researched shark behaviour, and what happened is what they do with seals – attack it, give it a bite, then swim off and wait for it to bleed out and get weaker. I am a hundred per cent convinced that's what it was going to do to me, if it had the chance.

All the people who have survived have managed to get out of the water quickly. Those that haven't have either bled out from their wound or they have had a heart attack or the shark eats them. I could have been another statistic, for sure. In the water, that was the scariest I have ever been. I was in shock for days. That was the situation I was in.

The initial attack was something I had no control over. It was a massive animal. There was no way I could defend myself other than using the board as a shield. I was lucky I didn't have my leg bitten off straight away. Being in the water with it, I was just screaming. I thought I was a goner for sure. It was like being stalked. I have the scars, some loss of flexibility. Then there's the mental scarring, which I am on top of.'

With surfing such a big thing in Mick's life – something that has been important for his mental wellbeing – a huge hurdle for him to overcome was the fear of getting back into the water for the first time after the attack.

'There was definitely anxiety with it and some mental issues but I've tried to keep strong. My daughter started surfing around the same time and I didn't want her to go in the water. But I made myself go back to surfing a year after. I made myself do it. My family and friends have been supportive, so it's been a good outcome.

It is one of those primal fears of man to be attacked, especially by something that wants to eat you – and I've lived through it. Over the years, the flashbacks have waned, and when I go into the water I'm a bit smarter now with what I do. Every day I still deal with that anxiety and the feelings associated with it, but surfing is something I love doing and it's not going to stop me from doing it. It's a total release from normal life. If you're thinking about anything else while you're surfing, you can't surf. You have to break away from any thought pattern and – although this may sound stupid to non-surfers – become one with the wave and one with yourself. I think it is fantastic. Surfing allows you to break away from your day-to-day routine, family stresses, pressures at work, whatever they are. It's selfish in a way, but I can come home from a high-stress job, go for a surf and it's all washed away.

I feel calm and relaxed. It's good for your mental health and physical health as well.'

At the time that Mick was bitten, there was no such thing as Bite Club. It was many years later that Dave Pearson reached out to Mick, and he has been grateful for the support the group offers.

'I joined Bite Club in 2021. I've found it really good to talk to people who have gone through similar experiences. It's amazing, in fact, that so many people are out there in the same situation. There are more recent cases where people have just been attacked, and there are ones that were attacked years ago and still have no feeling in their legs or arms or are struggling to get back in the water. I have tried to help people and

CHAPTER 3
AMY TATSCH

JUAN PONCE DE LEÓN LANDING,
MELBOURNE BEACH, BREVARD COUNTY,
FLORIDA, USA, THURSDAY 15 MAY 2014

*'God, please let me get back to shore
so they know why I am going to die.'*

Mum-of-six Amy Tatsch loved living by the sea. Since moving out to Florida from Dayton, Ohio, in 1984, the beach had been her happy place. Just a short stroll from her home, it was her favourite spot to bodyboard (or boogieboard, as it's also known), go for six-mile walks or just sit and soak up the rays while her children played. One day, in May 2014, all that changed.

'It was 11.20 a.m. and we'd been at the beach since around 9.30. I was there with my dad Richard, my brother Rick, my youngest twins Ava and Charlie, and my aunt and cousin who were in town from Texas that day. My cousin Abby was training to be a nurse at the time.

My aunt Lori hadn't wanted to go into the water because a great white shark that was being tracked, called Catherine, was off our shore, but I told her not to worry as it was so far out. So, she came boogieboarding with my brother and me. She rode a couple of waves but my brother and I were still out there. There was no one else in the water.

I got an eerie feeling. Everything kind of went weird and quiet and I sensed that I needed to get to shore. A huge wave approached that I was going to take, but then I saw the wave behind was even bigger, so I decided to wait for that. Right as I was ready to ride the wave, I lifted my left leg to pivot around to take the wave, and that's when a shark bashed into my leg above my knee with his nose. It then reached under and ripped half my calf off.

I saw the blood just gushing out and then I saw the shark as he left. He let go and swam away. At that point, all I could do was try to scream to get my brother out of the water. The pain was so excruciating, I couldn't get anything out, no voice would come. I couldn't scream, it was just like a whisper.

I just wanted to get my brother out of the water. I was afraid he was going to get attacked as well. I stood there, looked at my leg and wrapped my skin back around. I held on to my calf. But I was in shock so I didn't move.

All I did was look up and say, "God, please let me get back to shore so they know why I am going to die."

I didn't want to drown and have them think I wasn't a good swimmer. That was the thought in my mind. I figured I wasn't going to make it. Finally, I told myself, "Amy, get on your boogieboard and try to get back to shore."

And that's what I did. With one hand holding my calf on and the other on my boogieboard, I managed to get to the shore.

I had drifted down the beach but there was a beachgoer coming up, so I said, "Please go back there and tell my family to get my brother out of the water and call 911. I got attacked by a shark."

He went off and did that. I saw my cousin Abby run over to me. I told her to get Rick out of the water. She told my dad to do that and, once I saw Rick was out of the water, I lay down. I didn't pass out but I didn't speak again.

My dad, cousin and another beachgoer made tourniquets out of T-shirts and Abby tied them to my leg. My aunt called 911 but it took them a while to figure out what beach I was at because they were going off her cell phone area code from Texas. As we waited for the EMTs [Emergency Medical Technicians] to come, I remember my dad poking me in the chest, trying to make sure I stayed coherent.'

Amy's right calf had been bitten severely; a large chunk of muscle was removed and her Achilles tendon was torn. Brevard County Fire Rescue EMTs arrived on scene.

'By the time the EMTs got there, it had started to rain, and as they were walking me on a stretcher, the medic who was walking backwards slipped in the sands. I fell and my head hit the ground. They said they were going to have to call the helicopter to airlift me.

At that point, I started trying to say anything I could. They were trying to figure out my age and the first words out of my mouth were, "Thirty-six."

I didn't want to go in the helicopter. I just didn't.

They were asking me my name but all I could manage was real slow talking. When the ambulance arrived, my blood pressure was 270/185. They were afraid I was going to stroke out. [The reading suggested a hypertensive crisis that could also lead to a heart attack or other life-threatening condition.]

I got to the hospital and ended up in the trauma unit. They had to do five surgeries to save my leg. I still have half my calf missing, but they saved my leg. They did a good job sewing me up but there was a real possibility of amputation. I had so many bacteria in my bloodstream, I had to have blood and plasma transfusions. I was in the hospital for a week and a half. Two days after I got out, I had to go back in. I was in so much pain because the Achilles tendon was severed. They had a splint on the top of my leg to make sure it wouldn't bend, and as the swelling went up and down, the splint was digging in and hitting a nerve. They took me back in to refit me for another splint.'

Amy was confined to a wheelchair initially, and it was four months before she could walk without crutches. It was extremely hard for her, a single mum, to raise her children, Amanda, elder twins Christopher and David, Matthew, and younger twins Ava and Charlie.

'My babies wanted to know why I couldn't pick them up, get them out of the crib and take care of them. It was very difficult but my dad stepped in while I was in the hospital and recovering. He stayed at my house and looked after my babies. He ended up getting cancer not long after I started walking again, and died on 23 June 2015. That was tough because he was my best friend throughout. He was there for me through the whole thing.'

The psychological impact of the attack has been particularly hard. Amy suffered nightmares that took her back into the water with the shark and debilitating panic attacks that led to full-blown post-traumatic stress disorder (PTSD).

'I've tried to make a little light of it by saying that PTSD is "post-traumatic shark disorder". That's what I call it. It will soon be eight and half years and I still have nightmares. I'm back in the water, reliving it.

The beach is my happy place, or it was my happy place. Every time I go there, all I do is worry about everybody who's in the water. I can't stop worrying that something is going to happen to them. If something happens, what can I do to help, so they don't have to go through what I went through?

I walked with a limp for quite a while – I'm just a little bit shorter on the right side than the left now – and it still hurts every day. The nerve damage, the pain and my depression is really bad. I'm happy to be here and be able to tell my story, given I thought I wouldn't survive, but it has been an ongoing thing with the depression. I don't care about the scar on my leg. I'm happy that's there, but it is the PTSD that's really hard. It just doesn't go away.'

Amy joined Bite Club not long after it started, and being part of a global support group has provided her with much-needed comfort.

'Bite Club has been the most wonderful, most amazing family I could ever have wished for. We have private groups where we can chat. We've got so many different people all around the world with different degrees, whether it be in psychology or guidance counselling; while others were involved in an attack or have lost a family member because of an attack. Everybody helps each other out. I just don't know what I'd do without the group. It's amazing. People are actually coming together to help and support other people they don't even know. It's absolutely wonderful.'

Amy was too scared to go back into the water until May 2016, one year after her attack. She forced herself to overcome her fears on a date she now calls her 'sharkiversary'.

'I had to get back to the beach on my own. Nobody saw me. The first time was a real struggle. I was in fear; I had tears in my eyes. I still go out on the water once a year, on my sharkiversary. I go out on the same boogieboard and I get myself enough courage to ride one wave, maybe two, and that's it. I'm a water baby. I love the water.

I know I was in their territory. I don't have any issues with that. I know where I was, but I've lived here since '84 and I never thought it would happen – but now that it has happened, I worry about everybody in the water now. I don't want anybody to have to go through that.'

One of the biggest impacts on Amy's life post-attack has been the financial burden. She was denied state assistance because she didn't fit the criteria for either physical or mental disability aid.

'I was working prior to the shark attack as a baker in the cafeteria at the school. I loved it because my four older children went to school there. I ended up taking a leave of absence when I was pregnant with my second set of twins. After my leave of absence, I was going to go back to work but I got attacked by the shark. I didn't have any more leave of absence, so I wasn't able to work there.

I have a hard time standing for too long, so it's really hard for me to find anywhere I can work and be able to sit down. That's not how it goes. I haven't been able to work and so, as far as finances go, that makes it really tough. I have a GoFundMe page because I'm trying to make ends meet.

I inherited my dad's house when he passed away but I still have to keep up with property taxes and bills. With me raising my children and my ex-husband working all the time, I didn't have enough work credits to get disability, so I was fighting for supplemental disability. I was denied after spending four and a half years fighting my case, so I have start the process all over again, which is very difficult to do. I'm not going to stop, though. I am going to continue to try to fight it.

One of the reasons the state doesn't recognise my PTSD is because I'm not going to a therapist locally to have it documented. But I don't have the money. I'd have to travel to Orlando, an hour and a half away [to see a state-appointed therapist], and I don't have the means to do that.

My brother has two master's degrees, one in counselling and one in psychology, so he's been a really good help for me to talk to. But they don't recognise that. I didn't wish for this to happen. It's not like I was on my motorcycle, driving crazy – I actually had to sell my motorcycle because I can't ride on two wheels any more because of my leg.

My vehicle hasn't worked for five weeks, so I can't even get to doctor's appointments right now. All I can do is pray every day that something's going to work out and I'm going to be able to keep my house.

I used to love work, I loved my job, and that's a big part of the depression because I am not physically able to do what I used to … I used to walk three to six miles a day on the beach. Every evening. Six miles if I was by myself, three miles if I had my children with me. I literally can walk to the beach, I live so close. It was my getaway from reality and now it's just something that my triggers my anxiety. I start having panic attacks.

The PTSD is a really strong thing that causes massive depression and I don't have an outlet. Everything triggers it because I live beachside. Everybody – even little kids and grown-ups – wears shirts with sharks on them. They're just little cute sharks, but the triggers are constant. I even tried to stop looking at the Facebook group for a little while, thinking that that would help me, but it made me worse. I maybe only went a month not looking at the posts, text messages and stories, but I went back, because the group has me doing something productive for others. I can explain to other people and let them know, just as everyone else in the group does, that we are all trying to work together, to work through, to support each other and be on each other's sides.

I met the parents of one girl who lives near me in Satellite Beach. She was only seventeen when she lost her leg to a shark. I wish I could have taken her place but she is doing great.'

When Amy reflected on the attack, she discovered there were potential indicators not to go into the water that day. And she has been able to identify the species of shark that bit her.

'I took measurements [the bite indicated a jaw diameter of 11 inches or 29.7 centimetres] and George Burgess, a now-retired fisheries biologist with the University of Florida, said it was a 6-foot [1.8-metre] bull shark, based on the attack.

There were factors. I didn't realise them at the time. That particular day was overcast, the water was murky, there were dark clouds and a little rain. The waves were quite big ... too big, maybe, even for surfers. When I went under the wave, I think the commotion is what drew the shark's attention to me. I guess it was just lack of knowledge on my part not to go out when it was murky and overcast.'

Shark attacks most commonly fall into three categories: Hit and run – or bite and release – is the most common. A shark will usually attack in an area close to shore where swimmers and surfers are the most likely targets. The victim often doesn't see the shark, and it often just inflicts a single bite and leaves, in a likely case of mistaken identity.

Bump and bite attacks are less common but can lead to most fatalities. The victims are often divers or swimmers in deeper waters. The shark bumps into a person before it attacks.

Sneak attacks are similar to bump and bites, but here the shark attacks without warning.

Amy is in no doubt what type of attack she suffered.

'It bashed into my leg, like it was stunning its prey, before it tore my leg. I think it let me go because I didn't taste good to him or her. It wasn't a bite and release. It was an inch at the bottom of my leg and an inch and half at the top away from losing my whole calf.'

Despite the hardships she has faced, Amy remains upbeat and is forever grateful to the many people – and objects – that saved her life that day and to the group that continues to offer hope and support.

'My cousin Abby and my dad used three different T-shirts as a tourniquet. There's a tank top from the beachgoer, my cousin's shirt and my dad's shirt. They've been washed; they're very stained but I just can't get rid of them. It might sound odd but I just can't. That's what saved my life. That and the boogieboard saved my life. I still have the same one.

When I got out of the hospital, my main concern was to make sure my brother brought my boogieboard home. Why I'm here right now is the boogieboard and those T-shirts.

My dad, who stayed at my house and looked after my babies and was there for me through the whole thing. My brother was in the water with me. He's Rick Tatsch. He's been helping me out and supporting me. And Abby – that was a huge learning experience for her. The fire department also did an amazing job that day. And the surgeons at the hospital – they did a really great job. And, as for Bite Club ... the bottom line is that this group has been the most amazing resource for the last eight and a half years of my life.

Despite it all, I keep my chin up. That's all I can do.'

CHAPTER 4
LAUREL-ROSE VON HOFFMANN-CURZI

LAKE TAHOE, CALIFORNIA, USA,
SATURDAY 30 OCTOBER 2021

*'This was endless terror. More and more pain
from many directions in the dark. I had no idea
what or where he would claw or bite next.'*

Laurel-Rose had been around bears all her life – just never in her own house before.

The sixty-seven-year-old retired physician is a fifth-generation Californian. Having a grandfather who owned a gold mine nearly three thousand metres up in the Sierra Nevada mountains, she was raised with a knowledge of how to exist in the wilderness and what precautions to take to prevent bears getting too close. She and husband Mario Curzi, a sixty-eight-year-old nephrologist (kidney specialist), acquired a vacation cabin in Lake Tahoe – a three-hour drive away from their home in the San Francisco Bay area. They were careful not to do anything to attract the black bears in the area, which had been growing increasingly bolder thanks to the carelessness of tourists and residents alike.

'The family gold mine was in the middle of nowhere, where we took water out of the stream, there was no electricity and just a very primitive dirt road to get there. Although the mine was not active when I was there as a child, there was a bear trap that had been there since the mining days of the twenties and thirties. When I went backpacking as a teenager and young adult, bears were always an issue. You would hang your food in a particular way so the bears wouldn't get into it and you were always cognisant that bears were in the forest.

Then, during a backpacking trip in Tennessee, where I went to medical school, I encountered a bear in camp that was fairly aggressive. One night, two days into the hike, we hung our food in the prescribed way, between two trees up on a rope, and the bear came into camp, went up one tree, jumped on the rope, which broke, sending the food swinging to the other tree, where it managed to retrieve the lot, leaving us to survive on dehydrated soup for the remaining two days of the hike.

While on a horseback trip into Mono Creek, in the High Sierras, we were meticulous about how we managed our food and toothpaste, and, even on a pretty steep pass, every night there were bear footprints about seven inches from my head on the other side of the tent. Anything with odour went into metal bear boxes.

When the bears came into camp, a little dog would start barking and the lead packer cracked his bullwhip. The startling sounds and a flashlight were enough to scare the bear off.

These bears were not habituated to human food because people were careful about keeping it locked up. But in the Tahoe area, which has one of the densest populations of black bears in the country, they have overpopulated because people have, unfortunately, been careless with food, trash and picnics. It's the big tourist destination for people in the San Francisco area. So, there are lots of bears and they are not afraid of people. And, in recent years, they have become much bolder. They are wild animals, but a lot of people have no comprehension of that.

I knew they'd been near the cabin because we'd seen some from our deck and we'd found some faeces. You'd hear about cars that had been broken into. A bubblegum wrapper will cause them to smash the windows and get into a car. Often, the car is completely destroyed once they are inside. They are always looking for food. They need over twenty thousand calories a day in the fall, getting ready for hibernation. And the ones that have grown up in the Tahoe basin have learnt to live off human food and garbage. They break into trash cans and scare people away from picnic tables. Their sense of smell is exceptional and can detect a scent from a mile away, which is extraordinary.

What is not well publicised in Lake Tahoe is that bears break into about one house a day up there, usually empty homes. The local, full-time residents of Tahoe maintain that tourists have "created" these bad bears. And yet, next door to us are full-time residents who rented and didn't have a bear box – the heavy, metal receptacle you need for your trash cans, the opening of which is too slim for a bear paw. They were putting their trash cans out and having the garbage spewed around every week.

Behaviour like that brought the bears right next to our house on a regular basis.'

'It was just ... awful ... absolutely terrifying ... this powerful creature attacking me in absolute darkness.'

Although the increasingly bold bear behaviour was a concern, Laurel-Rose and her family continued to enjoy their cabin, visiting regularly, on average, once a month and on major holidays. The cabin had been a particular place of respite for Laurel-Rose after she was diagnosed with B-cell lymphoma, a type of cancer, in March 2021.

'We'd meet our adult children and grandchildren there. And, since COVID has been around, it's been the only place I go because of my risk of infection. I have got a 50 per cent chance of dying if I get COVID so I've been isolating.

Although it is not curable, it is a slow growing type of lymphoma. In the very luckiest possibilities, it has a ten-to-fifteen-year prognosis, but it has a 20 per cent chance of turning into an aggressive lymphoma.'

The day before Hallowe'en in 2021, Laurel-Rose, Mario and their youngest son, Michael, thirty, who lives north of Lake Tahoe, arrived at the cabin in the evening after dinner. The property is spread over two and a half levels, with ground-floor entry and steps to the first level. The main living area is another level up. No food was kept in the garage or lower level.

'We put all the food we brought in the refrigerator. There was no trash or cooking, so no particular odours. The only thing left out was a bag of unripe of avocados. When we went to bed, I was in the master bedroom, which is on the opposite side of the stairway from the great room that encompasses the kitchen, dining area and living room.

At five in the morning, I was awakened by a loud crashing, banging sound. I couldn't imagine what it was. I thought perhaps it was our son, doing something in the kitchen. It was really loud and it sounded like something was going to break. I was a bit annoyed, so I got up and came out of the bedroom. It was dark. I came across the top of the stairs into the great room area.

The only light was a very dim glow from the open side-by-side freezer door, illuminating the back of a standing – and very large – black bear. It was taking things out of the freezer and flinging them on the floor. That was what was creating the loud, pounding, crashing sound.

The bear, apparently, did not like frozen meat. That was very clear.

It all happened in a moment.

It turned, saw me and flew at me. There was no real pause, no real time to do all the things that people counsel you to do. I opened the door, walked over, saw it was a bear and it just flew at me. I saw one large paw before he started tearing me up. I couldn't see anything. I could just feel what were like knives and blades gripping at me. He tore my face wide open and right all over my neck – my breast, my abdomen, the back of my arm, my back. It was just … awful … absolutely terrifying … this powerful creature attacking me in absolute darkness.

I started screaming and screaming. And I don't scream. I've had various situations where I've had broken bones and all kinds of things, and I've never screamed for any of these things. I couldn't stop screaming. I had suffered pain before, but this was unending terror. It was not the worst pain in my life – that was when I suffered a shattered right femur [thigh bone] in a skiing accident in 1998 at Alpine Meadows Ski Resort by Lake Tahoe, which almost cost me my leg. Childbirth was nothing in comparison to that pain. But this was endless terror. More and more pain from many directions in the dark. I had no idea what or where he would claw or bite next. I could not see anything. I had no idea when or how it would end.

Then he stopped mauling me.

I was able to get over to the wall where I knew the light switches were. There are two of them. I kind of groped around – and later saw where my bloody handprints had been on the wall. I got the lights on and could see him going down a few stairs. Then it stopped and turned around to come back up.

All the dogma you read about black bears says, first of all, if you encounter one in your home, speak softly and get out of their way, and they will go out the way they came in. I hadn't been in his way. He had flown at me anyway. I didn't say a word until he started flaying me, and then I screamed. That is a perfectly fine thing to do once they attack you, as they will go away – they say.

But he turned around to come back at me, which is a predatory thing to do. And that terrified me even more. I was standing at the railing above the stairway. There was a quilt hanging on that railing and I threw it over his head. It was the only thing that was there and the only thing, at that moment, I could think of to do. It must have startled him, as he turned around and went back down the stairs. He got most of the way to the bottom and stopped. Then he turned around again and started to come back up.

I was screaming the whole time; I just could not stop screaming. At this point I had awakened my husband, who had been sleeping with me upstairs in the bedroom, and my son, who was sleeping downstairs. They both appeared from their bedrooms.

The bear, I guess, decided three-on-one was too much. He turned back around and slowly sauntered out the hallway towards the front door and left …

I'm really lucky to be alive. The blow to my head and face was pretty horrific. He got me right between the carotids [arteries on the left and right sides of the neck]. I have a port that's used for my chemotherapy – a line that goes right into my heart – that he just missed. He bit and crushed my breast, which subsequently led a week or so later to an abscess.

I took a substantial blow and puncture to the abdomen. Even though my face was torn wide open, it was the abdominal injury that concerned me the most because of my enlarged spleen. I'd been warned by my oncologist to cease all activities that would put me at risk of a splenic rupture – so all sport, or any activity where I might fall or rupture it, were out because a splenic rupture can cause death immediately … he didn't mention getting a blow from a bear in the belly!

After the bear left, I briefly saw myself in the mirror. It was pretty horrifying. From my nose to my mouth was just wide open. I thought, Boy, I'm going to be wearing a Phantom of the Opera mask for the rest of my life!

As my son called 911, my husband got some facecloths to compress the wounds to stop the bleeding. The paramedics were there in minutes and carried me in a sling down to an ambulance. When I left the house, I was covered in blood. It wasn't clear that I was going to live; it wasn't clear that my spleen hadn't been ruptured. I left the house bleeding everywhere in an ambulance, and people had already gathered outside.'

Within thirty minutes of the attack, Laurel-Rose was at the local community Tahoe Forest hospital, where doctors conducted a CAT scan on her head and abdomen, irrigated her wounds and gave her a tetanus shot and antibiotics. But, in many ways, they were ill-equipped to deal with trauma of this nature.

'That was a story in itself. The folks at the community hospital had not seen bear injuries like this. There had been a few bear maulings before, but they're not that common. The staff taking care of me were horrified, fascinated, curious. On the surface, I was joking around with the nurses about various things, but inside, I was focused on self-preservation.

In the emergency room, they did give me a tetanus shot but didn't think to give me antibiotics. I raised that as something I really wanted. The doctor in me was running through a checklist of what needed to be done. I was furiously going through things like infections and the fact I had lymphoma and the risk of internal bleeding risk. Pain-wise, it definitely hurt, but my biggest concern – after the risk of splenic rupture – was how was this going to play into infection with the lymphoma, because I certainly was at very high risk.

One thing nobody seemed to know was what bacteria are in the mouth of the bear. The best guess was that they treat it like a dog bite, which was pretty much what was done, with a little bit of broadening of the antibiotics. I wanted the CAT scan immediately to see if I needed a splenectomy. Fortunately, the puncture was just to the peritoneum but not through it, so my spleen was OK.

The facial laceration was so complex and deep it was not something they were prepared to handle at this hospital, and they frantically went to look for a trauma centre that could care for that. They were able to find the University of California Davis Medical Center in Sacramento. UC Davis is a huge hospital – with at least a hundred-bed emergency room.

I thought I'd be seen by plastics [plastic, reconstructive surgeons], but they had the trauma team and then the ear, nose and throat specialist to see me. The doctor who sewed me up did an incredible job. He did multiple layers of sutures to pull things together very nicely. They also gave me different antibiotics there.

I was released at about 7p.m. A daughter of my close physician friend was training at Davis and she came by to check on me. She sent back a message to her mother that I was fine because I was entertaining the doctors there! If that was the case, they must have been doing something right.

But there were some things they missed, though. When I had time to analyse what happened, it occurred to me what needs to be done in situations like this: to protect my modesty, they had thrown a gown on me in the ER, but, in doing so, they actually missed some of my injuries. It wasn't until I was home later that we discovered that I had been clawed up on my back and upper arm, and one on my upper chest. The hospital didn't even know about those. They should strip somebody completely naked and look all over, but everybody was so concerned about the bigger injuries that those were missed.

I was actually lucky I stayed standing when the bear attacked. Some of the dogma says that if a bear attacks, you should drop down and play dead. But that applies to a grizzly or brown bear. With a black bear, you want to stay standing and make yourself as big as possible and fight back. I did stay standing and made a noise. That may well be what saved me. I feel lucky that it was me and not one of my grandchildren or somebody smaller.

I tried to get information from the state about what they knew from their biologist about the bacteriology of bear bites and bear mouths. They never got back to me. I did some research online and there is information about grizzly bears, and what's there is dependent on the season and what they are feeding on. I did get some information about various bites back from a cousin who is an infectious disease doctor, but that was the best I could get. It was interesting that there was not much else there.'

'People gathered to harass us, to blame
the victim, which was something I was
more unprepared for than the bear attack.'

Like many animal attack survivors, Laurel-Rose's physical injuries were only one part of her trauma. While victims whose stories have attracted media attention often must deal with negative online comments, Laurel-Rose and her family were immediately targeted by animal activists outside their door.

'One of the very worst parts of this whole thing was that within a couple of hours, my son, who was still at the cabin at this point by himself because my husband had followed me to the hospital, was being harassed by neighbours, being shouted at and called a "bear killer". People gathered at the front of the house to harass us, to blame the victim, which was something I was more unprepared for than the bear attack. It was unbelievable! The impact on me was much, much worse than from the bear. It happened when I was still in the hospital.

There is an organised group that love the bears and have that feeling that the bears were here first and they can do anything they want. What they forget is that the bears co-existed with the Native Americans for thousands of years. There was a balance there. A bear that came into camp was immediately killed and worshipped – and eaten. The fur was used for warmth, for bedding; the skin was used; they made ropes. The Native Americans honoured the bear. It was not exterminated but neither was it overpopulated.

Right now, the deer population in California is at its lowest number. It has been beaten down this far because bears and mountain lions have been allowed to overpopulate the state. The bears eat the baby deer and the deer eat the foliage, the fronds and grasses. So, the wildfire danger goes up with this overpopulation of bears. But the organisation, which has over twenty thousand members, has this misguided sense of letting the bears do anything and everything – including letting the bears attack you in your own kitchen. This is the bears' place and this is the way it has been, they say – but it's not. It is a fantasy. Within a matter of minutes of what happened to me, they pulled our address and had large groups of people coming to our home.'

While Laurel-Rose was still in the ER, a warden from the California Department of Fish and Wildlife visited to hear what had happened. He then went to the cabin to take DNA samples to try and track the bear responsible, as the law in California prescribes that the bear be euthanised if caught. A baited trap was put outside the cabin to lure the animal back, but activists sabotaged it.

'Two things can be done once the bear is caught – either relocate it, which is done in many states, or euthanise the bear.

When bears that have been raised by their mothers on garbage and human food are relocated way into the wilderness, they will either become somebody else's problem – because bears can travel hundreds of miles into another community – or they will starve to death because they don't know how to live on wild food. So, it can actually be cruel to take a bear that's been purely raised in Tahoe basin and put it out further into the wild.

There was a bear known as the "Safeway Bear". About half a mile from our home was a Safeway grocery store with automatic doors. This bear figured out that if you walked up to the door, it opened, so he could walk in and help himself to – guess what – avocados. A sign was put up in front of the store: "Beware of bear". Eventually, they captured the bear and relocated him. Over the course of a winter, I believe, the bear stumbled into a camp where there was a group, including a number of children. The bear was extremely aggressive, appeared quite dangerous, and a man shot and killed it. A biologist subsequently found the bear was extremely emaciated. It was basically starving because it hadn't known how to survive in the wild. It was concluded that this was an example of why it was cruel to relocate a bear that was used to living in Safeway. There have been other bears in the Tahoe area that have learned the same thing. One used to go into convenience stores.

Other bears that happen to come into a human-bear conflict and know how to live in the wild can be relocated. For them, that's not a bad solution. The law in California states that a bear in this situation should be trapped and euthanised. Therefore, in the eyes of some, it is my fault that a bear should die. The trap that was set was sabotaged. Bears don't like certain chemicals, like bleach or ammonia, so they put chemicals on it. The trap was replaced and guarded and it caught a female bear and cub. It was the wrong bear, so they were released.'

After a few days, the Department of Fish and Wildlife removed the trap without informing Laurel-Rose's family.

'They had cameras there to make sure the protesters didn't harm our home. They removed those and just disappeared without telling us anything. Finally, Fish and Wildlife were so bullied they became impotent. The warden involved with us moved out of town because he and his family had been so harassed with death threats. This happened to Fish and Wildlife and basically rendered the department impotent. This was the biggest surprise – a shock and real trauma to me was what was going on with the politics. We had human faeces smeared in our driveway and bear scat thrown against our cabin. This "hate the victim" was unbelievable.

I contacted the spokesperson for the Department of Fish and Wildlife. He told me the bear that came into our house was clearly frightened and undoubtably long gone. I don't believe that. Once a bear has found a source of food, they come back. They don't leave the area. The state has an obligation to find and euthanise a bear that has attacked a human.

There are different kinds of encounters. If I had been dangling a piece of food in front of a bear and been mauled, that would have been a different encounter than having a bear enter my home and mauling me. And being in front of the bear's exit would be different than not blocking the bear's exit. Which I wasn't. And having the bear exit versus having the bear turning around a couple of times to come back in, is a different kind of thing. This bear, on multiple counts, is a much more dangerous animal than a bear that claws somebody because they are dangling food in front of it.

The problem has been increasing and somebody is going to die. I am one of the few people that have the nerve to speak out about it openly.

There have been several other encounters this summer [2022] and people refused to let their names or details be released. They did euthanise a bear. I think the writing is on the wall that someone is going to die: a woman went out of her home at noon to take the trash out. In that brief period, a bear entered her home, and, as she went back in the house, it came back towards the front door, scratched her up and left. The bear climbed a tree and ended up being euthanised. The Fish and Wildlife Department actually acted in that case, which they haven't done in a long time. The bear was easily found, and they were able to do it before the Bear League could stop them.'

The Bear League is a non-profit organisation based in the Lake Tahoe basin that believes in 'people living in harmony with bears'. The league acknowledges, 'Too many bears now believe they can roam neighbourhoods and even come into houses,' but claims bears do this because of 'humans reacting inappropriately during bear encounters, which often results in the death of a bear'. In a response to Laurel-Rose's attack, the league posted an article on its Facebook page, remarkably, telling the story from the bear's point of view. In the post, the 'bear' claimed to have smelled the 'ripening avocadoes', did not know the cabin was occupied, found a door that was not secure, went inside and found the ice cream, which it was happily eating until Laurel-Rose disturbed it and started screaming. The post also claimed Laurel-Rose blocked the bear's exit in a narrow passageway, leaving it no option but to push her out of the way. The Bear League went on to state that it believed the story had been sensationalised to demonise bears. Laurel-Rose disagrees.

'It was the most absurd thing, saying that he accidently came in, didn't know it was an occupied cabin and was just trying to get something to eat because he was hungry. There were hundreds of comments afterwards: it was all my fault; I was making noise; we had all sorts of smells; we had tempted it with nice-smelling food on the windowsill; I did not have the deadbolt closed on the house.

The cabin door was closed and latched; the deadbolt was not closed, but the same night, a bear had pulled off the entire door of a house three doors down – the entire door off the frame – so it is not like the deadbolt makes any difference in the world. I did not make a sound until he sprang at me and started to maul me, at which point I began to scream. There was no narrow passage. I was not in the bear's way. He did not just push me aside. He clawed me multiple times, at least five times, and bit me twice, hard, causing deep punctures, crush injuries and a laceration on my breast. The clawing of my face went through from the skin into my nose to the corner of my mouth. There were punctures from the claws inside my lower lip. The bite stopped just at the peritoneum. About a week later, despite being on heavy antibiotics, I developed an increasing mass in my left breast where I'd been bitten and a smaller one in my left abdomen.

We had a hard time getting the ultrasound we needed. It was going to take days in the medical system. I ended up getting my husband, who had a machine he uses for kidneys, to ultrasound my breast, which found the cyst. So the assertion that everything was fine medically was not quite true. It was a little dicey, in fact.

This bear was not fearful.

The Bear League minimises the bear as a problem. They say that if you do everything right, there is no problem. You should just back away, not block the bear or the entrance, and there is no problem. Bears don't attack people, they say. There are things that the Bear League stands for that I agree with, like educating people about how to manage their garbage and food correctly. I totally agree with that.

I think there are legislative and municipal ordinances that should be enacted with penalties about how to manage your trash cans and what to do with tourists. For instance, with Airbnb you have a deposit for damage to the cabin. They should have a deposit for mismanagement of your garbage, a trash-bear deposit. If your garbage gets thrown all over the street because you didn't manage it correctly, you lose two hundred dollars or something. You should sign something that shows you are being aware and you know what you have to do. You can educate people. They did this in Yellowstone Park and the bear-human interactions went down.

The use of bear spray, which is like a powerful Mace, should be advocated more, to make them less comfortable around people, especially if you are hiking in the area, because bears have become very complacent with people and vice versa. It's not a good thing. People think they are so cute – they want to take a selfie with a bear. Bears are wild animals. Bears might want to be close to you but that is not a good thing.

The Bear League should not go around bullying the Fish and Wildlife Department. The Department of Fish and Wildlife had a complaint in the South Lake Tahoe community. Thirty-six homes had been repeatedly broken into. The community was in an uproar and wanted the bear to be euthanised or removed. The bear was called "Hank the Tank". The department did some DNA analysis and found it was actually three bears causing the damage. The Bear League got involved and were going to remove them and take them to Colorado where they had a place for bad bears, but that turned out not to be the case. So, nothing was done.

The reality is there are 300–500 bears in the Tahoe basin and only a handful of bears cause damage and are a threat to people. So, it is not like you are going to eliminate the species if you take away the handful of bad bears.'

Contrary to what she was told by the Department of Fish and Wildlife spokesperson, Laurel-Rose is convinced the bear that attacked her is still at large and was responsible for other incidents in the area.

'The one that was in our neighbourhood broke into the house across the street three times. She has a large dog, and he was there on two occasions. She happened to be in a different room when the bear came in and she was able to get a hold of another neighbour who has some large, aggressive dogs. The bear left, knocking a six-foot fence down as it tried to get away from the dogs. She thinks, like the Bear League do, that the bears belong there and wanted their assistance. They told her it was because she had peanut butter in her kitchen and had dogs living in the house. Now she has mixed feelings because she was being blamed for having the bear come in.

It is my suspicion it's the same bear. My nephew is living in my place right now. He is a hunter and very cognisant of different bears in the community. It is his sense that it's the same bear. He has seen this bear several times, and, by the way it behaves, he is fairly sure it is the same bear. It is very aggressive. It is very unusual for a bear to go where there are dogs. They tend not to like dogs. This is the kind of behaviour the bear that mauled me exhibited.

She did not want to report it to the Department of Fish and Wildlife because she did not want the bear euthanised. That's the kind of confused thinking people have. The saying is nobody has died in California from a bear; but it is just luck that it hasn't happened.'

The attack has not put Laurel-Rose off from staying at the cabin but she and her family now take precautions to mitigate against further incidents.

'I have a several deterrents around the place at this point. We have put ammonium Pine-Sol [household cleaning product] in jars with perforated lids around the cabin. We have a quick-release gun safe by the master bedroom. We also have a trip wire with a very loud shrieking noise device that we can hook up outside the front door. The bears are clearly in the neighbourhood.

It is a divided community – the pro-Bear League and the anti-bear-in-my-kitchen. It is not that I dislike bears, but I feel they belong outside, not in my kitchen.'

LAUREL-ROSE VON HOFFMANN-CURZI

'Bite Club people understand.
They respect each other and respect you.'

Faced with the negative reaction from bear activists and the failure of the wildlife department to take decisive action, Laurel-Rose found solace in Bite Club. She hadn't heard about the group until a member saw her story in the media and got in touch through Facebook. From then, she was immediately encouraged by the support she received.

'Bite Club is huge. Once I was put in touch, I described what had happened to me and what was going on with the reactions from the community. But then I heard from people about their interactions with conservation groups that had given them the hate – death threats and the same kind of things.

I received so many messages saying, 'Ignore these ignorant people,' and, 'Atta girl, stay strong,' just all kinds of reassuring support when I really needed it, from people who really understood what was going on. Because you can talk to people about an experience like this and they are sympathetic, but it can be abstract to most people. But it is not abstract to people who have survived an apex predator attack. What these people say is that it really matters, it really means something. They say, tell your story to who will listen, and appreciate the chance to help others who want to learn.

Part of my way of coping with things is to talk about them. But to talk to people who don't get it or who make light of something that's very important, that's the worst. Bite Club people understand. They respect each other and respect you. They may not have experienced exactly the same things, but the thought that somebody respects what you are going through

81

is valuable; the encouragement to stay strong and the acknowledgement that it takes time to heal, and that healing is not just physical but also emotional. It's also coping with different people's reactions. There is a sensational and voyeuristic element to something like this. Everybody wants to have a piece of you because you are interesting. It's useful to get other people's take on these things.

People also share little bits of their humanity – their families, how life goes on. This is nice to see too, because I am not just a bear bite, they are not just a lion bite, not just someone who has lost a leg. I have children and grandchildren. I have a life. I am not defined by my attack. I'm more than that. All of those things come out in the group.

I think Dave [Pearson] is the most amazing person. He has put together something really big that has helped so many people in so many ways. He always seems to have the right thing to say, the right piece of advice for each person. I have nothing but admiration for Dave. He brings out the best in people – and puts people together who can best help each other.'

Laurel-Rose might be the only bear attack survivor in Bite Club but she has one thing in common with other members. She bears no ill feeling against the animal that mauled her.

'There is no animosity against the animals that attacked the members of the group. Quite the opposite. There is more of a sense of balance about it. It's really interesting.'

And Laurel-Rose will continue to tell her story in the hope that it helps educate people on the habits that need to change if they want to avoid a similar attack. In the wake of rising numbers of predatory animals, she believes radical action needs to be taken if deaths are to be prevented.

'The main thing I would say to people is stash your trash. Grizzly bears are more innately aggressive, but black bears don't need to be made that way. Some black bears are naturally predatory, but that's the minority of them. When people are sloppy, wild animals become dependent on human food and get more aggressive as a result. We should be more careful. The bear that got me had thrown frozen meat on the floor but found a bunch of ice cream – Ben & Jerry's, Häagen-Dazs – he had high-class taste! That is what they do. In the cabins they break into, one of the first things they go to is the freezer for ice cream.

Before I was attacked, I had a series of preconceptions about bear conservation. And since I've looked into the issue, I've found things that are completely contrary to those preconceptions. When it comes to the issue of hunting, I thought the hunters would be the least balanced on this. Actually, they are the most balanced group as far as conservation goes, which is completely contrary to my preconception.

They understand the balance of the different groups of animals. You can get tags in California for the different types of animals that can be hunted. It is relatively easy to get deer tags. And the deer population is at an all-time low. You cannot get mountain lion tags, yet the mountain lion population is getting dangerously high. In fact, they are coming into the neighbourhoods in Silicon Valley. One was found in a school classroom. Mountain lions are huge, they are dangerous. The bear population is getting huge. They are getting out of balance. The hunters have a sense of this balance.

The Department of Fish and Wildlife, who I thought were the government organisation that should be concerned about the balance of the natural animals, are actually influenced by politicians and organisations like the Bear League. A lot of my preconceptions have been turned upside down.'

CHAPTER 5
ERIC SCHALL

KAIWI CHANNEL, HAWAII, USA,
MONDAY 18 MARCH 2019

*'As I swam on, I detected this wet,
burning sensation in my stomach.'*

When marathon swimmer Eric Schall was invited by his friend Steve Gruenwald, then a veteran of twenty-nine endurance races, to join him on a swim across the Kaiwi Channel (also known as the Molokai Channel) in Hawaii, he jumped at the chance. The twenty-six-mile challenge across the strait that separates the islands of Oʻahu and Molokaʻi is one of the illustrious Oceans Seven – a marathon swimming challenge that also includes the Cook Strait in New Zealand, the North Channel between Scotland and Ireland in Europe and the Tsugaru Strait in Japan. And Eric, a fifty-eight-year-old ready-mixed concrete producer from Pennsylvania who had by that time competed in fourteen swim races, couldn't resist the opportunity.

'I've been a long-distance open water swimmer for about ten years. I had no ambitions of doing the Oceans Seven because it costs a lot of money and I never envisaged myself swimming in the cold water of the North Sea, but when an accomplished open-water swimmer like Steve calls, you go. He and I share a lot of common interests outside the water. He manufactures high-performance cam shafts for high-performance motor sports vehicles, and I've been a fan of that engineering for a long time. We are the same age and our children have the same names. Steve's also been around marathon swimming for a long period of time, so when he calls to see if you are available for an adventure, it means it's an opportunity to swim with one of the best!'

Eric and Steve's plans were initially disrupted by the weather. High winds meant they were unable to attempt the swim for two weeks until the very last day they had set aside. They began at 6.18 p.m., supported by a kayaker and boat crew who were tracking their progress for social media updates.

'When we made our preparations for a swim, we knew going in that there was a possibility of a presence of tiger sharks and great white sharks in the area. We experienced dolphins, and the whales were breaching [leaping out of the water], as we were entering their migration season. And throughout the night, we were swimming into Portuguese man o' wars, which are like jellyfish and are quite painful. The best way I can describe what that's like is if you were in the forest and walked through some heavy cobwebs. The tentacles get wrapped up like cobwebs. Except, with the man o' war, when you brush them off, they sting you as they come across your body. We'd been swimming for about three hours when Steve was hit by a man o' war. Then an hour or so later, I was hit by them. I kept swimming but Steve got sick so had to come out of the water.'

Eric continued swimming and had made it halfway across the strait when, at approximately 3 a.m., he felt something else ...

'I felt this sharp pain right below by my belly button. I thought I was getting hit by another man o' war. I instinctively went to brush off the cobweb, but when I did, my hand came across a fish. I was able to grab it. It was a few inches in diameter. I could feel it wriggling in my hand when I threw it off. I continued to swim because I still thought it was a man o' war, and you have to put up with those when you're swimming. But as I swam on, I detected this wet, burning sensation in my stomach. I put my hand down and I could feel I had a significant amount of skin removed. I thought it was superficial, but I was concerned because it was burning a lot – maybe because I was in the sea water. I swam over to the kayaker who was escorting me. His name, appropriately, was Ocean.

The rules of open water swimming say that if you hang onto the kayak, the swim is over. I didn't want to touch the kayak, but I said, "Ocean, I think something's not right here; I think something bit my stomach."

He said, "Hang on to the bow of the boat and roll over onto your back and we'll take a look."

We were using red lights rather than white because we didn't want to attract more fish. He shone his light down onto my stomach, and as soon as he saw it, he got onto the marine radio and yelled over to the boat, "Cookiecutter shark! Cookiecutter shark!"

I don't know how he knew the bite was from a cookiecutter shark, but he is a waterman and there is a mystique and a valued relationship that the Hawaiians have with their water.'

The cookiecutter shark – also known as the cigar shark due to its cylindrical body – measures only between 42–56 cm in length and is found in warmer ocean waters. For its size, it can inflict serious damage in the shape of circular bites that look almost as if they were created by a cookie cutter.

'The motorboat that leads the kayaker stopped immediately, reversed its engines and came back to us. I then had to navigate my way over to the boat and try to get in. The swell was between one and three feet that night. I was trying to get in the boat with a shark bite, in choppy seas. One of the other paddlers, Nacho, grabbed me by the arm and lifted me up into the boat. We found a flat place for me to lie down on my back, and Nacho grabbed a compress, jumped on my stomach and stayed there the whole way back to Honolulu. Another crew member I used to assist me was Lynn Goldsmith, who was a nurse, thank goodness, and she held me until we got back.'

When the boat arrived in Honolulu, the Hawaiian capital, Eric still believed his wound was only superficial and he would soon be patched up and be able to go back to their rented accommodation.

'This is how stupid I was, but I still hadn't seen the wound and I didn't know what was going on. I got into the ambulance and could immediately tell there was urgency. We went from the boat launch to Queen's Medical Center in Honolulu. We went into the emergency room, and in the US, that usually means you will have to wait for two or three hours before you are seen. There was no waiting. We were right into surgery. I couldn't believe the urgency of it all.

I only had on a brief-cut bathing suit – as in marathon swimming we are not allowed a wetsuit. I had only worn it once, and as they prepped me for surgery, I said, "Please don't cut it off."

They cut it off anyway!

Before a swim, we cover ourselves in Desitin – baby rash ointment – to stop ourselves burning and overheating, plus it contains a lot of zinc and oil. The nurses couldn't understand why I was covered in this white ointment. They also wanted to know what I was doing out in the middle of the ocean. I thought ocean swimming was a thing in Hawaii, but perhaps it's not among the medical community.

They put me under and I went right into surgery. I had no idea what they were doing. I didn't know the severity of the bite ... When the anaesthesia wore off, I woke up and felt like I was in a movie like *The Hangover* or something. I was completely disoriented. I had been swimming for eight hours and in surgery for two to three hours, and there were lots of doctors and nurses about. My friend Steve, crew member Lynn, and Steve's crew member Janine had all gone back on the boat to the Airbnb we were renting, because they had to pack up to be out that afternoon. I had no phone because that was on the boat that had gone back to the house; I had no clothing because all my pre-swim gear was on the boat; I had no bathing suit because they had cut that off; and I had no friends because they were all back at the house. However, some other friends from the open water swim community stopped by and filled me in on what was going on.'

Eric spent two days in Hawaii recuperating but then had to fly home with an open wound.

'The cookiecutter shark has a mouth about the size and shape of a plunger. It has teeth like a guillotine. When it hits, it clamps its mouth down on you, sucks in and then the teeth slide up and take a chunk out of your body. The mouth turns and pulls and leaves a giant, circle-shaped wound. Mine was fairly deep – about an inch and a half to two inches [3.8–5 cm] deep, six inches [15 cm] across in diameter.

To repair that meant skin grafts, which would mean staying in Hawaii, or it would have meant approximation repairs, which means they undercut what remaining skin is left and stretch the overcut skin that's left together and close the six-inch gap. I wasn't able to take either option in Hawaii because I couldn't afford to stay there for weeks on end. I wouldn't have had the mobility to move if the wound had been sutured together, and I would have had to walk on to an airplane, and so I had to fly home with it open. I had to have an open wound for ten days until I was able to have it surgically repaired in Pennsylvania.

It was a pretty traumatic experience, and then the surgery was fairly traumatic. They went for the approximation option. If they had gone for the skin grafts, I would have had more wounds on my body because they would have borrowed skin from another area. So, they took my whole stomach and sewed it all together. I had to remain in a hunched-over position until the repaired skin that had been stretched over grew as it healed. I was not able to stand up properly because they took three inches [7.6 cm] off my stomach and sewed it back together. The skin couldn't stretch without popping the sutures. That took a while.'

Eric was then faced with a lengthy recovery process. He was left with an eight-inch [20 cm] scar across his belly button. The hidden scars took longer to heal.

'I thought I'd be fully recovered in a month or two, which was sheer insanity on my part. I did a long swim three months afterwards but I should not have done that. There was a period of six months when I thought I was fully recovered and I wasn't. A year went by and I thought I was recovered. It finally took two and half years to get to the point where I could really stand up straight and get full extension when I was swimming: when you are swimming you really have to extend your body, really stretch it out from the fingertips to the toes, and it took two and a half years to regain that sensation.

I still have numbness through my belly button and that whole region. I'm looking to get acupuncture and get that whole area rewired because the belly button is like a nerve centre for cross-body movements and I know that that area has been interrupted and compromised.'

While he recovered, Eric did some research into a shark he had never heard of until it bit him. Cookiecutter shark bites are so rare, Eric's was only the second recorded incident.

'They are nasty little buggers. It hit me like a freight train. They come from 1,700 feet [518 metres] down and they come up and just … boom. I felt like I was punched in the gut. The Discovery Channel did a feature on my attack and they called it "alien shark", because I was only the second person to be bitten by one. Two weeks after my episode, a young swimmer was bitten by a cookiecutter shark in the same channel, around the same location, and two weeks after that, a South American swimmer was bitten in the same channel and the same location. There was one other guy bitten, in 2009, ten years to the day before my attack, but in a different channel. Before or after that, there had been no other attacks.

After the Discovery Channel did their show, National Geographic did one, asking why these occurrences happened, and no one has really been able to come up with a conclusion. I thought it was maybe because I was swimming through whale migration season, or maybe because my friend Steve was throwing up, but the other swimmers didn't have anyone else throwing up next to them. That debunks that theory.

We were all in whale migration season. We might have been mistaken for a seal or a dolphin because they also hit on them and tuna and things like that, so we might have been mistaken for a fish.'

These unanswered questions, added to the unsettling aspect that Eric never saw the shark coming, mean he has never truly got over his attack.

'There are a lot of emotions still. Sometimes I will still wake up in the middle of the night hanging on the bow of that kayak, waiting for the boat to arrive, hoping I'm not going to get bitten by a bigger shark. That's probably the most frightening thing. For some reason, I'll never forget the angle of the moon. It was a half-moon that night. I remember looking up and seeing it. That image will never go away.

I never really had a chance to talk to anyone professionally about it. I would love to do that. But as soon as I got back, I got patched up and got back to my day job and back to swimming, because I figured that was the brave thing to do … just suck it up and keep moving.'

Although married dad-of-two Eric, now sixty-one, still bears the emotional scars of his experience, he has been able to get back in the water. And, although he admits there have been moments of trepidation, the rewards from pushing himself to the limit outweigh any negatives.

'There was no hesitation for me getting back into fresh water, but the first time I got back into the ocean I certainly had reservations. And on a night swim – the first since the attack – in April in Arizona, there was a little trepidation because, at that point, I hadn't swum at night and I didn't know what to expect.

I also had people with me on my first swims. When you have a long, organised swim, you always must have someone with you. But on the practice swims there is a lot of solo time, which is when you start thinking, What's my purpose? Why did this occur? Why do I keep going? Those are the soul-searching questions that come across, the deeper-meaning things. The swims are for fun, bragging rights and to say you've done these wonderful things, but there are times when you are in there you ask yourself, Why am I doing this to myself?

Marathon swimming is about as solo as it gets. Even though you have a kayaker nearby, you can be going through a whole world of emotions in a ten- or eighteen-hour swim. You're asking yourself, Why am I doing this to myself after I have been bitten by a shark?!

There is always an answer at the end. There's always a deeper meaning to it. It's spiritual. I've participated in a lot of sports in my day. I come from a cycling background – the Welsh Tour de France winner Geraint Thomas is one of my favourite athletes – but this is a different type of thing.

You can keep swimming for hours and hours and hours and it hurts and the mental game is so challenging, but when you are done, everything stops hurting, and all of a sudden you have completed what you set out to do. I've swum around Manhattan ... and when you stop swimming, you suddenly think, Thank God I didn't quit, because I made it. Yet, while you're doing it, your mind and body are saying, "Quit. This is stupid; you're hurting, you're throwing up." Then you make it and suddenly there's a whole new level of awareness and it's like more doors open up for you to experience. That's what it's all about.

My wife, Mary Ellen, has no reservations about me carrying on swimming. She knows how important it is to me. My two boys were more incredulous about what happened. They were like, "Holy crap, Dad, you've been bitten by a shark!"

The first time you do a big swim, it's hard; the next time you do it, there's a whole new set of circumstances that makes it harder, but you master those and you try it again and there's now a new set of circumstances to get around. The water is my medium; some people are painters, composers or cooks. It doesn't matter, it's all the same journey.

Fortunately, I have not encountered any more sharks or anything dangerous. I've been back to Hawaii and I've swam with turtles and bigger fish, and when I swam in Catalina [in California], we swam with dolphins. They are joyful creatures, and when you swim with dolphins, you know you are going to be safe – they have a protection factor. I have never seen any sharks – but then again, I never saw that shark because it was dark.'

Eric might not have been able to face his fears so quickly had it not been for the support from Bite Club members, who were able to monitor his progress at the time of the attack.

'When we're doing these long swims, the sanctioning body – the Marathon Swimmers Federation – provide a GPS tracker for your boat that people on the internet can follow. They were following our track, and we were getting all kinds of comments about how well we were doing. Then they could see the tracker was moving very quickly over towards Honolulu, so they knew something was going on. Texts started coming from the mainland to our crew asking what was going on and messages went back that there had been a shark bite. That all went out onto Facebook. Dave and other members reached out to me to check I was OK.

In the weeks following, some members reached out to me once a week or once a month just to check how I was doing. I thought, Wow, this is amazing.

The support is there when you need it. From that point, I swore that any time someone posts on Bite Club about somebody with a bite, I will always reach out and say, "If there's anything I can do, feel free to lean on me," because I would be glad to give back what people gave to me. That's how we get through this.'

Sadly, like many fellow Bite Club members, Eric witnessed some negative reaction online to his bite, but he remained philosophical about that type of comment.

The open water community has been very supportive, but there was a segment on the local Hawaii news and there were online comments like, "What are these a-holes doing out in the middle of the ocean in the middle of the night? What do they expect? They are going to get bitten by sharks."

What they don't know is that sixty-one people did it before me and didn't get bitten by a shark.

I didn't appreciate that commentary, but I guess it comes out of ignorance of what an open water swimmer does. Their own ignorance or fear or anger or whatever causes them to make those kinds of remarks. I refused to engage with that kind of activity.'

Since the cookiecutter shark cut short Eric's marathon swim in 2019, life has presented its own challenges but he has never given up on his goal of one day returning and completing his swim.

'There's twenty-six miles in that swim, and when I was done with my surgery, I had twenty-six staples; so we took the staples out, we put them in a cup and when I go back to do that swim again, I'm going to sacrifice those staples to the ocean. So, twenty-six staples; one for every mile.

I was in the best shape of my life. That was in 2019. In 2020, the world experienced the pandemic, and then in 2021, my parents got sick. My mom passed away and my dad was diagnosed with dementia. Since then, I have not been able to get back to that feeling of being in the best shape of your life, and when you're an athlete, that's what you want. So, I have no idea when I'll be able to do it but it's very much a case of unfinished business.

Before all this happened, before I went away, my mother said, "I'm worried about you going all the way to Hawaii for a swim."

I said, "Mom, what could go wrong? I'm only going for a swim!"'

CHAPTER 6
DAMON KENDRICK

INYONI ROCKS, AMANZIMTOTI, KWAZULU-NATAL, SOUTH AFRICA, WEDNESDAY 13 FEBRUARY 1974

'I stuck my head up to take what I was
convinced at that stage was my last breath.'

A shark attack on a lifeguard on 7 January 1974 at Amanzimtoti, south of Durban, South Africa, had shocked the local community. Cornelius 'Les' Pyper suffered severe injuries to his leg when bitten while swimming. It was the first incident of its kind in many years and highlighted that recent rough sea conditions had reduced the effectiveness of shark nets installed to protect the beach.

On Sunday 10 February, after the nets had been serviced and the beach reopened, tensions were still high. Damon Kendrick was a fourteen-year-old lifesaver at Inyoni Rocks. The youngest of three kids, whose mum was a swimming teacher, Damon had learned to swim before he could walk. He swam competitively, competed in gymnastics at national level and was the Natal junior champion springboard diver. Damon's family was heavily involved with the Amanzimtoti Surf Lifesaving Club. Such surf clubs teach water safety, including emergency first aid, CPR, shark attack protocols and treatment of cuts and abrasions, and warn of marine hazards such as jellyfish stings. They teach search and rescue techniques to members from the age of five upwards. His father was president, while his older brother was club captain, his mother was fundraising committee chair and his sister a committee member. Damon was nipper captain, which meant he provided lifesaving cover every third Sunday. That day, a nurse who lived across the road from Damon turned up at the beach with two friends.

'She walked up to me and said, "Is it safe to swim here?"

I said, "What do you mean, is it safe?" knowing exactly what she meant – because of the recent attack. She said someone was attacked at this beach just last month. I said, "It is a one-in-a-million chance. You have more chance being struck by lightning" – which is statistically true. "It'll never happen again." That was on the Sunday. In three days' time, the "it will never happen again" happened to me.'

Damon's lifesaving club was due to host the provincial championship at the beach the following weekend. On Wednesday 13 February, the club held its last training session ahead of the competition.

'We had done the whole lot, and the very last thing was a surf swim. It was about 7 p.m. when we swam out. At that particular beach there are two surf breaks. There is a shore break, right where the dumping waves come onto the shore. Then, moving further out to sea, there is a bit of flat, open water and another shore break – what we call a backline break because there was a bit of a sand bank and a break – which was very popular with surfers. We were out past that line.

It wasn't that far out, probably about thirty metres. There were about nine of us. One of those there was Johannes Kool, who we all called Joe Kool. He was nineteen. Suddenly, Joe said, "Everyone swim for shore." He didn't say why. We all just swam. It is part of the training – if someone senior says something, you do it.

What I didn't know was that he had actually been bitten. Not very seriously, but he had been bitten on his knee – some quite severe gashes on it that would later require stitches. Joe swam back towards the beach. I was just behind him. We were so close that every now and then, as I swam, I tapped his toes.

We got to shore – into water that was probably just less than a metre deep. He put his feet down and ran out of the water. I bent my knees to put my feet down on the sand, when the shark grabbed me from behind. It had the calf of my right leg and shook so incredibly violently that my whole body was flung out of the water, left and right, a few times. Then the shark dragged me underwater.

I remember the feeling of the water coming up. I stuck my neck and head up to take what I was convinced at that stage was my last breath. That's it, I'm about to die. I took my last breath – and the next thing I knew, the last wave washed me onto the sand. I was on my back, and I started pushing backwards, headfirst, landwards with my right leg held in the air. My calf muscle was hanging off the back of my knee. I can still remember the feel of the wobble in the back of my knee.

I was screaming, of course. There was blood – a lot of it. Two of the older guys came running down to help me onto the beach. And they put their hands around my leg just above my knee to try to stop the blood.

My brother, Miles, who was twenty-two, was in the showers. He heard the screaming and went out into the change room. He saw my towel hanging there – the only one still there. He instantly knew it was me. He grabbed the leash of his surfboard, ran down and, when he got to me, put the leash around my leg, which stopped the bleeding. He was – along with those two guys who took me out of the water – the first person to save my life. There would be so many people involved that day, though … '

The lifesaving club had a well-drilled shark attack procedure. Damon himself had earned the surf proficiency award, which meant he was a qualified junior lifesaver. People sprang into action, including one boy, Eric, who ran to get the shark attack pack – a trauma first-aid kit. He had followed Damon on shore.

'Eric was a friend of mine who I had been at school with since year one. He had been deeper out in the water than me. He watched the shark attack me and thought he was going to be next. He had to swim through my blood to get to shore.

The lifesaving clubs have a kit of dried human blood plasma. The plasma is in a vacuum and it comes with a bottle of sterile water. You put a double-sided needle firstly into the water and secondly into the blood plasma and mix it up. There were no mobile phones in those days so someone ran up to the payphone up on the road and called the local doctor, who came down and put the drip into my arm. Part of the thing that probably saved my life is I got the very best treatment I could, at the time, in those circumstances, with all the equipment available.

The protocol then was to make sure that some of the blood plasma had gone in to replace blood loss. The protocol was you did not move the patient for thirty minutes. So, the ambulance arrived and they were told they had to wait. The protocol has since changed, but the idea then was that if you put people into the ambulance immediately, they sometimes died of shock on the way to the hospital. If you replaced some of the blood volume first, it decreased the possibility of dying from shock.

Weirdly, I had absolutely no pain from my right leg, even though my right calf was hanging off the back of my knee. But when the guys lifted me and put me on the first bit of dry land, they put me down lying down in the direction I had been going – which was landwards. Only after they started bandaging did they say, "Oh, we made a mistake. We are supposed to have him head-down, towards the sea, so it helps with blood flow back to the heart." The protocol said they could not move me, so they decided to raise my legs.

Because of the thrashing of the attack, just above the inside of my left ankle there was a tiny bit of a skin graze, probably about an inch in diameter. When they held my legs up, one of their thumbs was pressing on that spot. If you've ever felt a shark's skin – if you stroke it from nose to tail – it's as smooth as a rubber wetsuit. But if you go the other direction, it is like the roughest sandpaper because of the scales. I had to ask them to please move their thumb because that was causing me pain – not the leg that had been half eaten!

People say when there is too much pain, your brain just switches off, but no. Because I could feel pain from the other leg, not the major one. I think that the reason

I didn't feel pain was because the nerves were severed, so there was nothing to transmit.'

While medics waited to move Damon, someone called his parents to let them know what had happened.

'I was being loaded into the back of the ambulance when my parents arrived. My father was ashen and my mother was hysterical. She wanted to come in the back of the ambulance with me, but I turned to my brother and said, "She is not coming." So, my brother and Joe rode in the back of the ambulance with me, with one of the ambulance officers, which at that stage was very unusual. Another thing that was extremely unusual for 1974 was that all three ambulance officers were female.

From our beach to the city was usually a forty-five-minute drive. They took seven and a half minutes. My parents were travelling behind the ambulance. At one stage, my father said, he was doing 180 kilometres an hour and they lost the ambulance. I remember everything. By the time I got loaded in, it was 8 p.m. and dark. There were times when we crossed over the central island and were on the wrong side of the road. I felt every bang of the ambulance. My brother and Joe held me down so I didn't bounce around too much.

Apparently, it was the first time that the emergency procedure worked like clockwork. As we got to one set of traffic lights, the following three were blocked off. And three ahead of every set we got to were blocked off, so we had a free run all the way through to the hospital.'

In the emergency room at Addington Hospital in Durban, medics conducted an X-ray of Damon's leg through his bandages. It confirmed his whole calf was missing and, although his foot was still attached, he had lost most of the major nerves and tendons. Three specialist surgeons examined Damon's injuries and concluded his right leg could not be saved and would have to be amputated below the knee.

'They took a needle, stabbed my big toe and asked, "Can you feel that?"

"No," I said, "I can't feel anything."

When I was on the beach, I suspected the leg was going to go, but it was at that point I knew. They pushed me into the operating theatre, and on the table, they cut off my Speedos.

"Hey, they are new Speedos!" I said, but it was too late. Next thing I was out, because they slapped the gas mask on me.

When I came to, there were people around. I thought they were surgeons but they could have been orderlies pushing the gurney from recovery to intensive care.

I asked, "Did you amputate?"

"Yes," they said.

"Oh," I replied. "OK."'

The next morning, there was a cage holding the blankets off my legs. I could feel my toes. I remember saying, "How can I feel my toes if they have been amputated?" I had never come across the concept of phantom limbs before. I lifted up the blanket but, no, it had gone. I lay back and thought, This is real. What the hell do I do now?

I didn't know what to do. I was a fourteen-year-old kid. Nobody tells you how you are supposed to behave when a wild animal rips your leg off. I remember going through the thought process: Do people expect me to cry? I suppose I could cry if I wanted to cry, but that's not going to bring my leg back. OK, let's shelve that. That's not going to happen. So, what can I do? I've just got to make do with the best that I have. I'm going to make a decision right now that I'm going to do what I always do – leg or no leg.

And that was a decision made in intensive care when I was fourteen. And it held right through my life and holds today.'

Sadly, Damon, Joe Kool and Les Pyper were not the only people to be attacked by sharks in Amanzimtoti in the coming months. Even while Damon was still in hospital, he would learn of another victim.

'There were five attacks involving six people in the space of thirteen months at our beach. My attack was the second and I was one of two people attacked that day. Then on 21 March, Jimmy Gurr – who had been a classmate of my brother – was surfing in the same spot when he saw a shark coming side on. He was sitting on a surfboard, picked his legs up and the shark bit his board, so he was unharmed. But Jimmy brought the board into the hospital to show me. He was physically unscathed but very rattled, probably more rattled than me.

I said, "You are really lucky."

"Yes," he nodded.

Then on 4 August, Tony Baker, who was a year ahead of me at school, was bitten on the foot while surfing at the same spot. And on 22 February the following year, Bretton Jones, who was in the year below me, was surfing nearby but on the other side of a rocky outpoint. He was sitting with his feet dangling in the water when a shark took his foot off.

I believe we hold the record for the highest number of kids at the same school bitten by a shark. It's not the kind of record you really want, though!'

Tragically, the incidents occurred even though shark nets in the area were intended to mitigate against such attacks.

'The nets had been there for quite a while, but there had been floods and the nets hadn't been serviced properly so they weren't effective. They were entangled with debris and found to be bunched together.'

Although Damon hadn't caught sight of the shark that bit him, and there were no witnesses able to identify the species, experts were able to study tooth fragments the fish had left behind. They estimated it was just under two metres long with a jaw size of 190 mm.

'They got two tiny fragments out of my leg. In those days, pre-DNA, they said it was either – in local terms – a Zambezi shark or a dusky shark – basically a bull shark. The water was murky so no one witnessed the shark. It was dusk as well – perfect conditions for such an attack.'

Damon spent the next six and a half weeks in hospital and had two subsequent operations because his flexor hamstring muscles went into contraction.

'It bent my knee. Apparently, it's quite common with an amputation. I had to have manipulations where they straightened the knee with brute force. It was done under anaesthetic but was quite painful for a brief time afterwards. About a week before I left hospital, I had to go to another hospital to be measured up and cast for my first prosthesis. They did a plaster of Paris mould of my knee. It is good to have a knee but every prosthetist I've ever seen has said, "Oh my God, you really don't have a lot to work with." It does make prosthetics a little difficult.

Around ten days after I came out of hospital, I got my first prosthesis. In the beginning, I could only wear it for a very short time before it started to ache and I took it off. I used to put it on for fifteen minutes, then half an hour, then an hour, and take it off. I would do that four, five, six times a day.

When I went back to school, I used my prosthesis on Monday, Wednesday and Friday and went on crutches Tuesday and Thursday, just to give it a break. I started off on two crutches, then one crutch and then two walking sticks. And that was awful because going to school, aged fourteen, with two walking sticks was not good. The comments I used to get, like, "Oh, old man with his walking sticks," kind of thing. They didn't last very long. After about six months, I went without crutches or sticks.

Generally, however, I had a really good reaction from the other kids. Before this happened, I had been bullied mercilessly at school. There were two major reasons – I was two years younger than the average age at school. I started school earlier, so when everyone else had gone through their growth spurt, I was still a little kid. I only grew later. I went into year twelve the smallest boy in the class and left the tallest boy in the class. I left at year twelve and went to university at sixteen. So, I was very slight, and because I'm gay, I suppose I was a bit effeminate and used to get really bullied for that.

Losing my leg was probably one of the best things that happened to me at that time because the bullying stopped. I think the attitude was, you can't bully the crippled kid.

A few months later, I was in school when the secretary came to my class and said, "Can Kendrick please come to the principal?"

Oh God, what have I done now? I thought. I was sure I hadn't done anything bad to be called to the principal's office. Jimmy Gurr was sitting there, and the principal said, "Jimmy says would you like to go over with him to the Natal Sharks Board and watch a shark being dissected?"

I said, "Yeah, absolutely," because I was a little bit of a nerd and enjoyed science and biology. Watching a shark being dissected wasn't really as interesting as I thought it might have been. I don't know whether the shark board contacted him or if he contacted them, but that was part of his mental and psychological healing process and he thought it might be good for me.

After that, there were huge differences in the protocols around the servicing of the shark nets. Bretton's attack was the last for quite a few years.'

Trying to adjust to life with a prosthesis was one thing, but for Damon, swimming and diving had been such a huge part of his life. He had resolved to make the best of what he had. The big question was how?

'About a week after I came out of hospital, friends took me camping to a very big dam. In the caravan next door was a girl who went to school with me and who swam at national competitions. She and I decided to swim across the dam. It was about a kilometre. It felt really good to be back in the water. It had always been my safe place. I kept up with her and we had a good swim, then a speedboat came and picked us up.

The first time I went back into the sea was probably around August or September 1974. My brother was quite high up in the country and had been national champion in a number of different events. He was really good, was well-known and was competing in a place called St Michaels on Sea in Natal province. We went down to watch his competition. I took my Speedos but had no intention of going in.

Then I looked at the sea and thought, This is ridiculous. I really love the water. I'll just go in a little way and stay with everyone else if I don't feel comfortable.

I went out and was in that zone where the waves wash and people bob up and down. I looked and thought, This just isn't me to bob up and down, so I went, "Oh bugger it." I swam out to where the waves started and bodysurfed in. I had an absolute whale of a time. Just loved it. There was never any conscious decision, "I am going to do this." It was just a quick, "OK, I'll get in and see what happens."

At one stage, I was furthest out in the water. I thought, If anyone asks me what happened to my leg, they will never believe me with the fact that I'm furthest out.'

Conquering his apprehension about being back in the sea was one thing, but it was going to be a whole other challenge for Damon to dive again with just one leg.

'About three weeks before the attack I had won the junior springboard diving competition. When I was attacked, I thought, Oh, well, I'll never dive again. It just didn't seem possible or feasible. No one does one-leg springboard diving.

About four or five months after the attack, there was an opportunity to do a course to become a diving judge. I said to my mum, "You know, I really enjoy diving and would like to stay involved. Maybe, how about I become a judge? That way it would keep me in the sport and in something I really enjoy."

"OK," she said, "I'll take you there."

The course was at a private girls' school. There was training in the morning, then in the afternoon there were videos and practice diving. At lunchtime, everyone went off. Mum had packed a lunch for us. There was a pool with a diving board. She said, "Let's go to the pool."

I had taken my swimming costume with me and I dived in the water. She said, "Do you want to have a go on the diving board?"

"Hell, yeah," I said.

For some reason, I didn't go onto the one-metre, I immediately went onto the three-metre board. The very first time, I got down on my hands and knees and crawled to the end. I stood up, rocked up and down without bouncing – because you weren't allowed a double bounce on the thing – and did a one-and-a-half somersault. I thought, You know, I can do this. I went through a few more dives, got out of the pool, and Mum said, "Would you like to dive again? I can take you to training."

"Hell, yeah!"

It was in the city – a forty-five-minute drive in each direction – but she drove me three or four times a week for diving training. She used to make dinner and I would eat it in the car on the way home.

A year later, I competed in the senior championships, because now I was past juniors. I got the bronze medal, beating some people with two legs. The next year, I went to Cape Town University and was selected to represent the university at the South African championships –

which was quite big. South African Universities is second only to the national championships. I was selected to be on the South African Universities team for three years.

From there, I represented the province at the national championships. I did that for nine consecutive national champs. I think in the first year I was round about tenth. Then I rose up the rankings and was always somewhere between fourth and seventh position. In 1984, I had my best year when I was second in the country. By that stage, I had developed hopping, not crawling, down the board, and developed a hurdle so I would hop down the board and take off.'

The spate of shark attacks might have been in the forefront of people's minds in Damon's hometown, but the fear that such incidents could take place at family beaches was soon to reach hysterical levels around the world. In June 1975, Steven Spielberg's movie thriller *Jaws*, based on the 1974 novel by Peter Benchley, about a killer great white shark terrorising a tourist town, hit the big screens. It meant Damon's story was once again in the limelight.

'The newspapers took Bretton and me, because we were the two people who had lost legs a year apart, to see the opening night of *Jaws*. I bought a box of chocolates and waited for the most gory scenes and then offered the journalist a chocolate. The first time he accepted, but then I think after that it made him feel queasy because he went, "No, no, no!" I may look and sound like a nice person but I can be quite nasty! Both Bretton and I agreed that it wasn't terribly realistic. We could see it was fake, so it didn't really affect either of us.'

As Damon continued to adapt to his new reality with his rigorous training regime, it not only helped him excel at diving, but led to a chance to fulfil a childhood dream.

'As a kid, I used to have a circus fantasy. I strung up ropes between two trees in the garden and walked the tightrope. I had a very good sense of balance. I think that helped, but I trained very hard. When I was at university, I did springboard diving training for an hour in the morning before lectures. The afternoon was taken up with practicals, but I trained for an hour at lunchtime and, after practicals, trained for two hours more. I did four hours, five days a week and, on Saturdays and Sundays, I did between six and eight hours of training, starting at 6 a.m.

Our university pool wasn't heated or outdoors, so we couldn't dive in the winter as the pool was closed. I used to watch in the newspaper for when the temperature hit sixteen degrees, then I'd start training again, even if it just meant for twenty minutes to half an hour. The best we ever got was 21 degrees. Consequently, I used to do trampolining during the winter to keep the muscles going.

One day a guy came and was doing really amazing stuff. I could see he wasn't a gymnast, diver or trampolinist and I couldn't work out how he had the ability to do the tricks that he was doing.

One day I asked, "OK, come clean; what do you do?"

"Oh, I'm a trapeze artist," he said.

"Wow," I said, "that's always been a fantasy of mine."

"Come along!" he said. I didn't need a second invitation!

I went and for a long time just did it on weekends and only in winter when I wasn't doing diving training.

I did that on and off for a few years. When I finished diving, I went into it more seriously and was asked to join a trapeze troupe. The catcher spoke French and gave us the name Les Maîtres du Ciel – the Masters of the Sky. They asked me to be part of the troupe. So, for a very brief time in my life, I was a full-time professional trapeze artist. That was from 1989 to 1991, or thereabouts.

I really feel privileged to have been able to do that – how many kids grow up wanting to be a train driver, a racing-car driver, a spaceman, an astronaut? And they never live up to their childhood fantasies. I had a childhood fantasy of being a trapeze artist and I did it! How great is that?'

Damon didn't stop there. An opportunity to try horse riding led to a new area of expertise.

'I was working in a gym in a very upmarket area of Cape Town, when someone said to me, "It's such a pity you don't ride horses because I've got a spare horse you could come ride."

I agreed to take a lesson.

I had one lesson a week and went on two outrides a week. Within a month of having lessons, I had organised a half-lease of a horse. Within four months, I competed in my first show-jumping competition. Within two years of learning to ride, I was selected to represent the province at the national championships in three-day eventing – like Princess Anne and her daughter Zara Tindall do.'

After completing a medical science degree, majoring in physiology and the history and philosophy of science, Damon went on to do postgraduate studies in exercise physiology. He has lectured in health science for thirty years and in 1994, he and his partner decided to move to Perth.

'When we got to Australia, we couldn't afford a horse each, so my partner said, "How about carriage driving?" So, we bought a section C Welsh cob pony and took up carriage driving. I had been trained to drive carriages by Joy Clacton, who taught Prince Philip to drive six-in-hand, meaning the reins of the six horses pulling the carriage could be held in one hand. Philip actually wrote the international rules for carriage driving. Joy was one of only three women in the world who could drive six-in-hand and she taught him to drive that style, but not for competitions. We bought a little two-year-old stallion and trained him up. In our first Australian championships we came fourth, in our second we came first in the dressage phase but second overall. We enjoyed quite a lot of success in that.

While I was doing that, however, it wasn't doing anything for my fitness. So, at the age of around thirty-eight I decided to go back to swimming. At first, I did sprint events and managed to get close to podium places. As I'm an exercise physiologist, I knew that as you age, your endurance capacity increases and your sprinter capacity decreases. I decided to start entering longer events. I tried four hundred metres and won the state championships – competing against able-bodied swimmers. That progressed to eight hundred, then fifteen hundred, which led me to open water swimming.

While in Perth, I joined an Ironman squad training group, but for the swim part only. [Ironman is a triathlon consisting of a 2.4-mile swim, 112-mile bike ride and a full marathon distance run – generally having to be completed in seventeen hours or less.] At that stage, the Busselton, Western Australia, Ironman was the only one in the world that had a team event. It's since been cancelled but, back then, it started when one guy was injured so was only able to cycle. He assembled a team and found a runner and he asked me if I would do the swim. I said "OK."'

Damon excelled at swimming, winning gold medals at two World Masters Games. In 2010, he won a bronze medal in the Pan Pacific Masters Games, and in 2011, he won the 20 km Geo Bay Swim from Quindalup to Busselton, Western Australia, against able-bodied people, breaking the record by 22 minutes. He is also the current Queensland record holder for the 800 m freestyle, which he set in 2021. However, ocean swims meant the risk of encountering a shark once again, something Damon had managed to avoid in all the years previously.

'I was competing in the Rottnest Channel Swim, the 20 km swim from Cottesloe Beach in Perth to Rottnest Island in 2011. The rules state you must have a kayaker and boat supporting you. I lucked out because I had a 75-foot flybridge cruiser as my support boat and also a Zodiac inflatable [boat], which we call a rubber ducky. I swam mostly between the rubber ducky and the canoeist. I could see them looking at each other and looking at me, and I thought, Oh, I don't like the look of this. I couldn't see anything in the water – but a 1.5 m hammerhead shark came within ten metres of me. I only found out after the swim what had happened."'

Now sixty-three, living in Queensland, Australia, and working on a social science PhD on engagement in lifetime physical activity, Damon has witnessed significant advances in the technology of prostheses – and in people's attitudes towards those who need them.

'I've seen a huge change in technology and attitudes – interestingly, particularly among children. Kids are absolutely honest and it is a product of their upbringing. When I was younger, kids would stare, they would ask questions. Some people would be terrified of me because I was different.

Nowadays, the kids go, "Awesome! Bionic man!"

It's a complete and utter change. I suppose that change occurred somewhere in the early 2000s. I don't know whether it was movies like *Transformers* that led to changes in attitudes but it was really interesting. Another thing I found interesting was going places where people are not as socially aware. In Bali, for example, when I went there for the first time, not only did the people stare at my leg, but the dogs stared too! It was really funny. I wasn't used to being stared at by dogs.'

Some things, however, have not changed. People are still being attacked by sharks, despite measures taken to prevent such incidents.

'I'm really conflicted about some things. Shark nets work up to a point. They are not perfect. But they do kill creatures that I care about, like dolphins, turtles and other things caught as bycatch. I'm not mad about the baited drum lines, either, where they kill the sharks. I have an intellectual preference for the smart drum lines. And I do feel safer within a netted area, on an emotional basis.

The one thing I really can't stand is when there is an attack and people go out in boats to try and find the shark that did the attack and kill it. When you have a car accident – and let's say it's not your fault – do you go and ask for the offending car to be crushed? It's just not logical. That aspect of retribution against the animal, I don't enjoy. I don't blame the shark. The shark is doing what the shark does. We are in their territory. We do need to take responsibility. By the same token, there has been a population explosion of sharks; and Australia being very much a beach-culture nation, I'm all for some sort of shark mitigation procedure.

How that plays out – I'm probably undecided. I do look at the science. The wrist and ankle bands [that generate an electromagnetic field causing sharks to keep their distance] looked very promising but apparently they only work for a metre and certainly don't work for great white sharks. There are also disguised wetsuits – camouflage designed to be either less visible to sharks or to not look like their prey – which are apparently quite good, but they have not yet developed them for a speed suit, which, as a swimmer, I would wear. I wouldn't wear a wetsuit.

But there are correlations to attacks. When I was attacked, it was dusk and it was a couple of weeks after major floods. The flood waters had brought debris down that got tangled in the nets, which hadn't been serviced properly. The floods had also made the water murky. So, there are things to look out for.'

Remarkably, given he sustained injuries that could have been life-changing, Damon developed a coping mechanism to help during moments of anxiety.

'I never had flashbacks or nightmares or anything like that. There are times when I do get emotional. I never really started getting emotional until a few years ago. So, there is something lingering there. If I go into the water, there is always the thought ... and I hate it if a piece of seaweed or whatever touches my foot. I'll freak out.

I was training with a triathlon squad and one of the guys was a fairly good swimmer. He was eighteen and at that stage I was in my fifties but I would beat him all the time. One time we were doing backstroke kick and I was on my back, kicking. He was swimming regular freestyle and I passed him. He stopped in the middle of the pool and said, "You are a fucking dolphin!"

"Yes," I said, "I'm a dolphin." Just as a joke, I told everyone at the end of the pool what he had said. One of the girls said, "You should make that your mantra." So I did.

When I'm having negative thoughts, when I become paranoid that there might be a shark behind me, that's what I do. That's how I get out of that mindset of thinking there might be a shark there. I go, "I'm a dolphin, I'm a dolphin, I'm a dolphin." I use that to push those thoughts out of my head.'

Although Damon has been able, largely, to banish negative thoughts and face his fears by continuing to swim despite being only too aware of the dangers, he has still benefitted from being a part of Bite Club.

'A friend put me onto Bite Club and I immediately thought they would not be interested in me because I wasn't bitten in Australia. But the next thing, I got a phone call from Dave Pearson. We had a chat and he came to visit me. We instantly hit it off like we were brothers. He is quite an amazing person.

It's a support network and you are just one part of the net. You support others and others support you. I've had a hell of a lot of support for the swims I've done, in terms of the psychological stresses – all of those kinds of support have been really good. I've had long phone calls with people from various parts of the world. It's really good. I hope I've done a little to help some people. I've said quite often that you can't change the past, but you can change the future. So, changing the way you look at moving forward, with whatever condition you have, will make a difference.

My sister, Brenda, died of breast cancer, and when she was going through the chemotherapy she said to me, "How did you do it and manage to get through everything without crying or whatever?"

I said, "It is not easy." You need to make a conscious effort to be positive. Positivity is sometimes quite hard. But you have to go, "OK, this has happened. I mustn't mind, and this is what I'm going to do in the future. And I'm not going to let things get in the way, and being positive is everything." She was absolutely amazing. She took that on board right till she drew her last breath. She was one of the most positive people I knew.

I never realised [anyone else could find my story inspiring]. I just did what I did. One day – long before my sister went through her cancer – I was chatting to one of the girls at university. She said, "You have made such a difference to my mum."

"How?" I said. "I've never met your mum."

She said, "My mum is going through breast cancer and when she sees you hopping down the end of the board, throwing yourself off and doing multiple somersaults and multiple twists, she says, 'If he can do that with one leg then I can cope with one breast.'"

That was the first time I ever had any inkling that I could have an effect on other people. It's quite a responsibility. I don't set out to be someone's inspiration. I set out to do what I want to do and not let things get in the way. Obviously, there are things I can't do, but I do push the boundaries a little bit.'

CHAPTER 7
MICHELLE 'MICKI' KOCH GLENN

FRENCH CAY, TURKS AND CAICOS ISLANDS, THURSDAY 14 NOVEMBER 2002

'One decision can change your life.'

It was a break between dives. Although it was just after 8 a.m. at French Cay in the Caribbean, the sun was already splitting the sky. Micki Koch Glenn, a forty-one-year-old radiology director from Florida, had not long surfaced from her first dive of the day, peeled off her wetsuit and marvelled at what she'd just witnessed.

'It was the most beautiful dive. My dive buddy Tim had the video camera and we went down on the wall, to ninety or a hundred feet, where a big turtle was eating coral. I scratched her back and we continued our dive. We were on our way back to the boat on top of the reef when another turtle came right up to me and started swimming circles around me, as I trailed my fingers on her carapace. Tim videotaped her swimming around me, circling around me with my fingers trailing on her back. It was an incredible dive – probably the best dive of the trip.'

Experienced diver Micki and her husband, Dr Michael Glenn, a keen underwater photographer, were five days into a week-long dive trip to the Turks and Caicos Islands, and were among twenty-one guests aboard the *Sea Dancer* boat, organised by their local shop, Scuba Tech. Also on board were a vascular surgeon and an intensive care unit nurse – very fortunately, as it turned out.

While that captivating moment with a turtle would live long in Micki's memory, it was sharks they had specifically gone to see. And already, throughout their expedition, they had encountered many and experienced the wonder of witnessing them in their natural environment.

'You can't imagine unless you have dived with them how beautiful they are. Underwater, where the grey meets the white, it's just so clear and beautiful. A straight line, where the milky white and darker grey meet. It's like a linen suit, it really fits them. They are gorgeous animals.

I had been diving with them for four or five days, and they would circle around us and underneath us and come close enough to touch. One time I did trail my fingers along the belly of a shark that was just passing over me. I just felt a kinship with them, and really wanted to communicate and interact with them. They didn't seem menacing at all.

There were usually three to four sharks most days just cruising around. Most of the time we were in around fifty feet of water where the boat would moor. So, we would do two dives in the morning, two dives in the afternoon and then an optional night dive, and the sharks would be either cruising down close to the reef or just off the wall or right underneath the boat.

MICHELLE 'MICKI' KOCH GLENN

It was really nice because at the end of each dive, we would go ahead and do a routine dive where we would drop down off the wall and go to our depth, so we would see turtles, fish and the beautiful coral and everything. Then when we came back to the boat; that's where we usually observed the sharks just cruising around in fifty feet of water.

The boat had a fifteen-foot bar that hung underneath it, and at the end of our dive, if we came back early enough, we would do our three-minute safety stop and then spend ten to twenty minutes just floating there, hanging on to the bar, observing the sharks. We did that on every dive, just watching the sharks. None of them seemed interested in us. They were just beautiful, just cruising around minding their own business, and didn't really pay any attention to the divers.'

On that blissful morning – their second last day of diving – the *Sea Dancer* had sailed six hours overnight to French Cay, a destination renowned for wall diving, where the depth drops like a sheer cliff down to several thousand feet.

'It is like this huge Devils Tower [famous igneous rock butte in Wyoming, USA]. When you swim on top of the wall, it varies usually from fifteen to twenty feet to fifty and sixty feet. And, once you go over it, it's like you are swimming over a cliff and you can look straight down into nothingness. That's our favourite kind of diving because it's dramatic and you can see all kinds of things.'

After her stunning early dive, as she sat in her bikini on the boat, Micki had made plans to practise sign language with her dive buddy Tim so they could communicate better under the water. But something made her change her mind.

123

'When we got back from that dive, I didn't have enough air in my tank to hang out for fifteen or twenty minutes like I usually did, to observe the sharks, before I came on board. I was on my surface interval and, as it was just such a beautiful morning, I had just stripped out of my skin, and saw a couple of friends were in the water snorkelling.

My dive buddy and I wanted to learn real sign language. That's what we had planned for that surface interval, but I said, "Oh, I'm so sorry, there are five sharks in the water and it's so pretty so I want to go snorkel, so … "

I was just in my bikini – which was probably stupid – but I joined them with my snorkel, fins and mask.

One decision can change your life.'

The sharks Micki and her party had seen most on the trip were Caribbean reef sharks, which share similarities in appearance with bull sharks. Below the boat were four reef sharks they had seen before that measured about five to six feet in length. Micki's husband, Mike, was in the water in his scuba gear with his camera. As Micki entered the water, they became aware of a shark they hadn't encountered earlier.

'She was a little bigger, around seven feet. Along her bottom jaw, on the white part, were vertical red marks. That's how we could tell we hadn't seen her before. All of the sharks were pretty heavy-bodied in the chest, and in the water, their chests looked similar in size to a bull shark's, which surprised me.

My husband was taking pictures and she came at him, right towards him. She bumped his camera housing and he pushed against it and bumped her with his camera housing. Then she turned directly towards me. I thought she was going to swim underneath my fins, because she was kind of on that trajectory. As soon as she got to me, she turned almost vertical in the water and her snout was about at the bottom of my fins. She just turned completely vertical in the water and stopped. It was almost like she just floated up. She made contact with my body at about knee level. My body was in between her right pectoral and dorsal fins, and she slid up my body very slowly – there was complete contact – and she slid all the way up my body until I was looking right into her eye. And she just hung there for a second. I was staring into her eye and she was still right up against my body.

You hear about sharks' eyes being black – and maybe some species' are – but her eye was so pretty, like a grey-green colour, flecked with gold. It was just mesmerising and really beautiful. My husband got a closeup picture of her and you can see the gorgeous grey-green colour.

I knew that it wasn't normal and the hair on the back of my neck was standing up, but I was more excited than frightened. I was thinking at that minute that maybe she felt how much I longed to interact with them, and she'd decided to come over, and chosen me to come over and have an interaction with. It was very gentle, it wasn't what they call a bump and bite. She never bumped me in that encounter. It was very gentle … at first.

I was in about fifty feet of water, facing the boat, which was another fifty feet away.'

While this was going on, some people on the boat were tossing peanuts into the water, which had attracted lots of small bait fish that congregated in little clouds.

'The sharks really didn't seem interested in the bait fish. When they made little clouds, the sharks meandered over. But something like that landed near me. I didn't feel comfortable with people throwing stuff into the water, but it wasn't stuff that the sharks would have wanted to eat. They weren't feeding the sharks. The bait fish were the ones that would come for the food.

I was actually enveloped in the bait fish when she turned up and started sliding up my body, and that may have been what attracted her to me. After she slid up me like that and we had our moment, she just flipped her tail and left me. As she went off to my right, I started to exhale, because I hadn't realised I had been holding my breath.

All of a sudden, before I could even get that breath out, she hit me on my right side. It was like being caught in a big bear trap or something. It was powerful, like metal jaws that just slammed into me and put me in a vice. There was no getting out of it; there was no getting around it. Once she clamped down on me like that, her teeth were at my spine on my back and they were all the way around at the front of my shoulder. She really had me in a grasp.

It took my brain a minute to realise what was happening, and then I did realise – I'm being attacked by a shark! It was terrifying. The power of it – I've never been able to articulate how powerful it was because it was just like being clamped down. I couldn't move – I couldn't do anything.

She started thrashing like you see on *Shark Week* when sharks go after prey; they just start thrashing their body back and forth. She was thrashing back and forth so violently that the front of my head hit the water, and then the back of my head hit the water. Front and back,

Dave Pearson, who founded Bite Club after being attacked by a
bull shark in 2012.

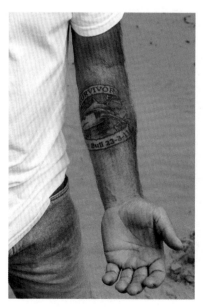

Dave's tattoo over his scar.

Bite Club members on a cruise in Sydney Harbour.

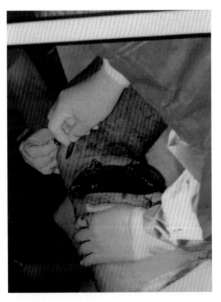

Mick Bedford's right thigh was torn open after being
attacked by a white shark in 2010.

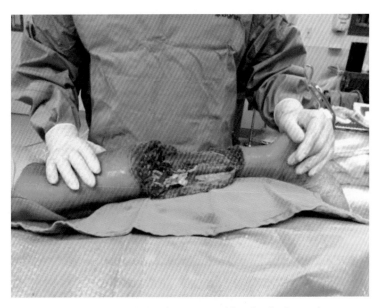

Amy Tatsch nearly lost her entire calf in the shark attack.

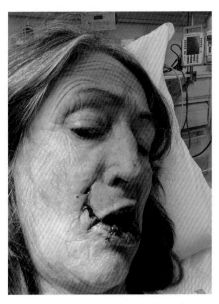

Laurel-Rose von Hoffmann-Curzi suffered a serious cut to her mouth, which required skilful suturing by a surgeon, after being attacked by a black bear in her own house in 2021.

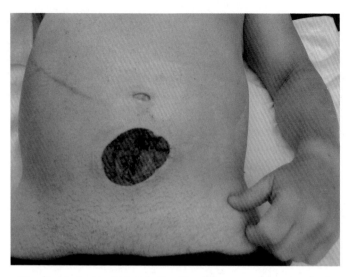

The distinctive bite Eric Schall suffered from a cookiecutter shark in Hawaii in 2019.

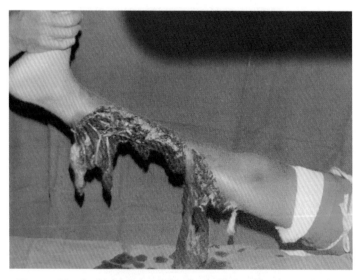

Damon Kendrick's leg was nearly taken off when he was attacked by a shark in South Africa in 1974.

The reef shark that attacked Micki Koch Glenn. Seconds later, it bumped her husband Mike's camera housing.

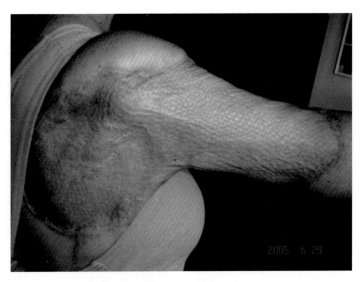

Micki's arm after the operations to save it.

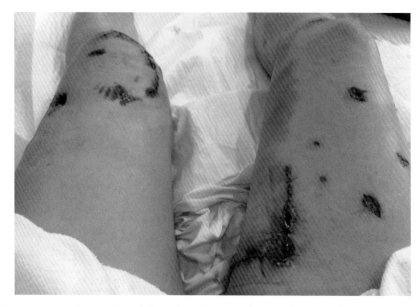

Lauren Fagen's legs after surgery to clean out her wounds.

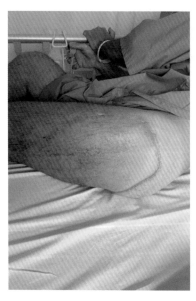

Cameron Wrathall's scar after surgeons managed to save his leg.

Julene Romsland's arm and shoulder were badly bitten.

The first shark's fin is visible above the water as it bites Chad Barker's hand.

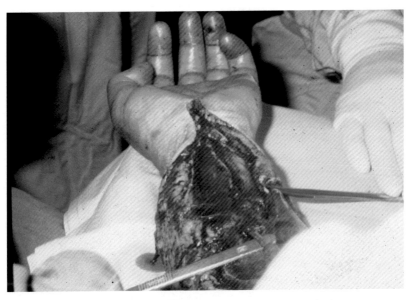

Meteorologist Mike Fraser lost his right arm to a great white shark in remote Campbell Island, off New Zealand, in 1992 and his left arm was also badly damaged in the attack.

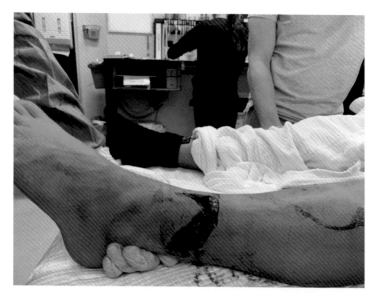

Anika Craney's injuries, after being bitten at Fitzroy Island, Queensland, Australia in 2020, showed she was bitten by a two-metre bull shark with a thirty-five-centimetre jaw.

Anika suffered extreme trauma but has been able to dive again, with sharks.

she was just slamming me back and forth, but her grip was so tight I didn't move in her mouth.

As it was happening, I was just incredulous. I couldn't believe what was happening but, of course, I recognised what was happening. I knew it was mortal.

I was so afraid she was going to drag me under the water and I would drown. I was thinking, Am I going to drown or am I going to lose consciousness before I drown? I expected to die. It was so violent, and there were four other sharks in the water. The level of terror I felt just being on the surface while she was attacking me, I really expected to be dragged under water. And I hoped that I would pass out from blood loss before that happened. Then she let me go. She swam off towards the boat, getting lower in the water. I could see the flesh from my arm and my back hanging out of her mouth as she left me.

For a second, I turned around to look at my arm and shoulder, and all I could see was ragged, bloody flesh. Already the water was red with my blood. When I saw that, I thought, I'm going to die, and this is how I am going to die, and I am going to die today. Then I thought, I want to get to the boat.

I had on fins, and just started grasping the water with my left hand and kicking as hard as I could, heading back to the boat because I wanted to die on the boat. I might be lost in the sea. That was terrifying to me. Suddenly, I started thinking about a conversation we'd had on the boat two nights before.

Randy – the vascular surgeon and diver from Texas – and I had stayed later after dinner, talking about ways you wouldn't want to die. He had said he wouldn't want to be attacked by a shark, and I'd said, "I don't think it would be so bad because you would bleed out so fast you wouldn't suffer." I'd said I wouldn't want to die in a fire. That's how I wouldn't want to die.

But he'd said, "Oh no, when you have a traumatic injury to an artery, it can really contract and clamp up. It can take you three to four minutes to die."

Now I'm in the water, seeing all that blood, I was thinking about that conversation, thinking that my artery didn't contract, I don't have three minutes. It seems a lot to think about, but if you have ever been in a traumatic accident, your body's response makes your thought processes speed up to the speed of light. Things seem to happen in slow motion and you have a lot of time to think when something like that is happening. It seems like a lot of time. It seemed like time had slowed down.

When I was trying to get to the boat, I turned around to look behind me and saw something white and chalky jerking along with me. It freaked me out. It looked like my hand was severed because it was really white – and it was my hand. But the water was full of so much blood, I couldn't tell if my arm was still attached. In my mind, I thought my hand was jerking along, following me through the water. It was another level of freak.

Then, all of a sudden, I thought about the other four sharks in the water. I thought about a feeding frenzy, everything you hear about when there is blood in the water. About that time, Nancy Birchett, who owns the dive shop that we dive with, swam up behind me, grabbed my waist and started to help propel me through the water back to the boat.

When we got to the ladder, my fins had to come off. I reached down with my left hand and took one off, because Nancy was holding me, and I held the fin up. The guy on the boat who was taking my fin, all he could see was my bloody shoulder and arm and everything.

He had just witnessed the attack. He didn't catch my fin and it went cartwheeling off into the water. Your brain doesn't really think like it should be thinking at these times – I actually pushed off the ladder to go get my fin! Of course, immediately my situation came back to mind: I had to climb that ladder.

The swim platform was only four or five feet wide. I could see the blood was pumping out of my arm. I thought, If I lay down here, nobody can help me. So, I climbed another vertical ladder to get onto the back of the boat – where there was room for plenty of people to crowd around me – and I walked several strides onto that platform. I lay down on my back and started screaming for my husband because he was still on scuba. I heard him come up the steps and drop his tank. I was screaming his name. People were all around me. But nobody was stopping the bleeding. They were all in shock.

But Mike came running up the ladder and knelt by my arm. He is an orthopaedic trauma surgeon, and the first thing he did was shove his hand up inside my wound and clamp the artery with his fingers. That's what stopped the bleeding. That's why I'm alive.'

When the shark struck, Micki's arm was by her side, and the bite, which had a radius of fifteen inches, engulfed her shoulder and upper right arm to her elbow, removing the back portion of her armpit and her triceps muscle and severing important nerves and the brachial artery.

'It wasn't in a place where you could put a tourniquet around it. It was up in a rich nest of blood vessels that's underneath your arm. She had actually taken that whole area of my armpit. It was gone and she had scraped the flesh off my back from my spine all the way across. She had taken my whole triceps, most of my bicep and slashed my breast.

Mike had brought a medical kit, as had the vascular surgeon, Randy, who ran and got his bag that had haemostats [medical clamps or forceps that can be locked in place] in it. My husband was holding my artery with his fingers and Randy clamped my artery with the haemostat. It was still bleeding, so my husband dug deeper into my wound, up above the haemostat, to find where it was still bleeding and clamp it off again with his fingers. Then Randy stuck another set of haemostats up in there and clamped it off. Then they packed it with four-by-four-inch gauze

The attack itself had been all about the pressure, then a crazy level of fear. But the pain hit the first time when Mike stuck his hand up into my wound. It was surgery without anaesthesia. It was horrific, horrible. I was screaming ... so high and so loud I couldn't even hear myself. It was terrible. The second time, when he had to do it again, it was the same. I would stop screaming and say, "I'm so sorry." I knew he had to do it.'

Faced with a six-hour boat ride back to the island of Providenciales in the Turks and Caicos, Mike and the boat crew knew they had to find a quicker way to get Micki to hospital.

'First they called and got a helicopter to come. They strapped me onto a stretcher from the boat. Their plan was to carry me on the stretcher up the spiral ladder to the top of the boat and have the helicopter land up there. Once they got me up, they realised there wasn't room for the helicopter to land, so they came back down the spiral stairs and put me in a dinghy. It was very frightening to be hovered out over the water when they were putting me in the dinghy, because at this point I was terrified of sharks.

The chopper landed on [a nearby small island called] French Cay, but it was just a little bubble helicopter, with room for a pilot and somebody next to him. There was no way I could sit up in the seat and fly anywhere. They came back and called in a police boat – I don't know where it came from.

We went full power, headed back to Providenciales. Both surgeons, my husband and Randy, went with me. The boat was going very fast but it seemed like a really long ride. My stretcher was on the floor of the boat, so when it hit waves, it jumped up and crashed down on the deck.'

The only care available back on the island was at a small clinic. Micki didn't know it then but she had lost half her blood. Although she thought her blood type was A-positive, she wasn't sure enough to risk the clinic replacing it with the wrong type, so they erred on the side of caution and gave her one unit of the universal O-negative blood type. An average person will have ten units of blood in their body. Micki ended up requiring thirteen units in total.

'They wanted to give me something for pain and I was afraid the pain was the only thing keeping me alive. I didn't have enough blood left and I feared if they gave me something to relax me that dilated my blood vessels, I would die. I was right, as it turned out, as I'd lost half my blood volume. I started a mantra, "Pain is my friend, pain is my friend, pain is my friend." They wanted to give me morphine, so

131

I said just a tiny little bit to see how it affected me. It took the edge off.

I couldn't fly back to Miami [on a regular flight] because I had been doing repetitive deep dives. That would risk decompression illness – for me and my husband – so a coastguard jet flew down to get us. It could fly low to get us back to Miami. On the way to the hospital, it was dicey, as Mike lost my blood pressure and couldn't get a pulse on me.'

A US Coast Guard Falcon jet flew Micki and her husband to the Coast Guard Air Station at Opa-locka, Miami. From the time of the attack – around 8.40 a.m. – to Micki's arrival was seven and a half hours.

'We landed at an airport in Miami and an ambulance met us there. They said, "We are putting you on the ambulance until the helicopter gets here." I remember thinking, I've come all this way and now I'm going to die in Miami traffic 'cos they didn't send a helicopter, but then the helicopter was there in just a few minutes and took me to the Ryder Trauma Center [at Jackson Memorial Hospital]. We landed on the roof of the hospital at Ryder.

Mike was with me, monitoring and reassuring me the whole time. I had a faint pulse, and one in my arm too. I had blood flow in my arm and, up until about two hours from the hospital, it was pink to my hand. But then I began to develop compartment syndrome, when you get swelling in the muscle, which Mike could tell was happening. When we landed on the roof, the surgical staff were there, dressed in their gowns. We got to whatever holding area was there and a surgeon came with a clipboard and a piece of paper. He wanted me to sign to have my arm disarticulated [amputated] at the shoulder.

Mike started telling them, "No, her arm can be saved. She had blood flow in her hand up until about two hours ago and her arm can be saved." The surgeon started to argue with him, and pretty soon they were shouting at each other across my stretcher. They were just yelling at each other back and forth, and Mike said, "I think I can save her arm, and if you are not willing to try, then either get somebody in here who is or let me do it. Give me temporary privileges and let me do it; I think I can save her arm." Mike is licensed in Florida, but not credentialled at their facility. The surgeon ripped his gown off and went storming out of the room.

At that point, I just wanted to get under anaesthesia. I didn't care if I lost my arm or not. I was just like, "You've just chased my surgeon away!"

I'm really glad he did because a woman surgeon, Dr Anne Ouellette, came in a minute or two later. Mike talked to her, she listened to him, and she said, "I think you are right, and I'll do everything I can to save her arm." And she did. Mike saved my life and he saved my arm because, well, it would have been taken off at the shoulder otherwise.

Mike also suggested to them that they do a muscle transfer – take part of my latissimus dorsi muscle on my back and flip it around and make me a triceps. Because my triceps muscle was completely gone. It worked. I can straighten my arm because of that. It's not real strong but I can straighten it.'

The first surgery to save Micki's arm took six hours. Because of the transfusions and trauma and the build-up of fluid in Micki's body, her face was so swollen her husband didn't recognise her. She awoke in intensive care to find herself on a ventilator, alone apart from one nurse in attendance.

'Although I'm a diver, I'm claustrophobic, and the scariest thing for me was waking up with that tube down my throat. It wouldn't let me breath on demand at all. I understand now that you are supposed to be able to suck in additional air when you are on a ventilator. I don't know if it was set for that. I tried to suck in air and it was like sucking into a dead regulator. Nothing came out, so I was in a panic. Also, I was having flashbacks of the shark attack. I was just a mess – a complete emotional mess – that morning when I woke up in the ICU.

There was a male nurse there, and the only way I could get his attention was to flutter my feet and he would come over. I felt like I was going to choke because you get saliva down the back of your mouth and they have to suction it out. The third or fourth time I did that, I was really in a panic. He leaned down and whispered to me, "If you keep pitching your little fits, I'm going to 'Pav' you." What he meant was he was going to give me a paralytic so that I couldn't flutter my feet. I couldn't do anything – he was going to paralyse me.

I started crying; tears were running down. He should not have been a nurse. He was threatening me. I'm on a ventilator and he is threatening to paralyse me.

As soon he saw the tears, his entire demeanour changed. I'm sure when he said that, he thought I had no idea what Pavulon was. But I was a radiology director in a hospital. I knew it is a paralytic [and in some states, it is one of the drugs administered during lethal injections]. I'm sure he did it for his own benefit and was giving me that little threat, but he didn't think that I would understand what he was saying.'

Unsurprisingly, especially given the seriousness of her injuries, Micki's shark attack attracted widespread media attention. As soon as she was physically able, she and Anne Ouellette gave a press conference at the hospital. Dr Ouellette described the shark bite as the worst she'd ever seen.

'The whole room was filled with reporters with microphones and everything. Dr Ouellette was in there with me and she didn't want to further traumatise me. She said, "If they ask a question that you don't want to answer, don't answer it. Don't say anything specific."

My doctor said if my artery had continued to spurt for thirty more seconds, I would not have lived. I was lucky because most people don't have a trauma team at the ready when they are attacked. My brachial artery was severed where a tourniquet could not be applied.

To my knowledge, I am the worst injured person ever to have survived a shark attack. I credit that firstly to God – many miracles – but the only earthly reason I survived is because of Mike, Randy, an ICU nurse who was also on board the dive boat, and Nancy Birchett, who swam into the blood bath and propelled me towards the boat.'

While in Ryder, Micki's wounds required daily debridement – a process in which dead or damaged tissue is removed. It took one and a half to two hours and was extremely painful.

'I cannot tolerate narcotics. They cause me to vomit uncontrollably. So, a Chinese alternative medicine doctor would come in about thirty minutes before the process and talk me down through levels of consciousness. Just prior to the debridement sessions, she would instruct me to leave my injured arm on the bed for the doctors to take care of, and to go to my happy places while they debrided.

Almost every time in my mind I went galloping with a horse I had, Gentleman Caller, or Gent. I rode him in my white dress on my wedding day. He was one of the greatest loves of my life. He was a Swedish warmblood and could jump a house! He was almost seventeen hands high and fast, fast, fast. I used to ride him at night on white sandy trails and open him wide up. What a rush. When Mike and I raced, I'd give him a head start for as long as I could hold Gent. He would get so excited, he'd leap off his hind legs into the air! Then he would pick up and put down his feet so fast his belly was only about a foot off the ground. Mike said when we would begin pulling them up from flat out, Gent was still leaping so high he could see under his belly from his seat on his quarter horse. Those were fun memories.

Other times, I sailed my catamaran in my mind, or relived sailing a trimaran I'd recently rented on Lake Tahoe. Never once did I feel the scalpels. The mind is truly incredible and most of us never learn even a fraction of its capabilities.'

The initial surgery was the first of six operations Micki endured to reconnect blood vessels and stitch various muscles and tendons back together. Although she had managed to combat the pain of her procedures, there was no such surgery or quick remedy, however, for the physiological trauma in the aftermath of the attack.

'I ended up on the surgical ward, and it was there I began to be assaulted with flashbacks. I was lying in my hospital room, and if I didn't keep myself busy every minute with my eyes or speaking to somebody, the walls would just dissolve into the sea again and it was like I was on the surface of the water, just before she attacked me. I'd relive the attack again over and over and over. In the flashback, I could see her teeth – but, of course, I couldn't see her teeth when she was attacking me. But in the flashbacks in the hospital, I could see her teeth coming at me. That was brutal.'

As well as battling the mental images, Micki had to deal with the reality that, although her arm and hand had been saved, it would take a long time for her to regain significant movement and strength – if it ever returned at all.

'I'm so happy to have this hand and my arm because my life would be so much more difficult if it had been amputated. You don't realise it but one of your hands is mostly your support hand. Your dominant hand does everything. Your support hand pretty much holds things so your dominant hand can cut or do whatever you are doing. But the fact that I've got that elbow means I can hold things in my elbow, like a bottle or a jar; I can hold it in my elbow and twist it with my left hand. I was right-handed before this happened. That was a whole different struggle.

They took a skin graft from my leg to put on my arm. They did two nerve grafts. The stump of my radial nerve was gone, so there was nothing for them to connect a graft to. My median nerve and ulnar nerve, they took nerves from my lower leg and grafted those. One of them worked.'

Remarkably, considering her surgeries and condition, Micki spent just twelve days in hospital. Her doctors allowed her to go home a week or two early because

Mike was able to care for her at their home in Destin, in Florida's Panhandle, changing her dressings and debriding her wounds. Once home, Micki wasted no time in trying to get on with her life.

'I got home from the hospital on a Wednesday before Thanksgiving, and that following Monday I went back to work. I missed that Friday for Mike to do my final surgery, then I was back to work full time that Monday.'

A talented equestrian, Micki was also desperate to pursue her other main passion, horse riding. In order to hold the reins, she designed a brace and hook, initially with mixed results.

'The first draft had a fatal flaw! My horse dumped me and dragged me behind it at a gallop through the woods by my injured arm. The release didn't work properly.

Three or four months after the shark attack, I competed in a horse show. I couldn't actually get on the horse until something like two weeks before the show because I couldn't use the arm. There was a big wedge that my arm was strapped to so that I wouldn't hurt the muscle transfer they had done.

By the time I could get on the horse, I didn't have much time to practise. I had a brace on my arm – and I went off with ribbons! It was amazing – and the biggest confidence builder. I was so proud.

Another competitor actually filed a complaint against me, saying I had an advantage in the dressage competition because of the hook on my right hand. I thought, I'll trade arms with you any day if you think that's an advantage ... I don't think the judge even knew I had a paralysed hand – because for dressage, you need two hands, and the hook was inside where my palm and my fingers were, and I had a long-sleeved riding jacket. But the other competitor obviously thought my hook won me all the ribbons.'

Micki had to wait months for feeling to return to her damaged arm.

'Mike and I were in Destin eating dinner, and I was constantly messing with my arm. I was holding my wrist down with my left hand and trying to move my fingers. All of a sudden, my index finger moved a tiny little bit.

I said, "My finger moved! My finger moved!"

He said, "No, it's just a … "

"No," I said, "Look! I'm moving it on purpose and my index finger just made a small movement."

Nerves are regenerated an inch a month, I think. So, it took a full year for it to get to my finger. After that, I really worked it, and I can flex my wrist really hard now. I can pick up buckets with it. That motion is really strong. But I can't lift my wrist. I don't have any individual finger function or anything like that. But I can bend the elbow with a lot of strength, and I can bend at the wrist with a lot of strength. So, I can ride my horses, I can saddle, I can do a lot. I use that a lot for tightening my girths and doing things like that. I'm constantly stretching my fingers – probably eighty or ninety times a day or more – and straightening my fingers and my wrist. And that's the reason those muscles haven't really clamped down so that I can't move my hand.'

As the movement began to return, so the mental scars also began to heal, if just as slowly.

139

'I had nightmares and flashbacks for a long time, probably for over a year. The last flashback I had was really unexpected: it was within a year after the attack and I was in Destin, at Mellow Mushroom Pizza. I have a dually truck [a vehicle with two sets of two wheels at the back] to pull the horses, and I was just sitting inside the place, waiting for my pizza, when I had a brutal flashback. When I became aware of where I was again, I was in the back seat, curled up on the floorboard where I load the feed and put the dogs in. I don't even know how I ended up in my truck on the floorboard. It was immediate – an assault on all of my senses.

Years later, I learnt that it was my mind desensitising to what had happened. It seems brutal, and it was brutal, but if you see something enough and live through something enough, you become desensitised to it. Within a few days, they became a little less frequent.

The flashbacks were when I was awake. At night-time, I had nightmares. But the nightmares were never about a shark. The nightmares were crazy scary. Before this happened, when I had a nightmare, I would wake up thinking I was screaming, but I wasn't really screaming. But since then, I would wake Mike up because I would literally be screaming out loud.

One of the worst nightmares I had, for some reason, was it was dark and I could see Mike working out of his office window with the light on. We lived near the horse barn and there were woods out the back of where we lived. In my dream, something was luring me out into the woods. I followed it until I was way too far, and then my hair stood up on my back and I felt in danger. I turned around and there was a wolf. He was half as tall as I was and he had these glowing eyes, saliva draining out of his mouth. He was between me and my home. It was so real. I didn't realise I was dreaming. I was screaming for Mike but in my dream he couldn't hear me because he was in his office with the light on. I was just screaming out loud and he woke me up. I was screaming out loud because the wolf was about to eat me.

Things like that. It was never like the flashbacks, which were about the incident. The nightmares were different.

Another time we were watching a James Bond movie. I don't remember which one it was, but it had a scene in it with a diver in a cage under water and, all of a sudden, a great white shark appeared with an open mouth and I completely came unglued. I was lying on the couch watching the movie. I guess I had seen it before but had forgotten there was a shark scene in it. I was crying, and it just really undid me.

For a long time, pictures of sharks would do that to me. I could see a picture of a shark on TV or something and it would just completely undo me. Mike talked to me and, just like the flashbacks desensitised me and they became less frequent, he said, "I think it would help you if I put a picture of the shark that attacked you on your computer screen as your wallpaper."

I trust Mike, so I said, "OK." For a while, I would walk around the corner of my computer and there she would be. I would start crying and become unglued, but, after a day or two, I could walk in and sit at my computer. It desensitised me, and I no longer have a problem with images of sharks or sharks on TV.'

Managing to desensitise her mind was a significant step forward in her recovery, but another major challenge would be facing fears about getting back into the water.

'When I was in the hospital, I told Mike, "I want you to sell my dive gear or burn it. I never want to see it again. I'm never going to dive again." By the time I got home and a week or two had gone by, I was like, "You didn't really burn my diving gear, did you?"

He said, "No, I know you better than that."

It took two years for me to want to get back in the water. Part of the reason is that I wanted to make sure the flashbacks were gone before I got back in the water because it would be terrible to have one at depth when you are diving. I needed to be over that. Almost two years exactly after I got attacked, the same dive shop planned a trip to Dominica and I wanted to go on that trip. It was really a weeklong trip, but Nancy, who owns the shop, said, "Micki, why don't we go down three or four days earlier than everybody else and come home three or four days later than everybody else?" So we did.

First off, she just took me for the first two days to the edge of the water. I just put my face in the water, and it was very hard. Then, pretty soon, we were diving at twelve, fifteen feet of water along the shore. The third day, we went out on the boat to do our first boat dive – and that's when everybody else was there too. I threw up my breakfast. When I put my mask on and everything and walked to the edge of the boat to take a giant stride to the edge of the water, I was just snotty. Tears were streaming down my face. I was scared to death.

It's interesting; I didn't have a flashback when I was riding on the bow of the boat to go out there. But once there, I looked down at the water and could see myself being attacked by the shark on the surface of the water. It wasn't like a flashback. And I was in it; it was like it was happening to me. I was watching it happen on the surface of the water. I just thought, I love diving so much I was at least going to try. At soon as I got situated on the surface and started to sink to depth everything was fine.

And I've been fine diving ever since. I love it just as much as I did before. It was that fast. The trouble was getting in, it wasn't diving.

I had a close-up encounter on that trip with a big barracuda. I was probably fifty or sixty feet underwater, right next to the wall, and I saw this barracuda. They sit on the water and open and close their mouths and you can see all their teeth. I came face to face with that and slammed against the wall. I started to have a panic attack and I started crying. All of a sudden, I just thought, It's a barracuda – it's not a shark. You have to solve your problems under water. You can't panic like that and go shooting to the surface, or you die. I just thought to myself, You have to solve your problems at depth. You can't run away from this. So, that was scary.'

Since that day, Micki has encountered many big fish ... and it was inevitable one day she would see a shark again ...

'The first time I encountered sharks, we were at Little Cayman Beach Resort. This was maybe four or five years after I was attacked. It was the first time I had really seen a shark. I was down on the wall, watching everything. For some reason, I turned round and looked off to the side of me. Probably fifteen feet off away was a big shark – a reef shark. She was keeping pace with me, diving parallel with me down along the wall. I watched her for a few minutes. She just seemed like a good omen or something. I wasn't afraid of her.

I was a little bit afraid when I was circled by a couple of sharks in Little Cayman. There's a lionfish problem in the Caribbean. It's an invasive species. Their numbers are increasing and they are harming the ecosystem there, so divers have started spearing them with little tripod spears to try to eradicate them from the reef. As a result, you see a lot more sharks in the Caribbean now, I guess because of the blood and the struggle and everything when they are spearing the lionfish. We had a reef shark that was circling me on the reef and that made me really nervous.'

Although Micki's attack predated the online comments that can be devastating for recent animal survivors, her ordeal did lead to discussion about what happened. Overall, however, her experience has been a positive one.

'I've read things that were speculative about the boat I was on, whether they were throwing chicken or offal off the boat. It wasn't a shark-feeding trip, but we suspect that they probably were throwing offal from the kitchen overboard. There was another dive boat nearby and, in the forums and everything that I read, they didn't have the shark activity that we did. A lot of the time we had three to five sharks cruising the reef in the vicinity of our boat, so maybe chicken and things at night were thrown overboard, but I have no idea.

I know sometimes people can be brutal. I've seen other people, like parents who've lost a child or something, I've seen really brutal social medial attacks on them. There may be something out there, but I've never had a negative response or any bad experience on social media because of it. I said something in an interview and had a couple of people say they didn't believe what I said. It's true – but I can understand why they wouldn't have believed me.

There are things that have happened in my life that were a lot harder than this. I would go through the shark attack again before I would go through some of the other things that I've been through, like my mother dying of Alzheimer's. There are things in life that are worse than some trauma. Also, I don't regret what happened because it really has been a positive experience in my life. I learnt a lot through this. Although I was never a person who, even when I was younger, has put make-up on or tried to enhance my looks, I think I took my looks for granted. I was always pretty and confident, and when this happened, I learnt that it doesn't really matter.

I'm horribly disfigured, but your scars are on the outside. I'm Micki, the same person I always was. That's been a huge lesson to learn. My dad had his bladder removed for bladder cancer. He had to have a colostomy bag. Before, something like that would have been horrifying. Now, if I had to lose a leg or have a colostomy, I would take it in my stride. It's physical; it's my body; it's not who I am. You are who you are inside.

The other thing I learnt is equally invaluable. You hear people say how powerful positivity is: the only thing I could control, when I got home, was my attitude. I was afraid of so many things, I was having nightmares and flashbacks, I was disfigured and I had to learn to do everything with my left hand. I know Mike loves me, and I thought he would love me anyway, but I did think he would be repulsed because I had this horrible disfigurement. I had a lot of fears. But I chose to be positive, because of my mother.

My mother would come walking into my bedroom in the morning and I knew if I started crying or complaining, she would have fallen apart. So, when she walked in, I would say, "Hi, Mom."

When she said, "How are you doing this morning?"

I'd say, "Oh, I'm fine." If you project positivity, even if you are not feeling it, it is so powerful.

The feelings come and I've learnt that. I learnt that every morning when you get up, you can either choose to be happy and positive and see your glass as half full, or you can choose to go into some dark place and feel sorry for yourself. It is a choice. That is a lesson that you don't learn unless you've been through something terrible and you've lived it and you've realised just how powerful that is. So, there are things that came out of this that have made me a lot better person.'

Micki, now sixty-one, has been able to pass on what she's learned. She shared the medical complications of her injuries with the US military at Hurlburt Field, an air force installation in Okaloosa County, Florida.

'A special ops [special operations] dive instructor is a friend of Nancy's. Around three or four years after my attack, he got in touch with her to ask whether I would be interested in talking to the new combat dive course classes that were coming through at Hurlburt. I was thrilled to.

A couple of nights before I was due to go, I was putting together my talk when my husband said, "Do you feel like you are up to seeing your injury pictures?"

I said, "You've got injury pictures? Yeah, I want to see my injury pictures!"

So, he gave me the disk of my injury pictures, and that night I created a PowerPoint slide. I gave my talk with a slide of my injury pictures. I've probably gone back five or six times to new classes. Not only are they taking combat dive courses, but they are also well-trained medics too.

So, it is a lesson of what Mike did to me. Even if you can't put a tourniquet around, you need to stop the bleeding. That's the first thing you do, otherwise you are going to lose this person. You've got to stop the bleeding first. I show them my slides and tell them the whole story. Some of the classes have taken me under their wing. They also took us on a night boat-ride, where they were parachuting into the water and we were picking them up and pulling them in the boat. I love those guys there.

Some of those who have been at my talk have been injured badly from IEDs [improvised explosive devices] going off. They've had legs blown off. I was injured doing something recreational; they were injured in battle, fighting for my country. And so, I'm always in awe of them when I go to Hurlburt and hear their stories.'

Yet, while Micki's experience has been wholly positive, she admits there were times when she found the road to recovery tougher than she anticipated.

'I went through a period of depression, which is really unlike me. It took me a year to figure out what it was. I would force myself to do things, to go to work, but I felt like I could have just curled up in bed and stayed there. I would have nightmares and things, at first at home. It was so bad that my safe place was my long walk-in closet. I consider myself a strong person, but there were nights when I would go and crawl up in a ball in my closet and sob. I'm not proud of that, but it took time to get past it.

I was having neurogenic pain in my paralysed arm and hand. It's like phantom pain if you lose an arm or something. They gave me Neurontin. It helped a lot with that, but it took me probably six or seven months to recognise it was depression. This wasn't like me. Was this just the aftermath of the trauma? Then I started thinking, What could I have done differently?

I started reading and found that it is a big side effect of Neurontin. When I got off the Neurontin, the depression went away. It had been the medication.'

Micki's understanding of what she had been through led her to Bite Club, where she identified with people going through similar experiences.

'I don't remember whether I found them or they found me, but I have been a member of Bite Club for three or four years now. I thought I could help people who were going through the aftermath of attacks, like I had. I can answer questions, I can give advice and I can tell them a little about what happened to me and what I felt. I can tell them if they have problems, I can answer questions about the purpose of flashbacks. I can tell them they do get less frequent and things do get better. There is tremendous support and a lot of love in that group.

I really hope to go to Australia one day and meet a few of them in person because they are a great support group for each other and their families. One family lost their son a couple of years ago and their grief is palpable. I can choose to private message somebody and offer to talk to them if they want to talk. We are a cheerleading group for people too. When somebody's suffered a shark attack and they want to get back in the water but have qualms about it, we cheer them on.

It is a great group of people.'

CHAPTER 8
LAUREN FAGEN

MOHOLOHOLO ANIMAL REHABILITATION CENTRE, LIMPOPO PROVINCE, SOUTH AFRICA, MONDAY 1 JULY 2013

'He had my right leg in his mouth.
I saw him go right through the knee like a blade.'

It was billed as an 'experience of a lifetime'. When Lauren Fagen read about the rehabilitation treatment the Moholoholo Centre provided for injured and abandoned wildlife, and the volunteer student programme that offered a 'unique African experience' for young people all over the world, she believed it was exactly the opportunity she was looking for.

Established in 1991, the rehab centre, in Hoedspruit, Limpopo Province, 420 km northeast of Pretoria in South Africa, was home to a variety of orphaned, injured or poisoned animals, under the stewardship of Brian Jones, who had been caring for wildlife since the age of four. Lauren had always felt a deep love for animals but, growing up in Montreal, Canada, had only really been able to interact with domesticated animals. She was keen to see how she'd adapt to a foreign country and whether she could help treat the animals at Moholoholo.

'I was eighteen and had never worked abroad before. When I finished CEGEP – the mandatory community college between high school and university in Quebec – I wanted to do something over the summer before starting university, and looked up volunteering opportunities with injured wildlife. It was my mom who actually found Moholoholo. It looked great. It was a rehabilitation centre for injured wildlife that doubled as a tourist attraction. As well as rehabilitating the animals, they charged tourists to visit the animals, learn about them and even have the chance to pet an ambassador cheetah with supervision.

Volunteers, like me, would pay for room and board and give up our time and services for free, doing jobs, mainly cleaning and feeding, around the centre. There was some education intertwined. I romanticised the idea a little bit but I had the right intentions. I looked up what I could, took the information they provided at face value and basically was paying seventy dollars a day to be a volunteer.'

In June 2013, Lauren flew to South Africa – her first solo trip outside Canada – and transferred to an internal flight before being picked up for a three-hour drive into the bush to the centre. She was due to be there for three weeks. On her arrival, Lauren found the volunteers were largely young women.

'My first impression was that it was cliquey. I felt like I was back in high school. For example, one of the first things I was told was, "Your name is Lauren and that's your bed. A girl that just left was also called Lauren and she slept in that bed and we hated her."

"OK," I said. "I hope I can be a better version of that."

I had this weird high-school desperation to fit in, and although I don't think I did anything outwardly weird, I definitely felt new, while everyone else was established. They might not have been, but that was how I felt. Very few rules, if any, were explained to me. It was a Sunday, the day off, so I was told that the next day I would become more informed.

One of the coordinators showed me around. One of the first things she did – when we came to a cheetah – was stick her arm right through the chain-link fence. She was petting him and encouraged me to do it too. I put my hand through the fence too and thought, This is great, you get to touch the animals with supervision.

I checked with her that we were only allowed to do this if she was there, and she confirmed: "No, we have to be here." She said I could put my hand flat against the gate without supervision. What I'd later discover is that this was just one of many inconsistencies in the way the reserve was run.'

As Lauren was shown around, she discovered the centre was home to lions, leopards, cheetahs, elephants, giraffes, antelope, vultures, rhinoceros and honey badgers. She was keen to know exactly what the rules were, given they were dealing with potentially dangerous animals. But, although that first coordinator had said Lauren could put her hand flat against the cheetah's gate, allowing it to lick her hand, not every coordinator agreed.

'Other coordinators said, "No." Contradictions started to arise and there was an overlapping. People were telling me different things. The park was quite big; it might have been classified as a reserve. I was told the animals that tourists came to visit were being rehabilitated or could not be released back into the wild for a variety of reasons – as opposed to a more classical zoo where healthy animals are kept captive for the sole purpose of tourism. Some animals could wander, while others were in medium-sized cages.

Getting to pat that cheetah on the first day – with supervision – was amazing, and it was cool to see the animals, but I was, most often, working or caring with them from afar. Before I'd left, I'd romanticised it as my first trip out into the world as a traveller, but the truth was that, although I had travelled to South Africa, I was secluded in one bubble. It didn't feel like I was exploring. I wasn't having that "Aha!" connective moment that a lot of people search for. It takes time, and when you are eighteen, with no experience and paying to volunteer, it's misguided to think that you're going to go in there and get that experience. It was overwhelming, like going to a new school.

One of the reasons I loved animals was because of the care I was able to provide for them or the interactions I could have with them. At the centre, those were quite limited. Sometimes, while I was there, I actually felt like I missed animals, which was weird, given where we were and why I was there.'

Over the next fifteen days, Lauren tried to make the most of her experience but discovered more inconsistencies in how the centre was run.

'The honey badgers were the animals I was assigned to feed every morning. Despite their small size, they can kill lions. Again, I wanted to know what the rules were while feeding them, for my own safety, but people were very vague. In a stack of old celebrity magazines in the corner of my dorm room, I found an outdated book with instructions on how to complete morning rounds. I was never shown this book – I found it – and it was so outdated it included instructions for animals that had left the centre years prior, and lacked instructions for many animals.

For the honey badgers, you fed them over walls, but when it came to cleaning the enclosure, you had an option – it seemed. You could quarantine the honey badgers by ushering them with a broom into one section, or you could jump in there with them if you were comfortable. Different staff were telling me different things, and different students were telling me different things.

More than once, a group of us students went out to walk a young rhino called Ollie. That was cool because it was a direct experience with this rhino. There were times, however, when he charged at us. Sometimes it seemed quite playful and the staff would laugh as he charged, but on other occasions, it seemed, like he was surrounded and overwhelmed. Once, it went too far and we had to hide in trees or run around the trees to avoid him. It was scary to a certain point. On another occasion, he swung his head and hit me with his horn, leaving a fist-sized bruise on the side of my thigh.

The coordinator I was with wanted to keep an eye on it, but said I wasn't to tell the owner, Brian Jones, and hide it from him, because he was uneasy about these walks. The staff also told the students not to tell him Ollie had been charging us.'

Lauren wanted to learn more about the animals at the centre and have a more hands-on experience with their care and treatment, but she found these were limited and unevenly shared among the student volunteers.

'The way it was advertised, you would get hands-on experience with these animals, but mainly it was cleaning. There were certain experiences that were more hands-on but you had to get chosen for it. I once got chosen by the vet nurse to hold a honey badger while she took a trap off while it was under anaesthesia. That was awesome. It made me want to be a vet nurse. But, for the most part, these jobs weren't fairly distributed. You could pretty much go through the entire experience with minimal animal interaction, outside of cleaning the feeding cages.'

On 1 July, Lauren got ready for her daily tasks and saw an opportunity to fulfil a promise she'd made to her employer back home in return for getting the time off to fulfil her dream.

'Every morning there was a system that did exist. Some jobs were mandatory – where small groups of two to four people would do certain animals. They called them the morning rounds. One of my rounds, among other animals, was the honey badgers. They were the most dynamic, the most hands-on of any animal activity I did there. Then there were big jobs, which would change every day, and that was usually for one of the bigger, more dangerous animals that we would take on together. It was often some form of cleaning.

On that day, I was instructed to clean the honey badger enclosure. I still wasn't sure if it was safe to go in there alone, so I asked one of the coordinators if I should go into it directly or usher the animals into a sectioned-off area first. He told me I could go into the honey badger enclosure if I felt comfortable doing so.

Back home, I worked as a waitress at a place called Jack Astor's Bar and Grill. They had given me the month off to do this on one condition – that I take pictures with cool animals with a Jack Astor's sign. I was like, "Done," and brought a sign. When the coordinator said I could go into the honey badger enclosure, I thought this was a Jack Astor's moment. I brought the sign into the enclosure. I was cleaning and looked up and held the sign and smiled and a volunteer snapped the picture.

But, just after that, the honey badger tried to climb my leg. I backed away and put the broom between me and the honey badger. I felt uncomfortable and wanted to get out. The volunteer I was with started laughing. I ended up jumping out of the enclosure and shocking myself multiple times on the electric wire that surrounds the top of the gate.

I never wanted to go in there again.'

Despite feeling deeply uncomfortable, Lauren focused on her next task – her 'big job' of the day. The outdated book of rules told her that if a volunteer had a specific interest in 'large predators', they should speak with one of the coordinators for involvement when possible. Lauren had shown this to a coordinator and at last one such opportunity had arisen.

'So that day, the big job was either cleaning the lion feeding cages or the leopard feeding cages. They asked us what we wanted to be part of, and up until that point I'd had less experience with the lions, so for me it was an easy choice. We were split fifty-fifty, and as we walked towards the lion cage, I was with the coordinator and we were tailing the group of people walking down the row of feeding cages, which are attached to the main enclosures. It's two people per feeding cage and people were already walking in pairs. As we all walked together, he assigned pairs to branch off from us into their respective cages to clean. By the end of the row, there were two cages left and three students. The other two paired off into a cage, so that left one cage and just me.

The cage we were at was attached to an enclosure that had two lions in there: Duma, a male, and Tree, a female. They were big lions, both around five years old. They were in a rectangular enclosure with a chain-link fence. Adjacent to that rectangle was a smaller, shed-like place that was the feeding cage. They put meat in the feeding cage, and it often got bloody and dirty on the floor, so you would have to go in there and clean any off food left on the floor.

They tried to find me a partner but, when no one was available and seeing the cage wasn't that dirty, said it would be OK for me to clean it on my own. He said not even to use biocide, which was the soap they used. I was just to wash it with water and call it a day. As he was saying this, Duma started rubbing himself against the main portion of the chain-link fence, pushing the top part of his head against it and rubbing it in a way that seemed like he was having a good day.

One coordinator asked us to come over. He knew I wanted more hands-on experience with animals. I think he took this as an opportunity because he said this was what I had asked for and pushed me in a playful way. It was an encouraging gesture and I was so excited. I put my hand flat against the gate with the other girls – because he encouraged all of us. I was petting this lion with a flat hand. It was sick. I'll always remember it. It was sweet to see the lion in a state I read to be happy. I'm not an animal whisperer, I don't know how animals are feeling, but it seemed like we were all having a good time. None of us stuck our hands through the gate, and at a certain point the animal walked away. The coordinator then told us to move away and go and do our work.

I said, "OK," and he walked away. I don't know where he went but I got the sense he was just patrolling the volunteers in some way.

There were two doors: one for the lion to access the feeding cage from its enclosure and one for us to access the same feeding cage from the outside. To separate us from the lions, only one door was to be opened at a time. My door was open, so I went into the feeding cage with my bucket of water and broom. Duma was right next to the feeding cage and continued to rub himself up against the chain-link fence that separated the main enclosure from where I was.

Everyone was away, working in the other feeding cages they had been assigned. Suddenly, because I was in a confined space, Duma felt very close. I was thinking, Oh my God. But I didn't touch him. I felt particularly alone. I crouched down with knees bent to observe the lion better, with my broom in my arms because I had already spilled water on the floor. I looked at the lion. I was maybe a foot and a half away from the chain-link fence. The feeding cage wasn't very big. Length-wise, it was maybe ten feet, and if I extended both my arms, width-wise, I nearly touched the walls. I was a foot away from the fence but I couldn't have got much further away. I was cleaning in a very small space and I was thinking, If he does lunge, there is that foot of space; he can't get me because it's chain link.

Just then someone gasped behind me – another student, who was outside the enclosure.

"You are so lucky," she said, meaning it wasn't often the animals were that close.

"Thank you," I said.

She said, "Do you want me to take a picture?"

"Yeah," I said.

She took out her own phone and took a photo. I wasn't looking at the camera, I was looking at the lion. That photo would become my saving grace. She said, "Have fun," and walked away from my feeding cage.

I didn't move from my spot because I wanted to suck this moment in for as long as I could. But then Duma moved to the left to where his door was to our enclosure. Duma walked right up to the gate and sat down. He turned his head and looked at me. I noticed the width of the gap in the bars. Those are wide, I thought. Normally, that kind of door is not made of widely spaced bars, it's cut out of solid steel. Some other doors had steel bars that were very close together – a finger distance apart. My door was made out of bars much wider. I had not seen bars like that on gates directly separating humans from large predators at the centre before. I was always cautious around the direct barriers, and this one rang an internal alarm for me. Realising its width, while already feeling very close to the lion, made me feel weird. This now felt borderline other-worldly. It almost looked fake. I had butterflies in my stomach and felt like I was going to throw up. Instinctively, I took a step back. I was almost hitting the wall behind me. I decided to keep a bubble of space around that door because those bars were *really* wide.

He took his paws and started to piano, like when a cat is kneading on a blanket or the floor. He was stretching his nails. Oh boy, I thought. It was kind of cool but I still felt sick, and thought, Should I tell someone? I thought of the rules – don't touch the gate, keep a distance. I didn't think I needed to tell someone – why would there be a faulty gate? That would be gross negligence. It crossed my mind for a second to tell someone the gate was faulty, but I thought there could only be a problem if I didn't follow the rules. I was going to follow them to a T.

I kept that distance and started sweeping around, and he was following me with his eyes. I turned my back to him because I was trying to ignore him, keep my distance and do my job – trying to respect the imaginary bubble I had drawn for myself.

He stuck his entire leg through, nearly the full length of it because of how far I was away. Before I could react, he got me with the tip of his nail into the middle of my right calf. It was like butter, it went right in. I felt a thud – he had pulled me on to my back, I hit the ground and was looking up at the ceiling. What the fuck? I thought. I could see my full leg in his paws. He was almost stabilising me with his paws. I was wearing grey sweatpants and he sliced through them, like craft scissors through card. He sliced open my leg. It looked like what you would see at the butcher, like something from a dead cow that would hang from the ceiling.

I thought, That can't be my leg because that's not what … Wait, it is my leg.

It wasn't bleeding – because when you slice something that fast it takes a few seconds for it to start gushing. It was something I had never seen before. It looked super-surreal. I thought, Oh no. Then I thought, The coordinators are going to kill me; they're going to be so mad at me. Why was I thinking that? I hadn't done anything wrong. I had kept my distance, but I felt stupid because should I have told someone. Should I have kept more of a distance?

I was never warned to stay any distance from fences; I was only given conflicting rules on how I could touch or not touch the gates and doors in general. Staying an intentionally large distance from the gate in this setting was my own decision and not something that was discussed or warned about.

I started to scream for help and kicked with my other leg but he immediately pulled that one through the bars up to the groin. He did it one shot; he got it past the knee all the way to the groin. There was not like a tug of war, it was an instant pull through. I was a lean person at the time, but not abnormally small or skinny. A lot of people would be the same size. Even for someone a bit bigger, I think he would have been able to pull them through, at least up to their knee or even past it. A lot of people's legs could fit through the space in those bars. I was now on my back looking at him. He was not looking at me, but both my legs were pinned through the bars.

He had my right leg in his mouth. I saw him go right through the knee like a blade, though both legs remained attached. Someone ran in. Her name was Emma. She picked me up from under my armpits. Emma was my size and I could feel her pulling and I was like, "Yes, Emma! Do it!" It was not possible. She did not hold me for long. I think she recognised, "I can't do this, I need to get help." She ran to get help. That was best thing she could have done; she handled it beautifully.

I didn't know how long it would take. I needed to do something. I couldn't just lie there. I put both hands around my left leg – the one not in his mouth – and I tried to pull it out but I couldn't because it got stuck at the knee. I couldn't work out how he got the knee through there in the first place. I couldn't pull it out.

Now I thought, Oh my God, I think I'm going to die. I need to pull my leg out.

For some reason, I don't know why – the psychology of how this happens – the only pain I could feel was when I tried to pull my leg out. I could only feel it in the sides of my knee. I didn't feel any other pain. Even then, it was a dull pain. I somehow expected it to feel spicy, but this was "bassy", like an underwater pain. I could feel all the pressure, just no pain.

Now I thought, You need to be like one of those moms who lifts the car off her child in times of desperation. I am going to superwoman this and pull my knee out with every cell in my body. I want to believe to this day that I really did put in that crazy mother-car-child energy, but it still didn't come out. I fell back and hit my head on the ground, not hard but with a thud. I realised then that I wasn't strong enough. I couldn't get my knee out of there. Was I going to die?

I was getting really tired and had this irrational thought, What would be great? A nap. Then I realised, You can't take a nap, you're not allowed.

It was a weird fight in my own head of, nap – no nap.

Eventually, the coordinator came in. I could tell a bunch of people were now in the cage. The moment he came in and I saw him, it felt like: this is the grown-up, this is the person who knows what to do – and immediately I got tunnel vision. It's funny how the mind does this … It felt like I was at the base of a long, soft, grey tunnel. I could see him and his head at the top of it, and I never fully lost vision, but I think it's interesting: the moment when you know it's no longer your responsibility to get this thing off you or to keep living, you start to black out, basically. Prior to that, you have the adrenalin that keeps you going. That said, I never fully blacked out.

I heard him organising something. It was echoey and weird.

The other lion, Tree, jumped in and bit my foot multiple times. She was almost trying to pull my shoe off. I have no recollection of this and couldn't see because I was looking at the ceiling, but I was told later by people there. Up until that point I hadn't noticed what she had been doing.

From what I understand, partly from what people have since told me, they made a chain of people, with the coordinator first, holding each other under their armpits, and, step by step, they pulled me back. Other people took buckets and brooms to make a noise and stab the brooms through the bars to push the lions away. They eventually pulled me outside the enclosure. I looked at my hands, which were shaking, with all the blood on them, and I screamed.

It felt so dramatic, like in a movie. I heard them shouting, "Get her out, get her out!" They pulled me out onto the grass. I could hear the lions roaring in the background. I was lying on my back and the sun was so bright. It was beaming right down into my eyes. Suddenly it felt like that was the worst thing that was happening to me. I asked people to shield my eyes. I was confused – and not focusing on the right things, but asking stupid questions like, "Am I going to be able to walk again?" I should have been asking, "Am I going to die?"

Everyone started to apply pressure to my wounds, and at one point, a woman called Kate – who had been a nurse but now worked at the centre – ran in and was a massive help. I was spewing blood, like a little fountain, from my knee, and she took her thumb, stuck it in and stopped the bleeding. I was in shock and focused on my wounds.

While this was happening, they were saying, "We've got to get your mom on the phone."

I was like, "No, wait. Am I going to die?"

"No," they said, "we don't think so."

"Then don't call my mom!"

But the next thing I knew, a phone was thrust at me. I was thinking, I'm going to live. You should've called her after, or I should've been the one to call her. You're calling her while we're in the middle of this trauma, even though I'm going to live. You're going to ruin her life. And it did.

At this point, I started to feel the pain. It had moved from dull to spicy pain and it was the worst … like being in an arm-bar hold and tapping, "I'm good, I'm good," and nobody's listening and they just keep breaking your arm anyway. So, I was screaming down the phone. I told her I loved her and added, "I'm OK but it hurts."

My mom was saying, "OK, honey, I love you."

It was totally unfair to both of us.

Another medic came and gave me something for the pain, but it didn't help enough to make the pain bearable. I begged for more but was not allowed.'

Due to the remote location, it took around five hours to get Lauren to hospital. Staff at the centre put her in a van and drove her for two hours to meet an ambulance on the road and transfer her for the drive to Mediclinic Nelspruit, Mbombela. She had suffered multiple lacerations and wounds to her legs and lower abdomen. Lauren underwent surgery to clean out her wounds.

'Essentially, my left kneecap nearly came completely off and was hanging by a piece of skin. They were able to put that back on like a sticker. There were multiple stab wounds ... including a full pierce through the right tibia [shin bone] at the knee and out the back and a slice near the groin on the left side in the inner thigh. I had muscle and nerve damage, and actually caused quite a bit of damage to my anterior cruciate ligament myself when I was trying to get my leg out from between the bars. I could've been a lot worse: Duma sliced open my inner thigh so badly that my femoral artery was pulsing, and had it got pierced, it might likely have been lethal.

I've thought back to what the lions' intentions were. It's very possible that either one of them was messing around and not necessarily trying to kill me. Duma's canine went through my tibia [shin bone], and had he wanted to kill me, he could've just jerked his head and my leg would've come off. Maybe he thought I was food. Maybe he thought he was playing with his meal.'

Lauren's mother travelled for three days to be with her daughter. Lauren spent eight days in total in hospital, but a painful period of recovery lay ahead.

'I was unable to walk when they discharged me. I was wheelchair-bound, and getting onto the toilet took an exceptionally long time – it was almost impossible – and I couldn't shower. I needed full-time aid, and my mom and I went to a bed-and-breakfast because I couldn't fly home as there was a risk I might develop a blood clot at high altitude. We stayed there for just over two weeks. If she hadn't been there, I'm not sure I'd have been able to leave the hospital. I couldn't even get into a regular taxi.

It wasn't just a matter of picking me out of the wheelchair. My legs hurt, so it was like picking up a stiff, weird thing with a million bandages. After around two weeks I was able to take baby steps with a walker, but it was exhausting, so I could only do that for a little bit and had to go back into my wheelchair for practical purposes. By the time I got home, three weeks later, I still had a wheelchair but I was able to loosely hobble around.

After suffering so many stab wounds on my leg, the fact that I'm walking around right now is insane, but I do feel chronic pain in my inner thigh and my knee, although I'm used to it now. The nerve damage did cause some feeling to be relocated. Sometimes when I touch my leg, I feel it in a different spot. That's super weird, but it happens when you get a lot of damage to your leg. I also have a bit of a limp that comes out in certain circumstances. My knee is very effective and I exercise, so for the most part, no one notices my limp; but if the weather is cold, people will say, "Are you limping?" For the most part, though, it's not noticeable.'

Although Lauren surprised herself with how quickly she was back on her feet and moving around, she was unprepared for the disturbing psychological effects.

'I've had a ton of nightmares – not necessarily about lions; sometimes I get bears or cheetahs, but almost all of them have this theme of I'm in a cage or the animal is in a cage or that cage is breaking, and it's often like I'm trying to build an emergency barricade to protect myself. It's never just in an open field or the woods, there's always a mistake going on – me trying to plug a hole with my hands, as it gets bigger. I've also had flashbacks during the day – real PTSD. They happened quite quickly after the incident, often around animals like horses or dogs, anything that would stare at me for too long. Even today, if an animal looks me right in the eye, I think, OK, what are you doing now?

I still think about it, but I spend time with animals all the time – cats and dogs – and I'm not scared of them any more; but sometimes with a horse, I'm thinking how big it is and what it's doing. I carry bear spray with me and dog spray, ready to go at a moment's notice.'

Once back in Canada, Lauren found people were captivated by her ordeal – which had received considerable media coverage – but that led to some awkward interactions.

'At first people remembered I was "lion girl". In fact, they actually used to call me "tiger girl". Get it right, there are no tigers in South Africa. They would often come up to me at parties. I can understand the sensationalism and the shock around it, but I feel it's often followed by insensitive questions, like "Can you re-enact the event?"

I'll say, "I'm at a bar; it's someone's birthday; this was traumatic for me … Do you want to re-enact your parents' divorce? This is weird. We are not doing this here."

Even close friends will forget and start a gruesome conversation about animal attacks on a semi-regular basis. When *Tiger King* [Netflix TV documentary series about breeders of big cats] came out, I really don't think that helped the process.

There have been people who were super-intense about it. I have no problem with people asking me, but there is a bro'ness [macho curiosity] around it, like, "Oh, no fucking way, man."

For the most part, though, people are generally really nice, and if they say, "Hey, is it OK to ask this?" I'll thank them for asking. Often it is OK to ask, but I appreciate the remembrance that this is a traumatic event and I have flashbacks from getting triggered. I got really triggered when I went on an expedition recently to become a wilderness first-responder and to get some leadership skills. I really didn't appreciate it when people joked about animal attacks when we were actually in a scenario where it could happen again.'

As well as the physical and psychological challenges, Lauren had to deal with another kind of attack – from the Moholoholo Centre itself.

'This, to me, is the real story – because after what happened, I questioned whether it made me lose my faith in animals. But the answer was no, I lost my faith in humanity.

When I was in hospital, I was thinking, Are they going to apologise to me? Because people know what happened. There were eyewitnesses, not necessarily to me getting pulled through directly, but before and after. I was there for two days when the coordinator came to the hospital – before my mom got there – with three of my friends from the centre who brought all of my stuff. I was so lonely and sad then, but when I saw them, I was so happy they were there. For whatever reason, we didn't talk about the attack. It wasn't like I was avoiding it, I would have happily spoken about it, but it was just, "How are you doing? Are you OK? How are your injuries?"

The details of the attack weren't mentioned, and I guess I felt it was because we were all on the same page.

But we weren't, because two days later, Brian spoke to the media. He told them I had unlocked the cage or somehow climbed into the lion's cage, tried to kiss the lion, tried to hug him, and inevitably got attacked; and I was just this silly, young Canadian privileged white woman. That was not what I did at all.

I called up the news source and said, "You need to take this down," but they never did. It went all over the place, it spread like wildfire.

Brian came to see me and again said I made a mistake. He showed me two images printed from a computer of cages around the centre. One of them said "Beware of lions", and the other said "Be careful, they bite".

Am I in hell? I thought. "What are you talking about?" I said. Those signs were for the tourists. Obviously, they bite. I thought it was weird the images were printouts. This was 2013; he could have just shown me from his phone. The images appeared to have been printed on a larger page, but then cut out individually with scissors by hand, removing all the white border around the image. I found this odd. He mentioned the picture that was taken of me inside the enclosure. I asked to see the picture so I could show him the gate I was pulled through. He denied the gate was made of bars. He pulled out the picture but, again, it was a printout and cropped with scissors. I saw myself, sitting in front of the cage, about a foot away from the gate, with a broom and water on the floor; but the gate, which would have been to the left of me, was just cut out of the frame.

From then on, I went viral. Nelson Mandela passed away, which was front page news of the local newspaper, but I was there, underneath: CANADIAN LION-KISSER GETS MAULED.

Oh no, I thought, this has got way too big.'

Fortunately for Lauren, the student who had snapped her in the feeding cage posted the original photo online, which showed the gate – complete with the bars Duma had been able to fit his paw through.

'I was shocked because it was so clear. Oh my God: I could see all the details and to the left of me was the gate. His image had been cropped. I was a victim with evidence.'

Lauren found a gate like the one she had been pulled through and measured the width of the bars. They were 115.2 mm apart.

'The distance between them was the length of an iPhone 4. I know that now because I took my phone and turned it length-wise against the bars. The gate I measured matched the gate in the image the volunteer had taken of me in the feeding cage. They were the same. In the original image, you can get a good sense of the size of my leg compared to the size of the gap between the bars, so it was always clear I could be pulled through.

While we were there, we met Brian. We had framed the visit to seem like a final goodbye to the staff and centre, so he spent a lot of time with us and gave us a tour. He even called us lucky for getting such a private walkthrough of the centre. We went along with it because we wanted to eventually see the original attack site to take photos for evidence. During his tour, he offered to take me "on your dream and bring you around the reserve with a cheetah".

I said, "I've done that before, as a group. This is not my dream."

After what had happened, I didn't want to, but he was very insistent so I said OK.

So we did it – it was actually a baby leopard that he put me in a cage with. I had been less comfortable with leopards in the centre in general because we had been particularly warned about them. They are dangerous. I was limping, with casts and bandages all over my legs, and the baby leopard – whose name was Fagan, which was funny because it's like my last name, albeit spelt differently – started rubbing himself against my calves and looking at the bandages and being interested in them. I was hyperventilating.

I said, "I don't like this, I want to get out of here."

He questioned why I wasn't liking it when I had done it before. He said I had made a mistake and now I knew. I thought, Get me the hell out of here.

The difference was that I used to be OK with spending time with this leopard under supervision, but now I wasn't. I still felt the same about boundaries and rules: that they should be made clear, followed, and that judgement and common sense should be used. What had changed about my perspective on safety is that if something doesn't feel right, it's very possible something unexpected is wrong and you need to tell someone. And don't assume that the gate will protect you.'

As Lauren battled to have her voice heard against the centre's criticism, she also had to deal with the inevitable online comments.

'There were all these hate comments: "She deserved to die … that's what happens when you go volunteer as an eighteen-year-old girl."

I didn't do what they said I did. I did volunteer, but I didn't break the rules. Sometimes the media can do weird things, like quote you with something you didn't say. Isn't that illegal? But what are you going to do about it? You can't sue them. It was nuts what some people were writing.

My reaction at first was to try and respond to every comment and message news outlets. Then I decided to focus on my own community and put it on my own personal Facebook to get the truth out there. But even that was an unreasonably large task, so I gave up. I thought I'd just do one-on-one talks with the people that I really care about.'

Lauren's story attracted the attention of the producers of *I Was Prey*, a documentary series for the Discovery Channel. In her episode, she featured alongside a kangaroo attack survivor, which led her to meet a host of other people who'd lived through similar experiences.

'It was 2017 and I was in a Tim Hortons [Canadian restaurant] doing my university homework and finding a way to procrastinate. I wondered if there were other lion attack survivors out there. At this point, I had been on *I Was Prey* and I reached out to a kangaroo attack survivor who was in the same episode. I wondered if I could find more. I started googling it, and I found Bite Club and also found another lion attack survivor called Brendan Smith. He had also been attacked in South Africa, on a safari, when a lion jumped through his window and got his leg. A lot of the lion attacks had happened to people who were generally older men who worked on a reserve permanently. He was from Australia and a younger guy – it felt more relatable. I reached out to him – which went wonderfully – and to Bite Club.

I asked Dave Pearson, "I don't want to infringe on your group, but do you know where I can connect with survivors of large predators?"

He said, "No, welcome to Bite Club."

I brought Brendan and the kangaroo survivor into Bite Club, and then I went to Australia to meet them. It was the end of 2018 into 2019. My mom came with me and we spent Christmas there. It was absolutely sick. I got to meet a ton of people. They taught me how to surf. Bite Club has made the experience a lot less spectacular in the sense that I can tell my story and people's eyes don't widen in the same way.

There's a sense of understanding, a sense of empathy instead of sympathy, and I think, what was most important for me, there's a difference between being attacked by a shark and a lion, and a difference between being attacked by a lion and another lion, but it made it less weird and less showy. Often, when I tell people what happened to me, that spectacular element drowns out the fact that it was a really traumatising experience. That doesn't happen in Bite Club. Plus, it is really nice to be able to relate to people about the terrors of the media that ensued after. It made me become a more careful speaker because anything you say can be twisted or cut.'

The attack left lasting physical and psychological scars. To Lauren's credit, however, she found a positive way to use her experience. Although she was initially reticent about working with animals again, her ordeal sparked in her an interest in primitive survival, which led to another TV challenge. She had to survive in a hostile environment for twenty-one days with only limited resources. And she hasn't ruled out working with animals at some point in the future.

'When I got attacked by the lion, I remember, as they pulled me out and I was on that stretcher looking up to the sky, I thought, Damn, I guess I can't work with animals ever again. That was a thought I had but it's not true. At this point it's been nine years – I think I would consider doing rehabilitation work again. I think that my love for animals eventually transformed into a love for primitive survival.'

CHAPTER 9
WYATT RAYMOUNT

GOLDSMITH BEACH, YORKE PENINSULA,
SOUTH AUSTRALIA, SATURDAY 8 FEBRUARY 2014

'I looked up and the water was foaming red.'

Since the earliest civilisations, fishing with spears has been one of the most effective methods of artisanal hunting. Today, spearfishing is mainly done through free-diving and with snorkels, either from the shore or from a boat, using a specialised speargun. As an experienced spearfisherman, Wyatt Raymount knew the dangers of diving underwater to catch fish at close quarters. In 2014, aged seventeen, he'd already been doing it for six years – often travelling from his hometown of Adelaide across to the hotspot of the Yorke Peninsula. It is an area recognised as a shark migratory path, but in that time he had only encountered sharks twice before ...

' ... Both were on Kangaroo Island, about two hundred kilometres from where we live, and both were bronze whalers [or copper shark], a fairly placid shark but one which has been known to be aggressive. The first one just swam by and that was it. I didn't actually see it but the fella I was with did. The second encounter was when we were swimming in from a dive and it was just a very placid shark. We had a bit of burly [bait] and were diving on it and filming it, but it was very placid. It did a couple of passes and then never turned up again.

With the sport, you recognise the threat is always there, but you do it so many times and go on so many dives, it gets pushed to the back of your mind. I've been spearfishing since I was eleven. I got into it through my uncle. He was an avid spearfisherman on the east coast of Australia. My father also used to do it quite a bit when he lived in New South Wales, so it's been a bit of a pastime in the family. One day, I thought I wanted to have a crack, and eventually got my first gear and started from there.

In South Australia, there aren't many good spearfishing spots locally, so we used to frequent one area, called the Yorke Peninsula. The start of the peninsula is about an hour away from where we live but there is quite a big expanse of coastline. There are maybe a dozen spots that we knew were good, so we'd try and get there when weather permitted.

When we're out, we target King George whiting, silver trevally or pink snapper, all good table fish, the term given to good quality eating fish.'

On Friday 7 February, Wyatt headed over for the Yorke Peninsula Classic spearfishing competition, commonly known as the Yorke's Classic, to be held on Sunday 9 February. Entrants compete to catch different species of fish on a set list, scoring points for the amount and weight of their haul. He was joined by Sam Kellett, a twenty-eight-year-old English teacher at the prestigious Glenunga International High School in Adelaide.

'I'd met Sam about twelve months before on a dive trip in a place called Robe in South Australia, down the southeast of the state. It was a big trip, where there were about twelve of us. We got to know each other there and became quite good friends. We did a bit of diving together and went on a few trips. Then we spent two and a half weeks together when we were over on Kangaroo Island competing in the national Australian spearfishing titles. He lived in Adelaide as well, so we did a fair bit of carpooling together, where three or four of us would get together in one car to travel.

The Yorke's Classic is generally always held on a Sunday just because a lot of people have work commitments on Saturdays. I drove over with Sam and we met up with the other guys who were staying at the same caravan park at a place called Edithburgh. It was late on Friday night when we got in, and we woke up early on Saturday morning because we were going for a day's dive before the competition started.

The weather was very hot. From what I recall, it was about forty degrees and blowing really strong, warm northerly winds. We were going to a place called Chinamans Hat Island, which is in Innes National Park. We got there quite early but at the entrance to the park, a park ranger was turning people away because there was a serious risk of a wildfire that day. We'd had a hot, dry summer, and with the winds the way they were, and the temperature, there was just too big of a risk. So, we were turned away at the gate.

We agreed as a collective that we would dive at another spot close to where we were staying. We thought we'd drive out there, get a dive in, catch a few fish before the competition the next day, and all will be well. So, we went to this spot near Goldsmith Beach, about fifteen kilometres from Edithburgh and about a hundred kilometres from where we were.'

Wyatt and his group, including Sam, were free-diving, so had no scuba gear and were in camouflage-patterned wetsuits with a weight belt and hood, a mask, snorkel, long swim fins, speargun and a float with a flash on to attract small fish, which in turn might entice the larger species they wanted to catch.

'We suited up and got all our gear on. There wasn't a whole lot going on that day. Sam had a couple of silver trevally on his float. We had seen a couple of snapper hanging around, so we were looking for those. At one point, the water started getting a bit choppy. Aaron Whitaker – another of the guys we were with – and Sam and I had a chat about what we were going to do. We decided it was getting a bit rough, so we'd pack it in and make our way back to the other group. There was the three of us and another group of three guys closer inshore, and there was another fella, we didn't realise, who was down back where we started. We were going to swim to those guys to tell them we were going to call it a day, swim back to the cars and get ready, because we were going to have dinner that night at one of the local pubs. It was a tradition before a competition that we would have a social dinner and go through what we were going to do the next day.

We made that decision and turned to the shore ... and that's when it happened. I remember it vividly. I was on the surface, probably about four to five metres to the west of Sam. I was swimming along with him, facing out to the ocean. Aaron was maybe three metres to the east of Sam, but in front of us by about three metres. I could see the fish hanging around my flasher on the float. I was looking at those and just seeing what was around when I heard an ear-piercing scream. I looked up and the water was foaming red. Then I looked under the water and that's when I saw quite a big white shark in the exact spot where Sam had been.

I cried out "Shark!" to Aaron and we made our way to shore as fast as we could.

We were about fifty metres out from the shore. The tide was out quite far and there was a reef that that extended out another sixty metres. We were about fifty metres out from that low-lying reef where we'd be able to stand up. We were probably in about six metres of water. We headed to the shore, looking back to make sure nothing was coming for us. We didn't know if there were more sharks. We'd seen the one, but neither of us saw Sam. We were looking back behind us the whole way, just trying to swim as fast as we could.

The other three guys were already standing at the shore. We told them what we had witnessed.

We were all just in a state of shock and disbelief. We didn't believe it. When we first told the other guys what had happened, they just went, "Ah, right, OK ... " as though they thought we were making it up. But they could tell by our faces that we were being serious.

Then the other fella that had been with us, he was maybe half a kilometre back down towards the cars, and we thought he was someone coming to go in the water. I sprinted back down the exposed reef to alert him to what had happened. Then I realised he was one of the divers we were with. He thought we were joking. He also realised pretty soon that it was extremely serious and that it actually had happened.

It's a pretty barren place there, without much traffic, but we were lucky because, just then, there was a car passing the other way. Another good friend of mine, Nick, was there and he ran up, flagged the car down and got them to call the emergency services and let them know what had gone on.'

As Wyatt tried to process what he had seen, he was certain about the species of shark responsible ...

'There was no doubt in my mind that it was a great white. It was immediately clear, because I'd seen bronze whalers before and, in comparison, they are quite a small shark. A big bronze whaler is maybe twelve foot, and that's a big one. Four meters is quite large for a bronze whaler. But this was enormous. I reckon it was up near six metres, if not more. I was looking at it directly side on. It was maybe a forty-five-degree angle from the surface. Its head was up near the surface and its tail, I recall, was down pretty low on the bottom of the water – of the sand that we were on.'

Wyatt and the others shared a terrible feeling of helplessness and fear. All they could do was keep watch for any signs of Sam and wait for the emergency services to arrive.

'There was nothing we could do. No one was going back in after that. I guess you would say there was quite a large feeling of helplessness involved. We didn't see any sign of Sam – nothing.

The SES arrived, which is the State Emergency Service. The ambulance showed up, police showed up and the maritime unit of the police turned up. They had a boat and had divers searching the water, and then the police or SES also despatched a helicopter to scour the area.'

Wyatt and the others had been spearfishing for up to four hours when the tragedy happened just after midday. The ambulance crews checked them over for any injuries and shock, which everyone was feeling.

'We were there for a number of hours and that was mainly due to the ambos [ambulance medics] and the police wanting to make sure we were all right. Because we were quite young. I was seventeen and there was a sixteen-year-old with us. And the rest were all early twenties. I think the oldest fella there was maybe thirty. We were quite a young group of lads. We were there until maybe five o'clock. We alerted the rest of the people we knew that were coming over for the competition. A lot of those people showed up to make sure we were OK and show support.

I gave quite an extensive witness statement to the police. That was all to help the coroner's inquest into the death.

Eventually, we went back to the caravan park. We made the decision to go to the dinner that night. I think it was more of a support thing than anything else, because there were a fair few news crews and reporters already there. The caravan park wouldn't let them in. We had a little bungalow house for the weekend, so we just waited there to keep away from the reporters.'

As well as the marine police boats, the helicopter and police divers, the search for Sam also involved a Royal Volunteer Coastal Patrol vessel from Port Victoria and two smaller private craft, including a Jet Ski. Members of the public also joined in the search. The search was paused overnight. They recovered two lead weights, which bore incisions that experts concluded were caused by the teeth of a white shark.

'The only thing they found of Sam were those weights from his belt, his speargun and a float that he had. That was it. That was all they recovered.'

When Wyatt eventually made it home the following day, it took a long time to come to terms with what had happened.

'I was in a lot of disbelief, and in the week following, I convinced myself that it never happened. I woke up one night at about two in the morning and I had convinced myself that the whole event never happened, and that he was still over there and trying to get back. I got dressed and was going to drive over to the spot where he was and see if that was the case. I didn't end up doing that, but I completely convinced myself that it didn't happen. The whole incident used to go through my head quite a lot. But, over the years, that slowed down a fair bit, eight years on. But, when it happened, it was quite a frequent occurrence, the incident running through my head quite vividly.'

Such a tragedy inevitably attracted widespread media attention, which led to vicious online comments that Wyatt and the others had to deal with at the same time they were processing their own emotional response.

'It was at a very sensitive time because there had been a spate of shark attacks on the west coast of Australia. They were talking about introducing culling of sharks, trying to thin out the numbers of certain aggressive types of sharks. There was a lot of public uproar about it. So, there were quite a lot of negative comments on Facebook pages. There were a lot of remarks like: "Shouldn't have been there," and, "You are in the shark's territory," or, "Stupid to go in there."

There were even comments saying that we actually killed him! Some said, "They probably killed him and are trying to blame it on a shark." It was because no body was ever recovered. That was pretty confronting at the time.

I sifted through a lot of them and I read and replied to a few. I was angered at the time about the comments and remarks being made. When I did, they tended not to respond. And if they did, it was out of ignorance. It was stupidity. It wasn't facts. I could respond with the facts about sharks or about what actually happened ... but there was a lot of ignorance, a lot of naivety, people just not being aware of what the situation is or was. Some people do it for a laugh, some just because they can. They are idiots at the end of the day.

Everyone who was there reacted very differently in the aftermath of the attack. A few of the guys there really struggled after it happened.'

Contrary to what the online commentators might have believed, Wyatt says he and the other spearfishermen that day did everything they could to mitigate against such an attack.

'Nothing that we were doing would have attracted the sharks. We make sure the fish are despatched as soon as they are caught, and we bleed them so there is no blood trail to follow. We didn't have many fish anyway. I think Sam only had two fish on his float. It is more of a case of the wrong place at the wrong time.

We later learnt that some fishermen had seen quite a large white shark out there over the weeks prior. But we only found out about that after the incident.'

At the time, Wyatt was working as an apprentice electrician, and as part of his coping mechanism, he threw himself back into work immediately.

'It happened on the Saturday, and I was back at work on Monday. People were asking me, "What are you doing back here?" It was only the fact that it would keep me busy. If I didn't go back to work, I would be sitting at home thinking about it. In my opinion, that is a lot worse than coming to work. Coming back to work, I'm engaging my mind. I'm not focused on that for a good portion of the day.'

Sam's tragic loss was felt throughout the community. Being a popular teacher, news of what happened shocked his school, which held a memorial service in his honour. Wyatt and many of Sam's spearfishing friends attended.

'They held quite a large service for him at the high school, which happened to fall on my eighteenth birthday. Quite a large group of us attended. We tried to speak to the family and give our sincere condolences, but they were quite swamped. We made the decision that it was not what they needed then and there. I did end up getting in contact with his sister and explaining that I tried to come up and say hello. I still try to, on every holiday or anniversary, send a message to the family just to let them know that I'm thinking of them and sending them my condolences. The local spearfishing community erected a memorial plaque in the location of the attack, and my family and I go up every year to clean it, lay flowers, reflect on the years and toast Sam with a glass of champagne.'

The Yorke Peninsula Classic competition – postponed due to the tragedy – was rescheduled for a month later. Wyatt was sure Sam would have wanted them to carry on as planned and take part as if he were with them.

'I don't think Sam would have wanted me to give up diving. I could easily have sold up everything and left it at that and never done it again. But it was something I had to personally overcome as well. I wanted to continue and still wanted to do the sport I loved, and I wasn't going to let that deter me.'

The competition was Wyatt's first time back in the water since the shark attack. Although he was keen to continue, he did so with some degree of trepidation …

'I remember going out that day. I swam out to where I usually swim to. I did a few dives, and after about five minutes it hit me. I was still in the competition and I really wanted to win. I'm real hungry; I want to win. And then it hit me. I reckon I was in about ten metres of the water and I just thought, What am I doing out here? I made my way to shore, and I don't think I left the confines of about two metres of water for the rest of the comp. I was pretty jumpy and a bit on edge about the whole thing. I remember being spooked quite easily. Even small crashing waves made me a bit jumpy.

I ended up winning the juniors category in the competition that day, but although that was quite good, what had happened previously affected my diving for a lot of years. I don't believe I've ever seen another shark since that day, but on one trip we did to New Zealand, there was a number of bronze whalers that would hang around in the spot where we were diving. I never saw one but was told they were quite close off the end of my dive fins. They were within a metre of them, coming up and having a look.'

In the years following the tragedy, Wyatt, who is now twenty-six and has changed careers to become a truck driver, chose not to seek professional counselling. He did, however, have a desire to speak to people about what happened. And so, he turned to people who had first-hand knowledge of what he was going through, including Paul de Gelder, an Australian elite navy clearance diver who lost an arm and a leg in a shark attack in 2009.

'I didn't speak to any professionals per se, but I did speak to a few people about it, especially in the diving community, a lot of very senior divers. They went through various experiences that they had with white sharks. I also rang Paul and told him what happened. I found it helped a lot. When I was going through it all, I worked on the theory that a problem shared is a problem halved. So, I just talked to anyone and everyone who would listen about the incident. Being able to speak about it and know other people were listening was a great comfort, and I think it helped me lighten the load quite a bit.'

The experience of sharing his story and talking through the issues around what happened made him an ideal person to help others. Which was why Dave Pearson got in touch with him and his fellow divers to tell them about Bite Club.

'It was back in 2014 when Bite Club was still quite a new thing and not as big as it is today. Dave messaged me. I was in a group with Aaron and another fella called Nick. Dave wanted to get us involved, to be a bit of a support group. I got quite involved in promoting the Bite Club, because it was a place where people who had been through similar occurrences could offer support or advice. And I found it very helpful, even just to read things that other people had to say or offer others … just reading the comments on the Facebook group was helpful.

The insight that the other members offer is very useful in helping people deal with whatever is going on at the time. It's a really good thing to be part of.'

CHAPTER 10
CAMERON WRATHALL

SWAN RIVER, PERTH, WESTERN AUSTRALIA, THURSDAY 14 JANUARY 2021

*'A shark had me in its mouth,
attached to my upper thigh.'*

It was a beautiful summer's morning when Cameron Wrathall jumped off the jetty near his home in Bicton, Perth, for his routine early swim with his friend Richard O'Brien along the Swan River, a tidal stretch of water that occasionally saw the likes of dolphins and seals come up from the sea. The water was like a second home for fifty-five-year-old Cameron, who, as a keen swimmer had completed the 19.7 km channel swim from Cottesloe Beach to Rottnest in his home city of Perth, and, as an avid water polo enthusiast, both played and worked at the local Melville water polo club.

The conditions were near perfect as Cameron and Richard took off shortly before 8 a.m. They'd reached the halfway point of what they wanted to achieve that day and were treading water near Blackwall Reach, a limestone cliff running along the river that is popular with swimmers, paddlers, climbers and cliff jumpers.

'I was just talking to Richard, who was about three metres away. I had my back to the channel and the deeper part of the river. I was thinking how lovely a morning it was when I suddenly felt this impact and severe pressure. I looked down. A shark had me in its mouth, attached to my upper thigh from just above my knee to up around my buttock. It latched on and started to twist from side to side, trying, I think, to get a chunk of meat in its mouth. It had swum at speed and hit me and bit me ... all in one motion.'

A two-and-a-half-metre bull shark had come at Cameron from out of nowhere. Richard's first realisation that something was seriously wrong was noticing the tail break the surface of the water. As Richard fixated on the movement of the water behind his friend, a singular thought was going through Cameron's mind ...

'I have to get this off me before it kills me.

I didn't feel any pain. It was just the pressure. I hit it with the heels of both palms. I thrust as hard as I could on the top of the head. I didn't put a lot of thought into it. I just twisted my body and thrust down onto the part I could reach because it was right there. Almost immediately it let go and swam away.

Straight away and all around me, I could see the blood. I knew I was in trouble. I felt quite calm, however, very focused and singular. Quite basic thoughts went through my head, strong and clear. It was all about survival. Now the shark was off me, I had to get to the shore as quickly as I could in case I became unconscious. I was also thinking, Where's the shark? It could still be there – and still be hungry.

I turned to Richard and said, "Shark." Just the one word. *Shark*. The blood was everywhere. "I've got to get to the shore before I drown," I said.

"Do you want to hang onto my shoulders?" Richard said.

I just laughed and started swimming. I was digging as hard as I could into the water, trying to get to the shore. Right away I knew my leg was limp and wasn't kicking. I could feel water going through the chunk of meat that was hanging loose. It was a funny situation. We were both in a bit of shock. I didn't have any pain, just the feeling that I was losing a lot of blood. We both just swam as hard and fast as we could for the nearest part of the shore.

It was about a hundred-metre swim. When we got to the shore, I was in about six inches of water and leaning on one arm when Richard caught up, and I had a look at my leg. It was like a side of lamb hanging off, a big slab of meat hanging loose by skin – and a lot of blood. I could feel myself feeling faint.

"I think I've just about had it," I said.'

Richard grabbed hold of Cameron and dragged him a bit further up the bank. At the same time, he yelled out to a couple of kayakers nearby: 'Help, help! Shark! Shark attack! Help!'

The kayakers, Peter Towndrow and Kieron Hayter, and a standup paddle-boarder who was also nearby, hurried over and put Cameron on the board. By now, about six or seven people had come to help and call for the emergency services.

'Where I'd swum ashore was a little beach area, but there was quite an incline through trees and rocks. There wasn't a path to walk up to the road. One of the kayakers took off his rashie [swim top] and made a tourniquet and tied it up around my upper thigh groin area. I was going in and out of consciousness while this was happening, but they put me on the paddle board and walked through the water to where there was a path up to the road.

From there, they managed to carry me up the path, got me to the road and put me on a grass verge outside someone's house. Once they had me down on the ground, they wrapped a towel around me and one of the kayakers applied pressure to try and stop the blood flow. In fact, he was putting so much pressure, I had to say at one point, "You are leaning on my leg pretty hard." They were talking to me and trying to reassure me, but I felt calm and, in fact, really peaceful. It was a funny thing. I didn't realise I was dying. It was just a gentle feeling. There was no pain or anxiousness.

Maybe that's what happens when you bleed to death, but that was my recollection. I wasn't aware of my body shutting down, just that I felt sleepy, like I was going into a doze. I was conscious for most of it but for a couple of times when I drifted unconscious.'

Fortunately for Cameron, the incident took place in the city, so an ambulance arrived within ten minutes – just in time. Cameron was fading fast. The paramedics acted quickly, administering cardiopulmonary resuscitation (CPR) to bring him back from the brink of death.

'Apparently, my heart stopped and I effectively died from blood loss. But the ambulance was there and they got me inside and got some fluids into me. They restarted my heart and brought me back to life. I think that happened once more on the way to the hospital. I went straight into Royal Perth Hospital and spent the next three days in intensive care.'

Once in hospital, Cameron realised the full extent of the damage from the shark bite.

'The impact broke my hip, splitting the top of my femur – the knob part of the bone – diagonally from top to bottom, where it fits into the hip joint. I underwent a couple of surgeries and they managed to save my leg. I then spent about five weeks in that hospital on my back, not able to move, because I had a broken hip and had suffered a lot of tissue damage. The surgeons had to sew a lot of tissue back together and bits back onto bone, so they didn't want me moving. From there, I went to Fiona Stanley Hospital for rehabilitation, which ended up taking another five or six weeks. I had tissue and nerve damage and the sciatic nerve had been ruptured in a few places.'

Just as Cameron was trying to come to terms with the lasting physical damage from the shark bite, he was hit by the psychological effects of the trauma.

'I had been in ICU for a few days and had been kept in a suspended state while they were doing the major surgery. I was not really conscious. They wake you up every now and then, just to make sure they can, and then they zonk you out again. One afternoon, I came out of that and was on a lot of painkillers when I experienced the first of two flashbacks. I relived the experience and thought the shark was in the bed with me. I was wrestling it and screaming out. Apparently, I scared a few people a bit. They told me the next morning. The next evening, I had another flashback – and this one felt particularly real.

They were funny experiences. They were very real. They seemed to me to be my brain reliving the experience with the bits I had forgotten. The flashbacks showed me more information. At the time, I'd sort of blocked out a lot of what was happening around me because I was so focused on getting the shark off me. The second singular thought was that I had to get to shore before I drowned. But in the flashbacks, a lot of that other detail came back. I hadn't recalled it prior to having the flashbacks, which was interesting. I just put it down to how your brain integrates the experience so that it's more in context and easier for you to make sense of and put into perspective.'

As well as the psychological challenge of processing what happened, Cameron had to face the reality that the shark bite had caused lasting physical damage.

'I was in a wheelchair for a little bit and then progressed to a couple of big crutches and then onto little wrist crutches. Now I'm just using one crutch. I hope to get to a walking stick, and you never know, I might be able to walk unassisted in the future. I have a wheelchair for long distances but I don't use it a lot.

My leg will never recover though. There was too much damage to be a fully functional leg again in the future, so I've had to come to terms with that. I have limited feeling from my left buttock down the back of my left thigh, my left calf and foot. I can't feel my foot at all, I can barely feel my calf and, while I have a little bit more feeling in the thigh and buttock, I have no communication with any of the muscles down the back of my leg. I can't make them do anything. They don't work. And I have restricted blood flow in those areas now too.

I've done a lot of rehabilitation and physiotherapy and work with occupational therapists. That will be ongoing. I wear an AFO [ankle foot orthosis brace] that holds my foot up so I can walk. It also helps support my leg when I use a crutch. I had a lot of pain but I've overcome most of that. However, I still get some strange nerve pains. It's funny, the place I get the pain most regularly is in my foot, but I can't feel my foot.'

Before the shark bite, Cameron worked as a lifeguard at the polo club.

'I've not been able to work or go back to the job I used to do, as I can't maintain a qualification in it any more. I used to be a lifeguard, which was one of the reasons I used to swim all the time. I can't maintain that because of my physical limitations.

I was only working casually at the time, so I didn't have employee support and there's no insurance. If you have a motor vehicle accident or something like that there are things in place, but for something like this there's nothing. I was lucky in that I was a long-term member of a sporting club and they went out of their way to try and help me out and support me. Melville Water Polo Club is a wonderful facility where I worked for a long time – as a manager, lifeguard and water polo coach – and that community really helped. They organised a fundraiser, and the money people donated really made a difference.

I had support from other people too, who visited and made sure I was OK. Some even dropped off food occasionally. They were wonderful. I would've been lost without that help. I'm on a disability pension now, which took a while to process before I could get classified and only provides a low income, but it is better than nothing.'

Shark encounters in Swan River are extremely rare. In the immediate aftermath of the incident, a local police boat cleared people from the water and the nearby area was closed for a period by the city of Melville. But although Cameron did fear he might feel anxious about getting back into the water, it was the physical limitations rather than the psychological ones that slowed up that important part of his rehabilitation.

'I think I was the first person in over fifty years to have something like this happen to them here. I'd never seen a shark before in the water. I've seen plenty of dolphins, fish and bird life, all sorts of things, but never a shark.

The first time I went back into the water was in a swimming pool, so it was fine. But I wasn't able to get back in the open water for a long time. I had a something like a bed sore on the back of my heel from hospital, and because the blood flow isn't good in my foot, it took about five months to heal. And then, one afternoon, I fell over – because my foot drops and I can't feel it. It caught on something and I fell over, and, as I was going down, I shot my left arm out to try and grab onto the door frame, and took all my weight through my left shoulder and damaged my left shoulder. So, I've had a few challenges, which have kept me out of the water.

I only recently returned to swimming in early 2022, but I love it. I'm enjoying being back in the water. I've been for one swim in the river since it happened. I thought I'd try it out one day. I didn't go for a long swim because of the physical restrictions. I have one arm that I can't do freestyle with and one leg that I can't kick with at all, but I wanted to see what it felt like to get in the river and go for a swim. It did feel like I was getting over a psychological barrier. That was why I did the river swim. It was beautiful. It was during summer and it was a lovely day. I went by myself and I really enjoyed it. I had trouble getting out, which is why I haven't done it again since.

When the weather got a bit cooler, I went swimming in the nice, heated pool instead. I knew I would swim in the pool until I got some condition and mobility back and could swim using both my arms properly again, but I wanted to have that one river swim to see how I felt, to see if it was all OK and that I wasn't going to be hyper-vigilant and anxious. I wasn't. It was really nice.'

But while Cameron has been able to get over any feelings of apprehension, his friend who witnessed the incident has been more seriously affected.

'It was a big shock to Richard, in a lot of ways. I have got back to swimming, but he's not interested in swimming any more. At the time, he was a big help, getting on his phone and alerting people to what happened, but I have wondered if whether being a close witness has created more of a psychological barrier for him. I'm sure he has thought many times that it could have been him. It's a different situation to being the person it has happened to. For me, it was sort of grounding in a way and less psychologically damaging because I have lived through it.'

Now, over a year since his shark encounter, Cameron has had time to reflect on what happened and what the shark's intentions might have been.

'It was a funny thing. I didn't feel that the shark was being overly aggressive. It just felt like it was – and this is a hard thing to describe – just being a shark. I think it was very much having a taste to see what this is. When I hit it on the head, it let go and swam away. It didn't have to do that. It was much bigger than me. It could've done pretty much whatever it wanted.

There were quite a few shark sightings in the short period afterwards but I think it was down to people looking because of the incident. They were very aware of sharks being around. They are always there but now people are looking a lot more.

I have since found out that the female sharks come into the river to have their pups at that time of year. Generally, the males are out in the ocean, so if you come across a shark in the river – especially at that time of year – it will be a female coming in to have its pups. I believe it might have had something to do with that.'

While Cameron was still in hospital, members of Bite Club got in touch to offer support, something he found invaluable.

'Bite Club has been fantastic. Because it's a support group of people with similar experiences, some with the same type of injuries and some who have been dealing with similar issues over longer time frames, it has been really beneficial to be able to look and see how people have overcome things, what they've had to go through, different medical things they've tried, different pain mitigation measures, all sorts of things. I'm really thankful that Dave Pearson has created this group because it's a great service for people who find themselves in that sort of situation.

One Bite Club member, Greg Pickering, an abalone diver who has been through two shark attacks, and Della a psychologist associated with the club, came to visit me in hospital. It was good to talk to them, and since then I've met with Della a few times. It helps to talk about your experience and what you're going through and to gain some understanding. Not many people go through an experience where something tries to eat them.'

Another important aspect of Cameron's recovery has been his ability to retain a sense of humour, even in the face of his life-threatening experience.

'I have two daughters: Cian, twenty-eight, and Keely, who is twenty-six. One bought me a "Stay Positive" T-shirt. It is important to laugh about these things, to have a bit of sense of humour and to try not to take it so seriously. Everyone is different, however – but that's what works for me. You have got to have a bit of a positive mindset. There are enough challenges to go through without making them worse than they are. You have physical challenges with pain and mobility and the reality that things have changed in your life. It's easy to magnify those issues, but if you are able to make light of them it can help with the recovery process.'

CHAPTER 11
JULENE ROMSLAND

DEADWOOD, SOUTH DAKOTA, USA, SATURDAY 12 SEPTEMBER 2020

*'I could feel his fur, smell his breath
on my face, could hear his growling
as his incisors implanted in my shoulder.'*

It was already shaping up to be a good day for Julene Romsland. A former underwater acoustical analyst – a role that involved detecting, classifying and providing information on submarines and other contacts of interest for the US Navy – her interest in neutrino subatomic particle research – discovering how such tiny massless particles behave, especially underground – had been sparked by friends who ran a store selling gems, rocks and minerals. Through her friends' work in finding and recovering precious stones, Julene had been keen to learn more about the different densities of rocks and minerals and where and why they were located in the Black Hills near her home. That day, in September 2020, Julene, then forty-nine, paid a visit to Sanford Lab, the deepest underground research laboratory in the USA, situated not far from where her friends lived, in Lead, South Dakota.

'It was a fabulous day. Something had sparked in my head and I was taken back to that young age when you are eighteen and you're at college and it really imprints on you. The Black Hills are one of the most diverse places for rock and mineral specimens anywhere, and gold, silver, dinosaur bones and even prehistoric shark teeth have been found there. The Sanford Labs is an old gold mine now repurposed, and that morning I was up there to find out what they were doing in terms of neutrino research. I used to do signal analysis in the military, doing acoustical analysis underwater. What Sanford is doing is almost the same thing, except underground to analyse depth for the mines. It was an area I was keen to get back into.'

Julene's same friends who ran the gem store also had a property in Deadwood, in the Black Hills National Forest, where they kept animals such as huskies and foxes. That week they were out of town and asked Julene to stop in and check on the animals, something she had done countless times before.

'My then-husband and I had helped them out for four years. We would watch their animals, they would watch ours; we would trade pet-sitting. We had previously owned two huskies we had bought from this couple, and they also happened to own wolves. They started out with one or two and then ended up having as many as fourteen at the time. They owned about forty foxes, coyotes, you name it. We were friends, we helped out, you pitch in. That's what you do for friends.

Over that time, I'd helped hand-raise a coyote, a fox and a wolf. When you start handling them as a baby, you really get to know them.'

Julene got to the property at about 2.20 p.m. and began a thorough check of the kennels and pens.

'I always did my security rounds starting in the same place, making sure nothing was broken into. I would start with the huskies, then visit all the foxes. It was a lot of pen checking, making sure nobody has escaped, nobody has got in. There was a house to check too. I was always very thorough. I'd last been at the property a week before, while the couple were there. On this occasion, they'd been away for a couple of days and I never let it go longer than three before checking in. They knew I'd be there at some point.

I checked the animals all had food and water. It was a lot to take care of, so I had been there for about an hour when I approached the first wolf pen.'

In that first pen was a young Alaskan timber wolf called Echo, which the owners had introduced to a more mature wolf called Yukon and his sister called Trouble because of her tendency to bite.

'Although the new one was still in his youth, he was a full-grown dog. The wolves he was with were the largest on the property. In fact, Yukon was one of the largest male alphas in captivity in North America. The female in that pen was quite something too. She had bitten many people and had suffered a rough life where she had been picked on. Essentially, they rescued her.

When the owners were out of town, the wolves were more agitated, so you had to be careful walking by. There was just one fence between you and the wolves – not something you'd find at a zoo. They could stick their heads out and get out past their shoulders.

Knowing them for so long, they are like extremely smart dogs, but they want attention, like a child. If you are walking by and you don't know them, they will start snapping at you and biting.

If you have known them for four years and you are walking by, they will still snap at you but they want to play. They will tear your sweatshirt and you'll be all banged up. They'll jump all over you and knock you down. You'll be all bruised.'

Julene was walking past the pen, about to begin her checks on the wolves, when the young wolf suddenly lunged.

'It was a fluke, but he got hold of my hand. It was more shocking than painful – a complete surprise. That startled Yukon and, as the younger one pulled me closer, he got hold of my arm and began to work his way up. That's when I screamed. I don't think it started off as an aggressive bite, they just grabbed at me. Somehow, this time, they didn't stop, and it was the two of them.

They bit me and pulled me up to my neck through the fencing. One had about three of my fingers in his mouth. The other, on my right side, started biting my forearm. They were both biting and pulling at the same time. They pulled me in. Yukon was yanking me against the fence. I could feel his fur, smell his breath on my face, could hear his growling as his incisors implanted in my shoulder. He was right there, next to my face.

I was thinking, God, if he lets go of my shoulder, my face is right there.

All the time I was waiting for the other wolf – the one they called Trouble – to jump in. I couldn't see her.

I was thinking, It's not going to be him that does me in, it'll be her. She will just eat me. One wolf crunched down on my shoulder and yanked all at once. My bladder let go from the extreme pain and shock. Suddenly I thought, I'm going to lose my arm. I had no way to defend myself. I was just trying to make sure no other part of me went through the fence, like another hand to hit them off.

I remember thinking, All of me needed to be on this side of the fence. There was no one with me. No one was around. I didn't even have my phone on me.'

Just as she feared she might be dragged further through the fence, Julene had a moment of calmness and remembered what might make the wolves respond.

'I could feel the younger one back off. The large wolf still had my shoulder in his mouth. I couldn't get any more into the fence than I was, my face was right up against it. I switched up my tone and instead of calling him Yukon I used his nickname, "Yukie". I talked to him like you would a dog. "Yukie," I said, "it's OK, it's me, it's Jules." You always have to show them you're alpha. I talked to him like a pet and switched up the whole dynamic of yelling or screaming or being terrified. That flashed through my head as I was going to lose my arm.

I turned my face to face his. He let go long enough for me to push myself back, and I lay back to get away from that fence. He lay down and started crying. It was a pretty horrific scene. He had my blood and skin all over his mouth. And it was all over me.'

Bleeding heavily and knowing she'd suffered serious injuries, Julene had no conventional way of calling for help. She had left her phone in her car, parked some distance away, and no one else was at the property. She did have an emergency aid-call device she wore for a heart condition diagnosed years previously …

'It's one of those "I've fallen and can't get back up" buttons. I suffer from heart palpitations, high and low blood pressure, and high and low heart rate. Because of my condition, I'm supposed to avoid anything that causes extreme stress! I fought my medical team when they first said, "You've got to wear this." I didn't want to. But then I thought, You know what? This is going to save a life one day. If it doesn't save my life, it's going to save somebody's. I knew I should listen to them. I carry it on my waistband or hang it round my neck. It used to be on my wrist! That's what saved me – I had my button that day.

When I got the wolves to let go, I reached across and pushed it and prayed for a second that it would be able to reach a cell phone tower because in the Black Hills, it's spotty and iffy. I could feel the blood running down my bicep. Thanks to my military first aid training, I thought, OK, there is warm substance running but it's not gushing. It's the loss of my own blood but it's not pooling around me. There's no sign of a major artery being severed. I know he didn't get into underneath my armpit. I whipped off my T-shirt and applied a tourniquet on my arm.

I thought with the button, I'd push it and they'd locate me and come and find me. I didn't realise it was a two-way cellular. All of a sudden, a lady came on from 911 despatch and asked if she could help me. I said, "Yes, I've been attacked by two wolves." I gave her the most pertinent information they needed right away – my location, my phone number, the first aid

I had already applied – and, as we were talking, she said, "Help is already on the way; I'm going to stay on the line."

They located me right away, so I was very fortunate.'

Within six minutes, a sheriff arrived, swiftly followed by an ambulance and more police. Julene was able to walk out to the front of the property but was suddenly aware of how she looked – and how that might appear to people driving past.

'I walked out to where the first responder was. It was a busy highway. I felt like I looked like something out of a horror movie. I was worried about what would happen if a school bus drove by and I'm standing there without a shirt, a tourniquet on and I'm all bloody. That was wretched. I was thinking if I drove by and I had my kids or grandkids with me, I would be irate, as a parent, if I saw that. It was very graphic.

I was covered in blood and my own skin. It was all over my jeans. They tore into my fingers, up and down my arm and my wrist. My bicep was just hanging. My forearm was green and swollen from him biting on it. I had lacerations from my fingertips up to my shoulder by my neck, all on the back and front of my arm.'

The medics who attended Julene packed her wounds and tried to stem the bleeding. They took her first to a local clinic but facilities were limited and immediately it was clear she would require surgery. She ended up being taken to three different emergency rooms before an operating room was prepared in Rapid City, around forty-three miles away from Deadwood. Throughout that time, Julene was careful not to use language that might cause undue fear for anyone listening.

'I wouldn't say the words "bite" or "attack". They took me to the closest place but they were communicating I would need trauma surgery so they were already contacting the big hospital and making sure there was a surgeon in the area. My arm was blowing up like a balloon so they were trying to get the swelling down. There wasn't really anything else they could do at the first clinic.

I went to three different ERs, and I also wouldn't let them take me anywhere without being completely covered because I was such a sight. I was in one of the rooms, soaking my arm in ice. I had a ring on my ringer [finger] and they came in with a cutter to remove it.

I said, "It looks like I have been attacked by a great white shark." It would almost be better if I'd called and said I had been attacked by a shark because I thought no one was going to believe I was attacked by two wolves. It was insane, just unbelievable. You just don't think animal attack in South Dakota.

My emergency contact walked in the room and they just lost it and said the same thing, "You look like you've been attacked by a shark." It was very surreal, the amount of blood and everything else. But, from the first ER, I was thinking the same thing: Cover me up, don't let anybody see this, in case there were kids there.

We just have small clinics around here, and I thought, Don't say "bite", don't say "wolf", don't say "dog". I didn't want anybody to see me and get frightened of dogs because I had blood and skin all over me. I didn't want anyone else to have nightmares. People are curious, we all are, but that's also a great way to start a witch hunt, of, "Where did it happen? ... Are those animals going to be put down?"

I didn't want anything to do with that. I just didn't want people seeing this terrible scene and jumping to conclusions.'

Julene underwent surgery to save her right arm but, although she could move her fingers, it took a full year before any strength returned to her damaged limb.

'I was very lucky. I was blessed with wonderful doctors and everybody who helped me. They saved everything. I lost the use of my right arm. I could move my fingers but they were dead feeling. I couldn't lean on my shoulder and really couldn't use my whole right arm. It just hung at my side for a good year. I have been through a year and a half of physical therapy, working on my shoulder, my arm, my fingers. I go to the chiropractor and they do dry needling and I get massages on it. I've recently had further surgery. I'm working on repairing the nerve damage so I can feel parts of my forearm, my wrist and fingers again.'

As well as the physiotherapy to get the arm working again, Julene had to work on the psychological effect of her trauma. That would prove harder than she imagined.

'I got myself a psychiatrist, but I couldn't say "wolf" for the longest time. It was six months before I could say "wolves" plural, or that I was bit, that I was attacked by two wolves. That was an enormous breakthrough.

Flashbacks – they happened quickly. My triggers would be wolves anywhere. All of sudden, there are wolves on greetings cards, there are wolf memes. That was hard to get over. I had no idea that now dogs would be a problem, or when dogs fight, the barking and snapping. A couple of times I have just crumbled to the ground, and that is the complete opposite of me. I am not that kind of person. That was very hard to get through.

I was afraid of my own dog, Max, for a while. I was very apprehensive. He is a pit bull boxer, so quite large and loud. I knew it would be good to be around him. Instead of moving away from it, I had to stay in it, but showing him that I was alpha was hard, because I felt afraid of him, and you just can't show a big dog that they are alpha – all of a sudden they will be running the house. I knew it would be hard each day, but eventually I would work through it because I love that dog.'

As part of her rehabilitation, Julene underwent exposure therapy, a treatment developed to help people confront their fears. Although it can be a natural reaction to avoid animals or situations that might trigger the fright response, such avoidance can, over time, make the fear even worse. Exposure therapy has been used by the US military in helping veterans combat PTSD.

'We worked on that with a psychiatrist using exposure therapy, by walking through the attack so many times and talking about it over and over. It's not easy. I've been in special counselling for it ever since. You talk about the attack over and over and you feel yourself in the moment, and it's supposed to be the way to face it, instead of ignoring it. I relived that nightmare time and again. I could feel Yukon's fur and smell his breath on my face, hear his growling. They were so in my face … And it's part of my nightmares, not being able to see or know what the other wolf, Trouble, is doing.

The therapy sessions were every other day, and you don't just talk about your attack, you walk through your attack in your mind's eye and you explain it out loud. It's exhausting. You have to take really good self-care while you are doing it. I go swimming, I do yoga and I go for walks, but it really is a big toll on your mental wellbeing. I had to take a break from it eventually.

I love to run up to North Dakota, where I was born and raised, and sometimes I go there to think and process. It's a different setting. Sometimes when you're looking for an answer, you have to change your perspective. That's what I do. I drive to North Dakota, put myself in a different setting, surrounded by friends, and ask the same questions but in a different spot, in a different perspective.'

It was while she was back in North Dakota, seeking that new perspective, that she stumbled on the answer to her prayers. As a newly divorced mother of two, she was eager to find someone who could relate to her experience.

'I was really desperate. I was going through therapy and talking to my regular psych and another psych. I went back up to North Dakota and I was exasperated. I said to my psych, "There has to be someone I can talk to, a specialist."

They said, "No, you're the only one. You're the only wolf attack survivor. You're not going to find anything like this."

I kept processing it and I thought, That's impossible. We just have to find it. We just have to keep looking. I knew it was on me. I was up staying with friends and I kept searching on a bunch of different terms: "bite" … "attack victims"…

I finally came across an article in Australia about Dave Pearson. It talked about Bite Club. I thought, Oh my gosh, no way, how incredible. They're doing something about a predatory attack ... I hadn't thought of it that way. This same article mentioned that Bite Club was not just about sharks, but bears, lions and even a hippo. I absolutely froze in that moment and I thought, Oh my God, I'm going to get a hold of this guy and I'm going to ask and I'm going to pray, and all he can do is say no. If he says no, maybe I can start something in the States and mimic it, however he does it.

I thought I'd message him, tell him my story and ask if I could be part of the group. I'd even be the silent member that nods and says, "Yes." I've been through therapy before and you can only learn so much from somebody teaching a class, but when you're working with people who have been through it, then those are the people you really learn from. Group therapy can be so incredible, and I knew if I could just find the right group I would really learn a lot and hopefully have something to contribute. He messaged me right back and said they'd be more than happy to have me. I cried when he sent me that message. I never cry, but I cried tears of joy that day.

The wealth of knowledge and support that is shared in a trusting way all over the world from the survivors are a daily inspiration to me. Every single post I feel. It has absolutely changed my life. They get together all the time. I am absolutely heading to Australia. I am determined to meet Dave and for him to be the first person that I meet to shake his hand, give him a hug and tell him, "Thank you so much for creating this club because it saved my mind, my sanity and my family's sanity."

I go back and talk to my psych about things that come up, and everything's not put on your family or your friends. You have this exchange with people and there's no judgement with it. There's only support. There's never any negativity. It lifts you higher – it really does. It's inspiring.

I worked in a very scientific field in the military, and the combining of information with the healing process is so progressive. It's not just about someone asking whether anybody had a particular tendon repair done, it's above and beyond that. It's about recognising that PTSD exists after an attack, the mental impact on the survivor and their family. It can be someone whose child was hurt or who lost a spouse. Combining that mental health care and being a support system for people is like nothing I have ever seen before. It used to be that it was only when people were fifteen to twenty years down the road that PTSD was thought about. But here, Dave is already there, providing support.

Attacks like these change your life, change a family's life. It can change your appearance. Neighbours know about it; sometimes the media know. You feel like you're the only one who's going through it. There's stuff you can't explain to other people or even your own family. Yet, here we have people who say, "We are here for you. We are always going to be here for you. We have lived it."'

Given the extent of her injuries and the trauma she suffered, it might be reasonable to think the owners of the wolves – Julene's good friends – would have been keen to know what happened, how she was, whether the pens they kept their animals in were secure enough. As Julene discovered, though, their response was very different.

'When I was in the first ER, while there was still blood everywhere, I gave the hospital the number of the owners, because they needed to know what shots the wolves had. I also messaged the owners from my phone, saying, "You are not going to believe it. I got bit. I am in hospital because of the wolves."

The next phone call they would get was from the hospital. They said, "We know her but she's not supposed to be there." It happened so fast. I was in complete shock already from the attack, but then the hospital came back and said, "We called them and we can't get any info out of them. Zero. They said they want a lawyer."

I was in such disbelief. A lawyer? All we are asking right now is if they have had rabies shots so I don't have to go through those series of shots. They were getting a table ready, and a trauma surgeon perhaps might have to cut my arm off, and someone was talking about lawyers. It was so surreal, I was thinking, Did you call the wrong people? These were people we would see every few days and play with the animals. I can only assume they were worried something would happen to the animals.

I was not talking about a bite or an attack at this time. I must have been really extreme with it because the doctors and specialists were saying, "We are not a reporting agency. We're not going to report this. Nobody's going to get in trouble. We just have to know if you need rabies shots." I was not talking at all about it. I was obviously in such shock. I was really worried that something would happen to the animals. I was hysterical and crying about it in the ER. Nothing was ever reported to the authorities about the animals. In South Dakota, you have a year to charge somebody over a dog bite. I'm not even sure if the dogs or wolves were registered with the state.

I had seen many friends bruised and bit up there, but they used to say, "Until somebody dies, it's not bad." What we had been trying to do there was build better fences and enclosures, doing what friends do, jumping in and helping, just like they had looked after our huskies when we went out of town. I'd even said to them that they should look at building it into a wolf conservation centre. Right up the hill from where they are is Kevin Costner's Ta'Tanka, an interpretive centre on the story of the bison inspired by *Dances With Wolves*. They could have looked into moving up the hill there and creating a proper wolf sanctuary. We were in the process of helping them do that because they had really outgrown the place they were at.

They used to be very good friends, but they had no comment on what happened. They did not even check how I was. They charged me with trespassing and did not admit that I had keys to the entire place and was supposed to be there. I know they were acting out of fear but they are no longer friends.

In the end, I refused the rabies shots because of my heart condition.'

While Bite Club offers support and understanding of the like she never thought possible, Julene's road to recovery is still a long one. But she feels better equipped now to deal with the challenges ahead.

'It's been a bumpy, rough road since the attack, healthwise, and I think maybe my body is still dealing with that emotional release. When you are attacked by a predator, so much force is put onto your body it has to come out somehow. It takes a while for that trauma

213

to come out, for your brain and body to process it. I have a few scars up and down my arm and shoulder. I have some tattoos to cover up some of them, but they are very visible if I wear a short sleeve.

It surprised me that people would ask me about my scars. You don't know what to say the first time someone asks you about it. It feels strange to say, "This is from my double wolf attack." After a few people ask, you get your spiel down. It is really a strange beast. When I do tell people, they look at me in a certain way and say, "Wolves? Where the heck did that happen?" I say, "Up by Deadwood."

When I hear what other Bite Club members have gone through, I always feel so much more blessed and fortunate. I haven't had to deal with the media, the neighbours, the authorities. There is just the loss of a friendship. When I say this is from my double wolf attack, there just isn't a huge reaction.

I live in Sturgis, a small town of only 6,500 people. I walked around with open wounds and I think it was a bit shocking for people to see – so shocking that they didn't want to ask where it was from. But people were incredibly kind. They treated me with kid gloves. I consider myself lucky.

I always think shark attack victims have it harder. They all live on the water and have to deal with going back into there. For me, I have to accept I am not a dog person any more. I live with the belief that everything bites. At first, I would always carry a gun or a knife on me for safety. I don't have to do that any more but I still have that fear. I have been recommended a service dog, to help me go out in public more. What I have to process though is that it's still a dog. That is a constant.

Why would you be afraid walking down the street and a little dog barks at you? It's the same barking.

And it's the unknown. Is there a big dog with that little dog? Is it going to come out from somewhere? I'll always have that feeling … if there's one dog, there's likely going to be another. I don't see them as dogs any more. I see them as animals. There's one animal here, where are the other animals? I always have a high level of alertness. I work daily to keep that at bay and live with my triggers and not let them affect me.

Here, in the Black Hills, there are coyotes yipping at night. I can hear them as I sit on the porch. That's hard to hear. There are mountain lions in the area; they've been down the block. We have a wire fence and I don't think any fence can be big enough for me. I still have my button. I always keep it charged. I always have my phone on me as well. If my phone dials 911, it automatically lets my family know my location and that I am in distress. That's an updated safety feature. You don't always believe you have coverage, so you do anything you can to be safe.'

What happened on that day in September 2020 changed the course of Julene's life – one that had already taken many twists and turns. She's fifty-one now, but in a varied career, she completed four years in the US Navy, she's been a concert promoter, a massage therapist, a travel agent and been to college twice. And, although she bears the physical and mental scars from that day, she says she would not change a thing about what happened. The last two years might have been dictated by the injuries she sustained that day, but she hopes her future will be shaped by the research she began before the wolves struck. And she's optimistic that out of her trauma, something positive will emerge.

'I would never take away that entire day. I would never change anything about that day. If I hadn't had the

CHAPTER 12
CHAD BARKER

AMBERGRIS CAYE, BELIZE, WEDNESDAY 12 MAY 2021

*'When you're on the menu, it gives
you a whole different outlook on life.'*

For some people, the idea of finding themselves in shark-infested waters is the stuff of nightmares. Yet, for Chad Barker, a fifty-eight-year-old retired car salesman, and his wife, Sue, it seemed like an opportunity not to be missed.

The couple, from Decatur, Illinois, were holidaying in Belize, a part of the world they knew well and loved to visit. On their trip to the Blue Tang Inn, San Pedro, on the island of Ambergris Caye, they'd already swam at the barrier reef with turtles and other big fish, including some six-foot reef sharks. But on Wednesday 12 May, it was going to be the real deal – a forty-minute boat trip out into the Caribbean Sea to see sharks up close and – as it turned out – very personal.

When the crew found the spot they wanted, they baited the water with chum to attract the sharks, giving instructions to guests to stay on the other side of the boat. One by one, they entered the water with snorkels to observe the action. Soon it was Chad's turn:

'They had chummed on the starboard side and said if we stayed on the port side of the boat, we'd be all right. They didn't say what we'd see, just to stay on that side and to stay out of the middle of the sharks. My wife had got into the water before I did, as had a cameraman.

I wasn't in the water thirty seconds and they were on me. I put my mask on, looked down and all I could see was a mouth heading towards me. I stuck my hand out to try to stop it and two sharks hit my hand at the same time. They were two fully grown, eight-foot nurse sharks – the two largest ones out there. One got my hand to the left side and the other got my little finger and the finger next to it and they hit heads. I'm really lucky they did because they knocked each other off my hand when they hit.

The one that got my little fingers decided he was going to take them with him. He started shaking his head, and I ripped my hand out of his mouth. I raised my hand out of the water and said, "I've been bitten," but the guys all started laughing. They thought I was joking. I had been taking blood thinners for previous heart surgery and the blood just started squirting. Then they were like, "Oh my, he's not kidding. Get him out the water."

My wife's reaction was one of disbelief, but she came to me and tried to help me into the boat. I got over to the ladder but did no climbing at all. It was like – boom – I was in the boat. I couldn't believe how quickly they got me up. One of the guys on board must've been a weightlifter because he picked me up like I was nothing, and I weighed two hundred pounds [90 kg].'

Once on board, the crew gave Chad a towel to wrap around his bleeding hand and shouted for everyone else in the water to come back on board. Despite his injuries, however, Chad would hear none of it.

'They said, "We gotta go," but I said, "No, I'll just sit on the boat and bleed. These people paid a lot of money to do this." We'd all actually paid to swim with sharks. The guy looked at me like I was nuts and I said, "No, I'm serious."

The trip had cost $150 a person and I just wanted everybody to have a good time. I didn't want anybody's time ruined because of me. The cameraman and his wife were both professionals and they stayed in the water, but everyone else got in the boat and sat and waited. I just wrapped my hand up and sat there and bled.

So, I got bit by a shark. I didn't think it was a big deal – but I was still in shock. I unwrapped my hand to look at it. There was a shark tooth in my hand – and I picked it out and threw it overboard. As soon as I did, I realised I'd just thrown away the best souvenir I could ever have. It was the dumbest thing I have ever done in my life.'

Once the people in the water finished their swim, they got back in the boat and the crew headed back to Ambergris Caye.

'They called back to the hotel to let them know what happened, so when we got back in, it seemed like everybody on the island knew I had been bitten. It went like wildfire. There were possibly five hundred people on the dock waiting.

One of the guys from the hotel, who I'd got to know, came running and said, "I hoped to God it wasn't my buddy that got bit."

I said, "It was your buddy!"

They booked me for surgery but the only doctor they had available was a gynaecologist. He said I was lucky the sharks knocked themselves off me, because a lot of times, when you get a nurse shark bite, they suck onto you and will not let go. He said many times they expect the shark to come with the person because they literally stay on you. They won't let go, and they have to kill the shark and cut it off. It doesn't happen very often, he said, but nurse shark bites can be pretty extreme because of this sucking on.'

Nurse sharks are so called perhaps because the sucking sound they make when hunting resembles that of a nursing baby. Another theory is they take their name from the old word '*nusse*', meaning cat shark, or from the Old English word '*hurse*', which means sea-floor shark. They are capable of generating the most suction force of any marine animal. Although they possess small mouths, their suck and shake motion – which one tried to demonstrate on Chad – is highly effective when it comes to feeding. While nurse sharks might not appear as aggressive as other species, they rank fourth when it comes to the most bites on humans. The fact that he had been attacked made Chad very popular.

'When I was sitting on the table and getting operated on, a man from outside walked in and said, "Where's the guy who got bit by a shark?"

The doctor said, "Get the hell out of here."

It was hilarious.

Right between my index finger and thumb was cut deeply. That's where I pulled the tooth out. I also had numerous lacerations on the other fingers. When I was on the boat, it hadn't hurt. It didn't hurt until they started sticking needles into it to deaden the pain. It was weird. I couldn't feel the little finger at all. It was pretty mangled ... almost removed. I hadn't realised it was cut as bad as it was. When they got me to the emergency room, all the doctor wanted was to get the blood stopped on the little finger, and I didn't realise it had gone clear through the tendon and everything else. It was hanging on. He sewed it on.'

Many people at the hotel assumed Chad would want to get back to the USA as quickly as possible, but he was determined to see out the rest of his vacation.

'I said, "We're going to stay down here, have plenty of margaritas and I'll be good to go."

When I did return to the United States the following Sunday, I went to the local doctor. He looked at me and said, "What happened to your hand? Did it get stuck in a meat grinder?"

"You're not going to believe it," I said, "it's a shark bite."

He didn't believe me. "Really, what happened?"

"It's a shark bite."

"Well, it looks like a two-year-old sewed it up," he said.

I told him about the gynaecologist. He wanted to get some pictures of my hand to send to the surgeon. The surgeon came back with the same comment: "Did you get it caught in a meat grinder?" Anyway, they booked me in for surgery the following morning. The majority of the surgery was on the little finger trying to save it, which he managed to do. He had to sew the tendon back together. It still won't close all the way, but it's there and it operates and I'm happy to have it.'

The cameraman who was in the water had managed to capture the moment Chad was bitten. After viewing the video, Chad was still at a loss to explain why the sharks targeted him – but the footage confirmed that he had done nothing wrong to further provoke the fish that were already excited by the chum in the water.

'It wasn't anything I did. I thought maybe I'd swum over to them. But once I saw the film, I saw I didn't do anything wrong. I put on my mask, and, bam, there they were. They were that quick. I don't know why they came for me. I'd been in the water for twenty minutes prior to that on the other snorkelling trip, and there were other sharks there. I believe it was the chumming of the water. It got too big, and when I got, in it's like they went, "Fat guy in the water!"

On that previous trip, when we were at the reef, there were nurse sharks and reef sharks. We were warned about the reef sharks. The guy that ran the trip was keeping a close eye on them. He kept us all close together and, in fact, one of the sharks came over a bit too close and he had to run him off. At that point he said, "That's enough, let's go back to the boat." Reef sharks can definitely be dangerous. The ones we saw were about six foot. The one thing I did find out when they bit me was that human blood does not attract sharks. They scattered when the blood hit the water; they swam away … My attack was the first time they'd had anything like that down there, and one guy had been doing boat trips for thirty-something years.

I have good friends that live there, and they are not going to go back in because of what happened to me. The sharks are not supposed to bite, but they did, and one friend said, "I'm not going to be on the menu for them."'

Chad recognises how lucky he was that his injuries weren't more serious.

'If they hadn't hit me, it probably would have turned out a lot different. They knocked each other off me. I looked on the internet for nurse shark bites and saw pictures of a guy who was taken to the hospital with a six-foot nurse shark attached to his side. They took the shark and all to the hospital, because they couldn't get it to let go of him. They bite down like a pit bull. They will not let go. It's like being clamped on by a cheese grater, and it has such force that if you rip your hand out, it's going to cause damage.

I ripped my hand out of a shark's mouth. I probably did most of the damage when I ripped it out, but I couldn't leave it with the shark. He was shaking his head and he was going to take it. It was either him take it or me rip it out. I chose to rip it out. People ask me what I would choose again. You're talking a thousandth of a second to make up my mind, so I don't know. It was pure and utter luck that I got my hand out of its mouth. The other one that came, if I'd stuck my hand out, it would have gone right in its mouth up to my elbow, but it hit at the same time. I was lucky.'

Chad spent five years in the navy and three in the army, when he was encouraged to be in the water, before an injury suffered in an accident in Germany in 1988 forced him to quit the military. After being bitten by sharks, that feeling of security has gone.

'In December 2021, we went to Florida and we were on the shore, down at Siesta Key. It was my first time getting back in the water since the attack. I was only in up to my knees and I found myself being scared to death. I was shaking violently. My knees were knocking. I thought I was going to pass out. I was seeing things in the water and I had to get out. I was going to pass out if I didn't. In both the navy and the army, we were always taught going into the water is a safe place to be. Now I'm scared of it. I have not been in the water since then.

I haven't had nightmares, but I have had waking dreams when I think about it. They are kind of scary. I haven't even been in a lake because the water is brown, I can't see what's in there. This is from a man who absolutely loves water.'

Like many animal attack victims, Chad found it hard to find someone who could relate to what he had been through. Reaching out on social media led him to Bite Club.

'I put on Facebook that I was wondering if there was a way to track shark bites – to see how many there are a year and where they take place. Dave Pearson popped up, introduced himself and asked me a few questions. That's how I found Bite Club – the club that nobody wants to join and where tasting bad is a good thing!

It's been a lot of help to me, a tremendous help. I'm the only person in Illinois that's survived a shark bite. It's not like I can go out and talk to somebody about it. With Bite Club, I've been able to make contact with people who have been through the same thing I've been through. People have been able to overcome their fear, and they tell me, "Hey, it's perfectly normal for your knees to start knocking and feeling like you're going to pass out." When you're on the menu, it gives you a whole different outlook on life. It really does.

I like the fact that the Bite Club has taken on other types of bites. We have a woman who was attacked by a hippopotamus. Her husband was killed. She had to have something like twenty-six surgeries. I sit there and think, "I had my hand chewed on; I have nothing to complain about."

I've been told by other shark bite victims it just takes time. I'm lucky that I don't have nightmares – because a lot of people do have them. For me to think it's abnormal not to want to go into the water is wrong. It's completely normal *not* to want to go in the water after you've been bitten by sharks. Just like people who have been attacked by dogs become afraid of them. I've got to do it in my time. And when the time is right, I'll do it.

I tend to put expectations on myself, and in this case, I need to stop doing that. I am my own worst enemy. I know that. But I know I will never go shark diving again.'

Chad has experienced some negative reaction to his attack – but even the most critical comment made him rethink his own position.

'A lot of people said if it happened to them, they'd have been madder than hell and would want to kill the shark. I said, "Why? The shark was doing what a shark does. I was in his environment. He didn't come into mine." They're not pets.

I think there are two types of people – people who have been bitten and those who are about to.

One gentleman on the internet said it was my fault and I was bringing bad publicity onto sharks. At first, I got kind of mad, but then I thought, He is right. What would have happened if one of the guys on the boat had killed one of the sharks? They could easily have done it. There would have been a dead shark and it would've been my fault. That was an isolated comment. Most of the other comments have been very supportive. Even that one wasn't meant to be hateful towards me. He was correct.

Sharks and people don't belong together. We shouldn't be doing that. If you want to go diving with sharks, go diving but don't chum the water. That's just getting them into a frenzy and I don't believe that's the way to do it. On the way back to the hotel, the guys on the boat were talking about not chumming it again. I don't know if they were saying that because they were worried we were going to sue, but my wife and I are not the type to sue people. We signed up for what it was and we were dumb enough to get in the water that had been chummed and I learned my lesson.

I could have seen them in their environment from the boat. That's the way people are meant to see sharks.'

Although Chad will not pay to swim with sharks again, his ordeal has not put him off returning to Belize, where he hopes he will overcome his fear.

'I'm going to go back to Belize, probably in 2023. I want to go there because the water is really clear. You can see what's in there very well, whereas in Florida it was murky and that's why I was seeing things that weren't there. I think in clear water, when I can actually see what's in the water, I might be able to overcome my fear.'

CHAPTER 13
MIKE FRASER

CAMPBELL ISLAND, NEW ZEALAND,
FRIDAY 24 APRIL 1992

*'I looked across to my right-hand side and
saw my arm was down the mouth of a shark.'*

Experienced diver Mike Fraser thought he was in no danger. Subantarctic Campbell Island, 682 km south of Invercargill, New Zealand's southernmost city, was believed to be so remote and its ocean waters so cold that the only sharks there were the less aggressive sleeper or Greenland shark.

Mike, the thirty-two-year-old leader of a team from New Zealand's Meteorological Service stationed on the island for a year-long stint, had other marine life on his mind when he and his four colleagues went out snorkelling at around 2 p.m. on a beautiful autumn day in April. Their daily meteorological tasks – releasing weather balloons twice a day, recording and transmitting data and performing scientific services – had the benefit of a lot of free time. And winter approaching meant the arrival of southern right whales, which came to the island's Northwest Bay to breed close to shore. Mike recalls:

'We had been down there for six months, and I was into diving and underwater photography. The southern right whales had started to turn up and I hoped to capture some good underwater photos of the whales, something nobody had done. The day had turned into a beautiful day with brilliant, clear blue water. We took our snorkelling gear and went for a reconnaissance trip to see how deep it was.'

Mike and his colleagues – meteorologist and second-in-command Linda Danen, conservation officer Jacinda Amey, electronic technician Robin Humphrey and mechanic Gus McAllister – swam out into the bay to see how deep it was. Mike knew the whales came in close to shore to scrape themselves on the bottom to get rid of barnacles, and wanted to see what the bottom was like. Watching them with curiosity from the shore were several sea lions. They had been in the water for around thirty minutes and Mike, in a seven-millimetre wetsuit and with no weight belt, was able to duck down to the seabed. He was a little further out than the others and about fifty metres from shore, yet still the water was only about four metres deep.

'Something caught my eye and I stayed out a bit longer on the bottom. I had just got back to the surface when I just felt this great big thud on my right-hand side. I didn't see it coming. I thought it might be a bull sea lion getting stroppy. There wasn't any pain or anything like that. Whatever it was, it pulled me down. Then, seconds later, I got brought back to the surface. That's when I looked across to my right-hand side and saw my arm was down the mouth of a shark. It all happened so fast. I think I tried to hit it with my left arm but it pulled me down a second time.'

The others saw the shark as it broke the surface with Mike in its jaws. Under the water, Mike fought to free himself, pulling his knees up to try and kick it.

'I then felt a hard wrench and managed to roll clear. When I got back to the surface, my right arm was gone. It had been bitten off. It was all one movement. I was on my back and when I looked across, the wetsuit arm was in shreds. I shouted, "Shark!" then flipped on my back and started to swim back to the shore.

I didn't see the shark again but the others saw it. There was a pool of blood by this stage. They could see the dorsal fin circling around in the blood. The others made a bolt for the shore, which is understandable. Jacinda swam about halfway back and stopped to look at me, by which time I was on my back swimming back in. I swam to her, and she tried to help me in after that. The others then helped me out of the water.

I had lost so much blood I was having trouble breathing. I still had the wetsuit on and couldn't talk properly. I was trying to tell them to unzip the wetsuit because there was too much pressure. Finally, they got onto that and unzipped the wetsuit and I could breathe again. Once I was breathing and settled down a bit, I was sort of OK. I didn't even think of the time it would take to get me back to Invercargill. At that stage I just thought I'd be fine.'

After the others unzipped Mike's wetsuit and removed his mask, Robin applied pressure on what was left of the right arm, as Gus made a tourniquet from the mask strap and pulled it tight. Linda ran to a nearby hut in which was a first-aid kid, tent and VHF radio, while Gus took off for base – three and a half miles away – to raise the alarm.

'By the time they started putting bandages on my arm, the bleeding had just about stopped. We can put that down to the water being so cold. At the time it was only 8C. My arm was cut off about three inches below the elbow. When they cut the wetsuit off, I looked across to my right arm again. Jacinda tried to tell me not to look but I just said, "I know it's gone."

What saved my life more than anything else was the cold water. The stories you hear of people who have limbs bitten off in temperate tropical waters, they tend to bleed out and die in the same time it took me to get back to shore.'

Although the bleeding had stopped, the team faced a logistical nightmare to evacuate Mike from the island. Radio communications at the time allowed the team to make calls to phones through an HF [high frequency] radio, so Gus phoned Tony Quayle, the immediate contact, who then phoned John Funnell, the helicopter pilot the Met Service usually used to ferry contractors to the island. John, who the team had known for years, was the go-to person in case of an emergency and knew the remote location.

Any rescue helicopter would have to fly 682 km from Invercargill and, as night fell at around 6 p.m. that day, it would be impossible for it to land at Northwest Bay. There were no lights and by then the area would be in near total darkness.

When John received the call, he was at Taupo Airport, which was located way to the north on New Zealand's North Island. He called paramedic Pat Wynne and long-distance pilot and navigator Grant Biel. Their six-seater Aerospatiale Squirrel helicopter was fitted with long-range fuel tanks but had a total range of only 655 km. They would have had to first fly 917 km to the very opposite end of New Zealand's South Island. From Invercargill, on the southernmost tip of South Island, they'd then be faced with another 682 nautical miles further south still, over the open ocean. They began making arrangements to get to Campbell Island as day broke.

Mike's colleagues, therefore, had no option but to try and make him as comfortable as possible and wait it out until daybreak. Linda replaced the tourniquet with a pressure bandage, but the focus now turned to Mike's left arm.

'They strapped a snorkel to my left arm because they thought it was broken. It was so limp. I wasn't sure what the damage to it was. I still had the sleeve of the wetsuit on, although it was shredded. They put a snorkel on there because they thought it was broken, because it was so limp. I am at a loss how it was done. Did it go in on the first bite and straight out again without me even knowing about it, or was I trying to hit it? I can't remember.

I have tried to think how. Was I floating on the surface with both my arms out in front of me in order for it to take both arms? I know it hit me from the right-hand side, but that's the one thing I can't figure out – how my left arm got mangled.

The tourniquet was only on temporarily to stop the bleeding. You can't leave a tourniquet, otherwise it cuts the blood flow and everything downstream goes rotten and it would have killed the remaining part of my arm. They removed the tourniquet, put some pads on and wrapped it up tightly with bandages.'

Using a sleeping bag from the hut, an oar and some driftwood, the others built a crude stretcher to carry Mike to level ground and erected a small tent over him.

They hauled him into a sleeping bag, wrapped two more around him and elevated his limbs.

'I was lying on my back in the tent all night. During the night, Linda put something sharp on my fingertips and asked me if I could feel it. She was obviously wondering whether nerves had been cut. At that point I could still feel them.

The strongest drugs we had down there, as far as pain relief goes, was pethidine. We didn't have morphine. Linda was talking to Wellington Hospital regarding how much drugs to give me and what to do, medically wise. There was a bit of a communication breakdown, though and they gave me twice as much pethidine as I should have had. A few minutes after every pethidine injection I got, I threw up. We only found out later I'd been having too much. In fact, the paramedic told me at a later date that he had no idea how I had remained awake, as I'd had enough to knock out a horse.

The chopper wasn't going to arrive until about 7 a.m. The shark attack happened at about 2.30 p.m. so we had about fifteen hours to wait in the pup tent. I can remember most of the night in the tent. They were telling silly stories trying to keep me awake.'

Throughout the night, Linda gave Mike sips of water to prevent dehydration, but because he was vomiting from the pethidine, he could not keep the water down and his body was drenched in sweat. When morning broke, Campbell Island was cloaked in a thick layer of clouds as the helicopter approached.

'Before the attack, when we were walking on the way over to Northwest Bay, a New Zealand Air Force Orion surveillance plane flew over. We had talked to them on a handheld VHF radio, channel 16, emergency frequency. After the attack happened and things settled down a bit, the others got on the handheld VHF just in case the Orion was still in the area because it had a short-range line of sight. Unbeknown to us, the *Tangaroa* [a government fisheries research ship] was just out on the horizon and they picked up the radio call. She came into Northwest Bay and some of the guys came ashore. I remember them coming up to the tent just in case they needed to give a hand when the chopper arrived, or – if the helicopter ran into bad weather and couldn't make it – they would get me on the *Tangaroa* instead and get me back to New Zealand.

I remember hearing them outside the tent and then hearing the chopper arriving and [paramedic] Pat Wynne asking, "How do we get in here?" because he couldn't find the front door of the tent.'

When Pat got to Mike, his blood pressure was dangerously low at 70/40, but he was unable to set up intravenous fluids due to the poor light in the tent. The decision was made to fly Mike to the main base.

'I don't really remember the flight from Northwest Bay to the station. I recall being in the sick bay at the station for a while, then getting carried out to the chopper and then the flight to Invercargill. Pat gave me some orange juice to drink, and just before we got to Invercargill he put the phone to my ear and my mum and dad were on the phone – the first time I'd had any contact with my family. Quayle, my boss at the time in Wellington, had rung my parents and told them what had happened. They must have had all sorts of stuff at the back of their minds, but once I spoke to them and said I was OK, it was probably a big reassurance to them.

Due to the limited range of the chopper, they had to squeeze me in the back with a forty-four-gallon drum full of Avgas [aviation fuel]. As they flew back to Invercargill, once the main fuel tank got low, they used a hand pump to transfer the Avgas from the drum into the tank. And when the drum was empty, they opened the door and kicked it out over the Southern Ocean. I had been a bit squeezed in there for a while because I had the drum hard up against my legs.

The funny thing is they [the Met Service] did consider how remote Campbell Island was. Six months earlier, when we went down there, we stopped in at the Auckland Islands [465 km south of New Zealand] and put in an emergency fuel dump on Enderby Island with Avgas specifically for an emergency. We had some Avgas at Campbell Island as well, the intention being that, if need be, they could fly from Invercargill to Enderby Island, top up and then get to Campbell Island, top up, then back to Enderby top up and back again. As it turned out, they never needed to go to Enderby to top up. On the way down, I was told, there had been a tailwind, and in those few hours when the chopper was on the ground at Campbell the wind changed around, so when they took me back to Invercargill, they had a tailwind going back as well.'

It took six hours to get Mike to Southland Hospital in Invercargill. First, the helicopter had to land at the city's airport as the chopper wasn't permitted to land at the hospital. By then, John Funnell had been awake for nearly twenty-four hours. An ambulance was there to meet them.

'They shoved me into an ambulance and, bang, that's the last thing I remember. Next thing I know, I'm waking up at Invercargill hospital. While I was in there, they did a bit of a temporary clean-up operation, just to get an idea of what was left in my arm.

After a few days in hospital, some of the skin started coming off my legs. That's when I remembered that while I was in the chopper, some of the Avgas spilt onto my legs and damaged some of the skin. I was only there for a few days before I was taken up to Hutt Hospital near Wellington, where the main surgery ward was.'

Mike had been transferred to Hutt on 1 May, where he received skin grafts and reconstructive surgery to repair his tendons.

'The main reason I got moved from Invercargill to Hutt Hospital is that I came from Wellington, I had my house there and my parents at the time were living in Napier. It's a lot closer than way down the bottom of the South Island, so my parents and friends could come to visit.

The first stint in hospital lasted four months. That was when they were putting my arms back together. I got out for a few months and then I had major operations to clear tendons on my left arm, which was another two months. And a few months after that, I had another tidy-up operation, which meant I was in for another couple of weeks. It was a total of six to seven months in hospital. Most of that was operations on my left arm, putting the nerves and tendons together. On the left arm, the tendons got cut, a couple got pulled out altogether. A lot of the muscle got pulled and the ulnar nerve was cut, which meant I have limited use of my left hand. The nerve itself got cut about halfway between my hand and my elbow, so when I was in hospital they found the two ends and put them together, but then the nerve had to grow back down that track again, and by the time the nerve grew back, all the finger muscles had wasted away. I have limited amount of use in that hand.'

While operating on Mike's arms, the surgeons made an unusual discovery, which they presented to him after the surgery.

'They took two teeth fragments out of my arm, which were given to me after an operation and I still have. I still don't know what happened to my left arm. Maybe it went in [the shark's mouth] while I was trying to hit it, but what I do know is that I tried to bring my knees up to push it away using my feet. I ended up getting a cut on one of my knees through the wetsuit. It was so fast. The whole time I didn't feel a thing. If my arm hadn't been bitten off, I would have been stuck under water. I would probably have drowned.'

Mike was fitted with a prosthetic arm. Not only did he have to get used to having an artificial limb, but he had to train his brain to recognise his left as the dominant hand.

'I got my first prosthetic arm when I was still in hospital. They got changed over the years because the shape of the stump of the arm changes. So, as all the swelling dies down, the shape changes; you have to get a different arm to accommodate the shape, otherwise you end up with sores.

I was right-handed so I had to try and get my brain to automatically do stuff with my left hand and not my right. It took a fair while to get some use in my left hand again, and slowly some of the feeling has come back on one side of the hand so I can do most stuff.

Some of the things people take for granted that used to be so easy to do I can still do but I have to concentrate and it can be frustrating.

The prosthetic arm technology hasn't really changed at all in the years since. You see the occasional programme on TV where people are trying out robotic hands, but what they don't show is you have to carry around a heavy battery pack. The technology is there to plug into your nerves. I met someone who wanted me to try something out but it involved carrying a battery on my waist and I wondered whether it was worth the hassle. I can get by with the prosthetic hand that I've got. It's only a thumb and finger. I've got used to it, but even today, when I'm doing shopping and holding my credit card, people are looking at me using my hand. I've had people ask me, "How does that thing work?"

You hear people talk about the phantom pain. I don't particularly like the term because it's not a pain, and, as I try to explain to people, I can feel my right arm any time I like. The main reason for that is the nerves that run down to the fingertips, they are still in the stump end of my arm. I can actually make my little finger move, my thumb move, my index finger move, and if you look at the stump of my arm you can see the little muscles in different places working. Those fingertips are at the end of my stump now instead of on my actual fingertips, but it still feels like they are there. It still feels like my fingertips. I can make my arm feel like it's there any time I like.'

Adapting to the physical challenges was only one aspect of Mike's recovery. He had to deal with the psychological impact – but found he was better equipped than many when it came to healing his emotional scars.

'To this day, I have this image in my head of what I saw when I looked across and my arm was down the mouth of the shark. My head was right next to its head and I could see its eye. That's a still image in my head I can still see today. On the first couple of dives since then, I was looking over my shoulder a bit, to be honest. It took a few dives to get that one hundred per cent confidence again.

Once, I was doing some diving up at the Poor Knights Islands [50 km off the east coast of North Island] and the water was crystal clear, so it wasn't a problem. But if the water is cloudy or dirty, you sometimes think something is sneaking up on you. It's happened a few times but nothing too bad. I've come into contact with a couple of small sharks while diving at the Poor Knights. They were probably only about a metre and a half long, nothing of any size.

In terms of speaking to anyone about what happened, two people came and saw me while I was still in hospital. The first was in Invercargill when a minister from a church I didn't know came to have a chat. He said it was all God's will and he was just testing me. I looked at him and told him to piss off. When I was at Hutt Hospital, a psychologist came and had a chat for twenty minutes. He left and I never saw anyone again. Whether they thought I was all right, I don't know.

It annoys me [to have lost a limb]. It's made life hard, but I haven't had nightmares or anything like that, whether it's because I'd done a lot of diving with sharks before and it wasn't the first time I bumped into a shark. I've done a lot of diving up in the Kermadec Islands [800 km north-east of New Zealand], and up there if you don't see a shark, it's a novelty.

As well as Campbell, we used to go to Raoul Island and man the weather station there for twelve months at a time. I spent all my spare time diving, and most of the time there were sharks around. I've also dived at Hawaii and bumped into sharks there – then I go down to Campbell and get munched on by a shark. That's why it hasn't affected me mentally – because I'd done all that previous diving with sharks and nothing happened. These were different species. I tried to get up close to them to get some photos and they used to give warnings. If you are annoying them, they certainly give off the signals and you back off. Reef sharks get very rigid, they arch their backs and their fins start poking out tighter. It's hard to describe, as it's more a visual thing you detect, but they start to swim funny. As soon as they do that, you know that they're getting a bit annoyed.'

Since the attack, Mike learned that the creature that bit him was a great white shark – and discovered that, contrary to what was previously known about them, such apex predators are quite accustomed to colder waters.

'I've had experts look at the teeth they took out of my arm, and they said, yes, those are white shark teeth, and going by the size of the serrations, they've put it at about a four-metre great white. The other interesting thing was how cold the water was. I've had a few shark biologists questioning whether it was a great white because the water was too cold, but we now know they can handle that temperature.

I've done a bit of research and I actually went back to Campbell a couple of years later, in 1994, and did another year down there. I found a bull sea lion that had been taken by a great white in Tucker Cove. That was in the middle of winter and the water temperature was 6C. They can definitely handle cold water.

The interesting thing for me is why they are there in the first place. Clinton Duffy, a marine scientist from the New Zealand Department of Conservation, has done some tagging of great white sharks around the bottom of Stewart Island [30 km off the coast of South Island], and from his tags, he thinks that during the winter they go north; but what I'm finding interesting with the Campbell Island one is that the sharks are there during the winter but not the summer.

I've gone through logbooks on what people have reported seeing [at Campbell] and there is nothing in the summer. They all turn up for the winter, and the only thing I can match that up with is that they are turning up at the same time as the southern right whales. Maybe they are turning up to feed on the whales.'

Finding the evidence of a great white attack on a sea lion at Campbell Island has led Mike to believe he was attacked in a case of mistaken identity.

'It must've thought I was a sea lion and it was lunchtime. Down there, there are lots of sea lions, seals, sea elephants. I was in a black wetsuit, with some red and blue on it, and it's a nice theory about the black wetsuit [that sharks can mistake for a seal], but even if someone was wearing a white wetsuit and floating on the surface, they would still look dark from underneath. I don't buy the theory about a black wetsuit. Sharks often attack from below, so even if you're wearing a light wetsuit, you're still going to look like a shadow. I think it was definitely a case of mistaken identity.

At the time, we didn't know the great white sharks were there. We knew there were sleeper sharks or the

Greenland shark. A year before I was there, the guys found a sea lion that had been attacked by a sleeper shark, and the bite marks are very distinctive, like shredded skin, not what you get with big bites.

And when I went down there in 1992, I was talking to the guys at Macquarie Island [further south-east, towards Antarctica] on the radio, and they found a sixteen-foot sleeper shark washed up on the beach there. And Andrew Leachman, the skipper of the *Tangaroa* research vessel, later told me they had caught a Greenland shark just off Campbell Island. At the time, they didn't realise the value of it and turfed it back overboard. What attacked me was definitely not a Greenland or sleeper shark. I know what I saw and I've since got the videos of the elephant seals and sea lions that have been bitten down there by the same sharks.'

Mike's injuries meant he could no longer do the same job he did at the weather station. His employer found him work, and being able to go back to places like Campbell Island helped his rehabilitation.

'My employer, the Met Service, was good. In New Zealand, we have the ACC – the Accident Compensation Corporation. If you have an accident, the government will cover 80 per cent of whatever salary you are on. The employer has to cover, at most, 20 per cent of what they were paying you. So I was still on full pay but it was only costing the Met Service 20 per cent. I just wanted to get back to doing what I wanted, and I got back to work quite quickly. I couldn't do the original job I used to do because I needed my hands for that, but the Met Service found me some work I could do on a computer, so it wasn't a problem.

. I got back to Campbell again in 1994/95 and it was while we were down there that the Met Service decided to close the station down to save some money, so we were the last ones there. I didn't think it was a good idea, and once there were no stations to go to, I stopped working for the Met office. I started working for myself because I found it too difficult to get employment as, although I can do most things, I am probably ten times slower. I predominantly do computer work now.'

Despite the impact the shark attack had on Mike's life, he bears no ill will to the animal that took his arm and despairs at the attempts to mitigate against similar attacks using shark nets and baited drum lines.

'You get people who want to go out and kill every shark there is for some reason, but I don't think it accomplishes anything at all. The way I see it, they were here first. We don't have drum lines in New Zealand but I don't think they achieve anything either. Most of the stuff they catch aren't the ones that cause the damage. If they catch something on a drum line and it's over ten feet, they'll kill it, and if it's under ten feet, they let it go. I can't see what that achieves.

Then they have the shark nets, which catch a lot of turtles, dolphins and porpoises and they drown as a result. The shark nets are not netting off an entire beach. It's not a single long net which might keep people safe; there are lots of short nets with gaps between them. I really can't see the point of the exercise.

Some people say there are more sharks now, the population must be getting too big, but I don't look at it that way. The sharks are there as they always have been, but with the advances in technology, the drones and other gizmos people have, they are recording and seeing more sharks. It doesn't necessarily mean there are more sharks out there. For instance, near the Bay of Plenty [on North Island], in the last few years there has been a big thing about bronze whaler sharks being fifty metres away from the swimmers, and they've cleared the beach. But that's only because someone has sent a drone up and can see them. There were bronze whalers there twenty years ago when there were no drones, and it wasn't a problem then. At Campbell Island, we had pretty basic technology, which was why I probably liked it.'

Mike's attack was unique in two ways – his case is believed to be the most southerly instance of a great white attack, and at the time, the flight to get to him was believed to be unprecedented in the world in terms of single-engine helicopter rescues. As a result, John Funnell received a bravery award for his efforts, while Jacinda Amey was also honoured for staying in the water to assist Mike.

'I was swimming back when Jacinda put her arm around my neck to help me in. Maybe in the long run that might have done me a favour because apparently I had lost half my blood, and perhaps by stopping me kicking, I saved enough blood to survive. The paramedic who treated me told me later that I had lost half my blood, so in that short distance back to shore, when Jacinda stayed in the water, it might have saved my life.'

And a lasting reminder of Mike's experience remains on the island.

CHAPTER 14
ANIKA CRANEY

FITZROY ISLAND, QUEENSLAND, AUSTRALIA, TUESDAY 14 JULY 2020

'I put my fins around its face, hoping that would bump it off but it was very quick and hit me like a steam train.'

Anika Craney was not in a good place. After three months aboard the *Barefoot II* catamaran filming a TV documentary series, *Bluewater Safari*, in the Coral Sea by the Great Barrier Reef in Australia, it was time for a crew change, and the challenging events of the past year were beginning to catch up with the twenty-nine-year-old.

'We'd finished filming two days before. It was my second year working on the boat, and the irony was that my focus was shark conservation. I had an interest in myth-busting shark interactions and highlighting the importance of sharks in our ecosystem. The very last episode of the second season was me talking to my boss Dean Cropp's father, Ben, who is a shark expert, about shark conservation, how sharks are being overfished and, especially, how much he has seen the lack of presence of sharks in Australian waters and how that has devastated the ecosystem, which includes the Great Barrier Reef.

Two days later the crew changed over. Everyone apart from Dean, the captain and me flew home. We had a new crew, one of which was Emily. She had been an intern as social media manager, had a passion about videography and marine education and was joining us on board for the first time. We were just off Cairns, near a place called Fitzroy Island, waiting for the winds to change so we could sail back to Sydney. In the three months since I'd been on board, we'd left Sydney in April and sailed south. We'd swam with seals, we'd sailed east to Lord Howe Island and Elizabeth Reef, Cato, Middleton, Mellish, Elusive, Lady Elliot, then up to Cairns, and we were meant to finish filming and then sail back to Sydney slowly. That was the plan.

Truth be told, on that day I was in a pretty bad head space. It had been a challenging trip, not just because you're on a boat with seven people and you're filming, which I find quite stressful, but only a few months before I'd lost my house in the bush fires on the south coast of New South Wales. This was very closely followed by a break-up with my life partner, and going on the boat was our way of running away from COVID lockdown and my way of escaping my life, I guess.

My boss had offered me a position on the boat, not just for work, but to live, as I didn't have a home, so it was my only place of comfort. I was still struggling a lot with that grief. And saying goodbye to the previous crew was tough because they had become a family. We were already quite close but especially so during that time, and it was quite hard to say goodbye.

However, Emily was very excited to join the crew and brought a new energy. She was excited for me to teach her about sharks and sailing and free-diving. Initially, I had joined the boat as a cabin buddy for my friend who was on the crew, but once on board they offered me a job. I was a deck hand but was working my way up to being a skipper. Back in Sydney, I'd run the safety boat when we organised events in the harbour.

On the boat, everyone had multiple roles. Since we'd been on expedition, I was also camera assistant, cook, dive teacher, onboard medic and what they called an "engine monkey", as I also helped with maintenance.

It was my first day off, not working and not filming. So, that morning, the crew organised to go to Fitzroy Island to visit the turtle rehabilitation centre there. Many of us did a lot of wildlife rescue and rehabilitation work, so we went and had a tour. While we were at the centre, one of the guys there, Shaun, said a lot of turtles there were found in the region and got released after they had been rehabilitated – often after fishing or boating accidents, shark bites or spearings by local indigenous communities. When they release the turtles in that region, they tend to hang around, so they suggested Emily and I go for a swim after the tour on the beach up at the north end of White Rock, as there was a chance we might see some of the turtles. So that's what we did. Emily also asked me to teach her how to free-dive.

We took our dinghy back to the boat from the island. Wearing a blue wetsuit vest and bikini underneath, Ocean Hunter fins with fish scale decal [sticker designs], fin socks and a mask, I jumped in the water off the back of the boat. Immediately, I wasn't happy. The water was murky. I was instantly on edge. My hair stood on end.

We had just come from the Coral Sea, which was very clear. We had been swimming with big sharks there but we always had a lot of safety measures in place for that. We had been swimming with tiger sharks, bronze whalers, grey whalers, Galapagos whalers, and every now and then, we'd see hammerheads and bull sharks and probably a few others, but always in clear water and we were always in a group. I felt uneasy but we were close to a local tourist beach that seemed safe and supervised.

I waited for Emily to come and we swam towards the shore. Once we got to the beach, I turned to her and said, "I don't feel comfortable. I think we should get out." She agreed. She was happy to hear that. She said she'd been following my lead and had been hoping this was just normal and was trying to brush away her feelings of discomfort for my sake. I was glad we had that discussion and we mutually agreed to get out the water.

Instead of swimming directly back to the boat, we went ashore and then walked up the beach to find the closest point so we would be swimming directly to the boat, rather than out at an angle. We walked down to the closest point so it would only have been a hundred-metre swim from the shore. As we went into the shallows, I told her what I was feeling, that I was quite lost, still grief-stricken and kind of unsure of the next leg of the trip. Emily told me not to worry. We were going to have a lot of fun, she assured me. She was very excited to be there. "We're going to see fish," she said, "and we're going to have a great time."

I didn't know if it was instinct or what, but my hairs were raised again as we stepped into the water. I was still on edge. It was one of the first times I'd ever got in the water and not felt better, so I knew something was wrong. I was waiting in the shallows for her, only about thirty metres from shore, only a few metres off the coral platform. Depth-wise, there was about thirty centimetres below us and then it dipped away to about three metres and continued to slope down underneath.

Emily had been behind me filming a fish. I thought she was still behind me, so I was just floating on the surface, waiting for her. She later told me she'd actually swum around and was underwater when it happened, practising her breath hold. I was on the surface, looking down into the water, crying into my mask, feeling pretty shitty. I saw a shadow in my peripheral vision. I raised my head and saw what, at the time, I recognised to be a whaler but now know to be a bull shark. I didn't know then how to identify the species and it was very quick, but it had a very wide, blunt – not elongated – face. It made eye contact with me and didn't part its gaze, which was unusual. When you keep your gaze on a shark, it usually indicates you are a predator, whereas prey will look away. That's what I usually did – kept my gaze.

Dean, my boss, who has grown up around sharks, had always taught us that if you feel uneasy with a shark, put your fins in its face, which I'd done many times before. Within three seconds, I realised I didn't feel comfortable with this shark. It was moving up towards me, then it turned, kept its gaze on me and then flicked its tail towards me, from depth coming straight up at my face.

I put my fins around its face, hoping that would bump it off, but it was very quick and hit me like a steam train. Initially, I thought it had just rammed me with its nose and I was jolted back with the push. I didn't feel the pain of the bite until I saw the blood.

I kicked with the other leg. I can't say that was a conscious decision. It was instinctual. It hit my left leg and I kicked with the right. At that point, my foot was in its mouth. I didn't feel sharpness, just pressure, like I'd been punched but on both sides of the leg. I kicked with the other leg and saw blood fill the water, from the surface beyond my arm's reach. From that point I realised this was a problem. It was not just a small bite for there to be that amount of blood that quickly.

I come from a nursing background, and subconsciously, I probably realised it was an artery and that my life was now in danger, not just from bleeding out but also the fact that there was now splashing and commotion in the water. The shark could come back from underneath me and I wouldn't be able to see where it was coming from because the water was so murky. I was on the surface now, not looking down but trying to kick backwards with my leg.

Instinctively, I grabbed my leg with both hands and held the wound closed. I kicked with one leg and tried to swim with one arm … intermittently with one arm and one leg, screaming for help, back to shore, which was closer than the boat. Also, I thought it was safer to go to shore than to the boat and deeper water.

I began to scream, "Help me, help me, get out of the water, get out of the water!"

I shouted my boss's name, Dean, because he is also trauma-trained and previously worked as a war correspondent journalist, so I knew if anybody was going to be able to help, it would be him. He is also very calm in serious situations. Emily then surfaced, saw the commotion and came towards me.

From that point my memory is very fogged. I've had people piece it together. Everything became blazed in a white fog but I also became quite tunnel visioned. Emily was yelling at me, "What's happened? What's happened?" Then she saw the blood and said, "Was it a shark?"

I just needed to get to shore and to get out of the water and to hold my leg and try not to panic and slip under the water. She had my fin in her hand, which was confusing to me, because I didn't realise she had been that far deep. It meant that she had been around me and came back towards me as I was swimming towards the shore. She then helped push me towards the beach.

I looked around for someone to help. There were quite a few people in the water. There were kids playing at the shore. There was a man and his daughter on kayaks, but they paddled away from me as they saw me. I realised people were looking at me strangely, like I was faking it. I actually thought it, too. It hadn't sounded real as I was screaming. Now I found it hard to have power in my voice and to make sense. I think I was repeating myself and I didn't seem to have cognitive ability, just actions. I was looking for life, but when I realised that people were not rushing towards me to help but moving away, I thought, Fuck, I am a bit fucked here ... if this shark comes back underneath me, I am about to die.

In that very moment, I honestly thought I was going to die. I have never felt so scared ... just not to have control of the situation and not knowing if it was underneath me or not. Then I turned and saw a woman on a standup paddle board and her son in a kayak. She started swimming towards me, screaming, "Are you faking or are you serious?" I don't remember what I responded but I think she screamed, "Was it a shark?"

Apparently, I said yes, but I don't remember this conversation at all.

I would later find out her name was Jacqui Gibson and her son was Mackenzie. Then she saw the blood in the water and screamed for Mackenzie to get to shore, run up to the resort and ask the staff to call for the helicopter. She told him to make sure they called the helicopter and didn't send for the boat as it would take too long. She couldn't see my foot and saw that Emily was holding my fin, so she thought my foot was gone.

Ten-year-old Mackenzie did that. What an amazing kid. He ran up and made sure they got a helicopter and not a boat. Jacqui then paddled towards me and got down low on the paddle board. I tried to get up onto the paddle board but slipped off into the water. At that point, I began to lose consciousness. I guess because there were people around, my adrenalin was starting to wane. I was also losing a lot of blood.

I felt a sense of peace, of just wanting to close my eyes and slip into the water, but then Jacqui started yelling at me. She is an ex-firefighter, so was unbelievably amazing at trauma response. She yelled, "Get up, get up, you have to hold on, you have to hold on, you have to keep kicking, you can't stop kicking, you have to keep kicking!" She later apologised, but that was what kept me conscious and focused. I probably would have lost consciousness without that energy.

Emily helped me up a third time after I couldn't hold myself on the back of the board. I held my leg on the back of the board, held it shut, while holding on. Emily got underneath me and pushed me and the board towards shore because Jacqui was falling off and I wasn't stabilising very well. Emily was an absolute hero as well. These women were just incredible.

For her first day, what a rough introduction to boat life!'

Anika was bitten around 11.45 a.m. and paramedics were called to the island around midday. As Jacqui had correctly predicted, it would have taken them forty-five minutes to cover the five kilometres to the island by boat from Cairns and a helicopter was on the way instead. Fortunately for Anika, several trained medics were also staying at the resort and now came to her aid.

'After Emily pushed me to shore, I could see a crowd of people crowding around the shore and running down the beach. First-aid kits were coming out. One man came running into the water. He was apparently on the scene a lot quicker than I remember. He would rather I didn't use his name so I'm using a pseudonym, Stuart. He's an ex-medic who was also on holiday and he pretty much saved my life. He was one of the first people to hear my screaming and run into the water.

He said he waded in up to his board shorts and the shore of the beach was completely red – and if he'd been wearing white shorts, they would have stained red. They were dark blue but already they were beginning to stain. He got under my arms, Jacqui held my legs and they carried me up the beach and placed me on the sand in the shade under a tree on the sand.

People then crowded round with multiple first-aid kits, pulling stuff out and arguing with each other. It was an incredible miracle there were so many medically trained people there. I pray to the universe for sending them, but it was kind of a hilarious comedy at that point because they were arguing over who was more skilled. There were two paediatricians, a nurse, an ex-medic, an ex-firefighter, two or three medically trained staff from the resort, and they were almost bickering with each other. One woman yelled at me, "You need to calm down!"

I thought she was the one who needed to calm down!

I think they were panicked, not knowing how to organise themselves, but they raised my leg and were trying to bandage it. They were bandaging over my wetsuit sock, which was over the top of the wound, but I was still bleeding profusely and they hadn't looked at the wound yet. The bottom of a bull shark's jaw has more space between the teeth so it can hold onto its prey, while the top of the jaw, where the teeth are closer together, does the grinding. They saw that wound and thought it wasn't that bad, just a small flesh wound. But Jacqui and Stuart said there was too much blood coming from such a small-looking wound. Jacqui and Stuart were trying to keep quiet as the doctors took over but she eventually spoke up and said they needed to cut the sock off and have a look at the wound. At that point, they'd only seen one side of my leg.

Stuart also said he wanted to cut the sock off. When he'd woken up that day, he'd had the feeling he'd need to have his pocketknife with him, which was an amazingly strange thing. People were arguing with him but he took the knife out of his pocket. He cut off the sock, the flesh of my leg fell off the bone and the artery sprayed him in the face and over his shirt, which he then had to take off because he was covered in my blood. He said it was very Tarantino! I didn't hear that part of the story until I met with him a year later. Part of me wishes I saw that but I was only semi-conscious.

He then said, "Sorry, guys, I'm going to have to trump you for a second. I'm an ex-medic and she needs a proper tourniquet." Initially, they tied a towel around the bottom of my leg and thought that was enough, but it wasn't doing anything. Stuart then turned to me, grabbed my leg and said, "You might want to take a deep breath or bite down on something. This is really going to hurt, mate."

He was bloody right.

He put a belt around my upper thigh, pulled it as high and tight as it would go, then put a stick in and twisted it. That was more painful than the bite itself. I could feel the sharpness of the pain on my leg but the tourniquet was more painful. It felt like I was being crushed by a truck. At that point, I started feeling dizzy and nauseous. I was sweating profusely and went white. I said I thought I was going into shock. They rolled me on my side and gave me oxygen. As soon as I hit the sand, I began to consciously breathe slowly because I knew it would keep me calmer, more present and prevent me from going into shock, which I didn't want. I could feel myself slipping in but managed to pull myself out, which was amazing. I owe that to my free-diving training and meditation practice. Just having control of the breath, I think, made a huge difference.

At that point, Emily was holding my head, crying on my face and stroking my hair, telling me I was going to be OK. She was incredibly comforting and amazing.

I was on my side when I saw Dean, the captain, was now on the shore, walking towards me. I had heard the dinghy from his boat come over. He said he had heard the screaming and thought it must have been Emily and that it was probably just something silly. Then he walked up and saw the trail of blood on the sand and thought, Shit, it's serious. Then he saw it was me and not Emily. I think it was lucky it was me and not Emily, as I don't think she would've reacted in the same way. She didn't have as much experience in the water as I did.

Dean was very calm, which I remember thinking was really curious, but it was the best thing he could have done. He came up, held my hand and said, "What's going on, mate?" He said later he did that on purpose, and I think staying calm was the best decision he could have made. If he had run up the beach, it would have just created panic in me, which would have made it worse: made my heart beat faster and I would have bled more profusely.

I was in a drunken state of adrenalin. Drunk is the only way I can describe it. I said, "I saw a fucking shark and it came and it bit me. What the fuck!"

"It's not your year," he said.

"I don't think so. I don't know if I'm lucky or unlucky, but some bullshit is going on in 2020."

Then he asked if he could film me, which usually I would have said no to because I hated the cameras on the boat; it's not what I was there for. I was there for the adventure and I loved learning about diving and science. I hated the cameras and I always fought with him about that. But when he asked to interview me, I said, "Fuck, yes." Whether I was adrenalin-drunk or thought I would want to be able to look back on those memories for my own healing, I don't know, but I was right. It was very beneficial to look back on it.

He had a GoPro, and interviewed me while I lay there bleeding, talking about the pain. It was a good distraction, funnily enough, because I wasn't focusing on the pain in my leg, I was focused more on retelling the story and trying to piece together what happened. It really was a surreal day.

When they put the tourniquet on my leg, the sensation went from hot, rushing – feeling the blood rushing down my leg – to crushing. Although it was very painful, there was a sense of relief because I knew it meant I was no longer in mortal danger. I was no longer bleeding out. But the pain was real. As they lifted me onto a stretcher and carried me up the beach, they were talking to me, cracking jokes. Stuart said it was a good way to get out of washing the dishes and cleaning the boat – but I didn't have to go to this extreme to get a day off work!

It was great he had that sense of humour – a proper Aussie bloke. He was the only one capable of talking to me in a jokey manner. Everyone else seemed quite shocked, but he was the best person, because everyone else was behaving in a serious manner, which made me feel uncomfortable and unsafe. Having people joke was fantastic. Treating it like it's an unusual situation but you're going to be fine was more helpful than seeing people's faces looking like they were thinking, Shit, she's about to die.

They carried me up the beach towards the resort and I could hear the chopper in the background approaching the island. I could hear people on radios saying it couldn't land and it had to hover above the jetty. They lay me in the entrance to the resort and were all crowded around, reassessing me. They put a silver shock blanket on me because I was still quite pale and still on the verge of going into shock, which would have been dangerous.

They were playing Michael Jackson in the resort and I started dancing along to it, with my eyes shut, singing along. I thought it was funny. I think I was still quite drunk from the adrenalin. It didn't feel real. I felt like I was dreaming. I expected to wake up at any point and be back on the boat ready to set sail and continue the journey home. I remember saying to Dean, "Am I going to get stitched up and come back on the boat and we're going to continue?"

He said, "I don't think so, mate."

"What do you mean?" I said. "It's only a flesh wound."

They'd held up towels over my legs so I couldn't see what was going on – I hadn't seen the wound at that point. I had felt it but hadn't seen that it was to the bone and the chunk of flesh was hanging off. That was probably a good thing. I was curious but I remember I also made a conscious decision not to look. Another good thing about Dean recording me was that I was focusing on that and not what was going on. I was quite disassociated and not focusing on the pain.

The paramedics arrived and they offered me the "green whistle" [fast-acting pain relief methoxyflurane, commonly known by the brand name Penthrox]. I denied it because I knew it could induce more nausea and because I was in shock and already feeling nauseous. I didn't want to feel worse. I thought I'd rather manage the pain than feel like I was on mind-altering drugs.

The paramedics and doctors put on a second tourniquet below my knee and released the first one to ensure enough blood flow. If a tourniquet is left on for longer than two hours, you can lose sensation, cause nerve damage below and have to amputate the leg, so I was lucky that they got there so quickly. The paramedic gave me an anaesthetic and morphine-based pain relief, which reacted very well with me. It calmed me down and I became quite high and very happy. I was already in a daze but it really upped that level. I became very animated. I told the doctors and paramedics that with their helicopter gear on and helmets, they looked like James Bond characters.

"You guys are so fucking cool. I love you."

"OK," they said, "stay calm."

They strapped me to the stretcher, wheeled me down the jetty and winched me into the helicopter. I remember looking up at the helicopter that said "Rescue" on it, thinking, Is this a Bond movie? What is this? It was so crazy. It just didn't seem real. They had to hold me down in the helicopter because I kept trying to sit up to look out of the window. I was very excited.'

It took only seven minutes to fly Anika to Cairns Hospital, where a trauma team was waiting to treat her. As they came in to land, the paramedics told Anika a large media presence was waiting at the entrance to the hospital.

'They said if I wanted to be protected, they could put up sheets and cover me up, but I was pretty high and animated at that point, so I said, "No, it's fine, I'm going to say something."

They said, "Are you sure?"

"Yeah," I said, "it's fine."

As they wheeled me towards the entrance to the hospital, I sat up, looking like a crazy, with scrunched up hair, blood on my face and a half-open bikini. I screamed at the media: "I still love sharks! Sharks are beautiful!" That became a viral sensation. One of the paramedics, Terry, whispered in my ear: "That will make the news tonight for sure." He was right, but, oh my God, at the time I thought it was hilarious.

They wheeled me inside and there seemed to be around thirty staff waiting for me, but the only information they received was uncontrolled arterial bleed and shark bite, so they were assuming that meant a missing limb and quite a serious situation. But I came in laughing my head off, and they're all looking at me like, "What is going on?" I wondered why so many people were there to treat me. I didn't think it was that big a deal. I think a man who had been in a serious motorbike accident came in not long after me, so most of them dispersed, and I was left with three or four staff who were all very calm and amazing.

I became good friends with my emergency nurse, Melanie. She held my hand and asked if I wanted her to call my parents. I said, No, because my boss Dean would do that.

She said they were going to open up my wound to have a look and start treatment. They were going to give me some morphine because it would hurt. As she did that, I remember looking at her silver leaf necklace and feeling very fixated and soothed by that. I had been looking at my vitals on the screen on the wall, keeping an eye on my heart rate and blood pressure, trying to analyse it, but then I realised I needed to surrender to the care of these people and try not to be so in control. I could hear the doctor talking as he was looking at my leg, how the artery was now bleeding: "We have uncontrolled bleeding … I'm going to have to use forceps and close it off."

I remember being able feel that he was touching inside my leg but I couldn't feel the pain. It was a strange sensation. I had a profound gratitude for our medical system and the incredible doctors and nurses, who were so patient and kind. I burst into tears then, because I think I realised that it was serious and my joking manner had worn off. Melanie gave me a big hug and asked if I wanted to call my mum, and I said no, I'd rather just stay present and talk to them later.

They told me the extent of the damage and that I needed to go into surgery. I had lost a lot of blood and they would need to do a transfusion, which I didn't want to do because I know that it comes with its own dangers. The surgery was delayed because of the man in the motorbike accident, so they moved me into an emergency waiting room. For the first time, I was sitting there alone, really bewildered and confused. That's when it started to feel real. Before then, it had felt like a bit of a dream. Sitting there alone, hearing all the beeping and screaming and people rushing around the emergency department, I was quite bewildered and really hoped that someone would come and talk to me.

I was quite pleasantly surprised, therefore, when my doctor and paramedic from the helicopter came in. They'd taken off their helmets, and came to sit by my bed to have a bit of a chat. I burst into tears and gave them a big hug and said, "You guys are my heroes; thank you so much for being so calm and kind and patient – and for being so incredibly proficient at your job but doing it with kindness, which makes a really big difference. Not treating me like a patient but like a person made a really big difference."

My doctor, Emma, got a bit teary. She said no one had ever said that … it was nice for them to be appreciated for what they do. And Terry, the paramedic, was also lovely. I'm still in contact with him. He since moved out of Cairns. I met up with him once, when he invited me back to the helicopter hanger and I got to meet him and the rest of the rescue crew.

After they left, I was wheeled into the orthopaedic ward and I waited overnight while they discussed what sort of surgery I would need and where it would happen. Either I would have it there – or my family was fighting to have me transferred to Sydney so I wouldn't be stuck in Cairns Hospital and would be nearer to them. There were a lot of conversations about it being too unsafe to travel and that I needed to have surgery as quickly as possible because the nerves were damaged, three tendons were severed, the artery was severed. Because of the nature of the wounds and the fact that a shark's mouth is full of bacteria, I needed to have clean-out surgery before they did anything else. I had that the next day and then more surgery the following day. I stayed in the hospital for eight or nine days.

The care I received was incredible. The hospital was amazing. After surgery was when the real trauma began because the real, uncomfortable pain began at that point. I hardly slept for the whole time I was there – maybe just a few hours over a week. The adrenalin kept me awake, which was great for the first day or two, but that started to wear off and the pain kept me awake. It was a constant rise and fall of painkiller, then the pain rose again. I got quite sick, and it took a few days to realise that I was either allergic or had a bad reaction to the pain relief. That was more uncomfortable than the injury itself. I thought I'd rather be in pain than on these drugs – the side effects they can have like headaches, nausea, itching and insomnia. I felt like if I fell asleep, I would stop breathing, so I would wake myself up, which jolted my leg, which caused spasms. The pain would skyrocket to a "ten" and then I couldn't calm down again.

On top of that, because of the nature of the story, it then blew up. Even before I got to the hospital there were news stories saying, "Woman mauled by shark fighting for life." When I screamed, "I still love sharks!" that went crazy. The story went international and I began getting phone calls from journalists. I don't know how they got my number. It was horrible. I turned my phone off and got my boss to help manage it. He used to work in news and he helped protect me. My dad flew up and he was there the next day. He was amazing. But then a scientist went to the media, and that's when I would say the hardest part of the journey began.'

Anika was the first person to be bitten by a shark at Fitzroy Island – a popular tourist destination. A marine expert, Jamie Seymour from James Cook University, was quick to go public to say she must have been mistaken. Even in the face of contradictory evidence, he continued to dispute it was a shark when speaking to the media.

'He said it can't possibly be a shark; we don't have sharks in this region. The young girl was either confused, she doesn't know what she saw. The scientist said she was probably wearing a sparkly anklet which attracted the like of a triggerfish or a giant trevally, which have been known to be aggressive. The fish bit her ankle, she saw the blood, assumed it was a shark; she doesn't know what she saw. We shouldn't blow these stories out of proportion and scare potential visitors to this beautiful region.

That was then followed by a lot of other news stories saying that I lied to get attention for our TV show and filming. That's when the cyber-bullying began. People started sending messages through these articles or on social media and YouTube comments. I started to get trolls saying: "Stupid fucking blonde bitch, just trying to get attention for yourself" ... "You should have died" ... "What were you doing swimming there" ... "I bet my house cat could've done more damage" ... "I bet you were trying to get your five minutes of fame" ... "I hope you die from sepsis."

The ridiculous amount of horrific comments kept me awake and made me feel a lot more shit than I needed to feel. That continued for many years – it still kinds of affects me.'

Anika was able to dispute the claims from the marine expert because not only did her injuries indicate the size of the jaw of the shark that bit her, but doctors also recovered other evidence from the bone in her leg.

'I still have my fin. It has big teeth marks through it that match up with my foot. The thirty-five-centimetre jaw belonged to what was, approximately, a two-metre bull shark. I also have teeth that were removed from my tibia bone, which I then used during my first interview to say it's been determined to be a shark, not a giant trevally or a triggerfish. I didn't lie. I know what I saw. The bull shark tooth has been analysed, so that really helped me have some credibility – which I wish I didn't need, but it did help me. I know a lot of people don't have that luxury [of shark's teeth], which can be quite challenging, not to be able to determine what you saw. But the opposite is also true. I know a lot of people have lied about having a shark attack when it wasn't and that can be damaging to our community, so being able to prove it helped. Not that it stopped the trollers, who still said what they wanted to say, so I just had to switch off social media for a while.'

As someone who knows what it's like to be on the receiving end of online abuse, while still in hospital, Dave Pearson immediately got in touch with Anika when he learned about what happened and offered support.

'Within the first few days, Dave was on the phone and we talked for hours and hours. He was incredibly supportive and connected me to other people. I realise that through Bite Club we have all received similar comments and it's incredible how this group responded.

Multiple other people, not just shark attack survivors but friends and family, also responded. I have one friend who is a lifeguard and has been involved in multiple shark attacks, and he helped me in the very beginning when things started to go downhill.'

When Anika left hospital, she had a lengthy period of rehabilitation ahead, which presented not just a physical challenge, but a financial one too.

'In the first year, it was just focusing on the physical rehabilitation, and that was challenging enough … learning how to walk, using a wheelchair and crutches and a moon boot [controlled ankle motion boot] for four months. The wound itself took a long time to heal.

It was very painful doing three days a week of physio. I had to pay for it myself. I didn't have insurance. I was paying for everything from government-funded bush fire relief money, which I was lucky I had. Our health system is incredible, and I know that my medical costs would have cost more than $200,000 just being in hospital that long, with the surgeries and the helicopter flight. All these things are incredible, but it's the aftercare costs that I hadn't anticipated, like paying for psychology and physiotherapy, acupuncture and nerve damage treatment.

All these things added up, and if I hadn't had that bush fire relief money, I wouldn't have been able to pay for it. It went quickly, and I was not able to work sixty hours a week like I used to. Some people in Bite Club told me they'd set up a GoFundMe page or a relief fund, and I kind of wish I had, but I decided not to.'

For a year, Anika focused on overcoming the physical pain and on restoring strength and movement to her damaged leg, but she discovered that, although her injuries started to heal, the invisible wounds still needed to be treated.

'That's when it really started happening, later down the track when the physical injuries started to heal. I felt, in a strange way, that the physical pain helped me work through it [the psychological trauma], but when I started to get better ... whether it is the wisdom of the nervous system or the brain knows when it is in a safe enough place ... I started processing the trauma.

More than a year later, after the anniversary, I watched a video of me being on the beach. I had already been swimming with sharks by then. The very first swim after the shark attack was about three months later, after the wound had healed over, and was a swim I did with baby sharks. I found that was really healing and beneficial and I began to regain my confidence in the water again.

I had to learn to swim with one leg initially. I started training free-diving with one leg and one fin. I found an incredible family friend, Nathan Watts, who was a free-diving teacher and has been like my master guru, helping me through the physical pain and mental anguish. Diving with my eyes shut has been one of my best therapies, along with meditation practice. But come October last year, I had my first flashback. That's when things really started getting dark. All the online comments came spiralling back into my head and I couldn't get them out.

I was surfing with Dave [Pearson] when I had my first flashback. He was teaching me how to surf switch foot [using the foot not usually preferred], so I had to change to the other leg. My left leg can no longer take the weight in the same way and is not as flexible because the tendons – that had been severed and reattached – now overlap. He was teaching me how to surf and I fell off a wave. I jumped off and put my head under the water. I saw a bull shark swimming at my face at full speed with its mouth open. I shook my head, closed my eyes and when I opened them again, it had disappeared.

That to me was scarier than the real thing because it meant that now I couldn't trust my own mind. I didn't know that was going to continue to be an issue, but it did. That was October 2021, and from that point it was a very slippery slope.

I began to have more frequent flashbacks, hallucinations – auditory as well as visual. It started happening at work. I started seeing sharks in the water when I was working on the boat. I was about to be promoted to be the skipper. Initially, my job was the safety boat operator, so I was in charge of keeping people safe in the water – and I was seeing sharks; I was hearing people screaming for help, hearing people scream "Shark!" all the time. I became hyper-vigilant, I was having repetitive panic attacks, I was thinking people were talking about me, hearing people saying horrible things about me, but it was those comments I'd read online just spiralling in my head.

I stopped working and became quite agoraphobic for a while. I shut myself in and stopped talking to a lot of friends and family that just didn't get it. A lot of people said things like, "When are you going to get over it? It's more than a year ago now. What's wrong with you?" I was, like, "It's not actually that one thing, it triggered a lot of traumas that I had been through before which I had therapy for."'

By going back in the water and by returning to the pursuits she previously loved, like free-diving and spearfishing, it was almost inevitable that Anika would encounter sharks again. Only this time she was doing it as someone with post-traumatic stress disorder (PTSD).

'I have a lot of different coping mechanisms in place for my own mental health but also for physical health, like knowing how to defend myself. I've had to do it a few times since. It feels different. But since having worked through a lot of PTSD symptoms especially, it's a lot harder than it was physically ... just learning to deal with the panic. Physically, I had to deal with it within the first year. I began to spearfish again and I had a few scary moments but I dealt with them quite well. The scariest moment in the last few years has really been imagining there's a shark behind me when there isn't. To me, that's scarier than if there actually was a shark there. I've had quite a few scary incidents with real sharks and I've handled it the best way I can and it's been OK.

A few months ago [in early 2022], we were swimming with whales and a bronze whaler came up from the depths quite quickly. I swam down at it and it swam away, which is the best response you can do with a predator – show that you are a predator and you don't swim away. In the same trip, I had a panic attack on scuba. My mask clogged up and I couldn't see and I was imagining a shark behind me about to attack me and bite my head. That was scarier for me because I didn't have control of the situation and I had to get out of the water and calm myself down.

For me, it's more about being in control of my surroundings and the reality of the situation ... it's easier to respond to reality than it is to respond to a warped sense of reality, and that's where PTSD changes your life. It's definitely getting easier and it's better than it was, so I still have a lot of hope for working through these things. I do know from my group, though, that they say PTSD doesn't go away, you learn to deal with it. In the same way I have nerve pain in my leg and it's probably never going to go away but it does become less over time, you become more familiar with the sensation and the pain.

How I describe PTSD now is that it's like all the boxes that you've done a lot of hard work compartmentalising and categorising in your mind and putting into neat corners are now open and you have no control over when they start flooding out in public. They are inappropriate all the time. All these things I've been through since childhood were open and I couldn't control them. I've been through a lot before the shark attack. I've had physical and sexual abuse and a lot of death in the family. I've witnessed a lot of severe traumas and been through fires, earthquakes, floods and a twister, and then not long after that my best friend had an accident – a near-death incident at home – I was his first responder.

All these things came together and I was just falling apart mentally. Bite Club held me together. The people in the group understood. I started to realise that the responder could be just as traumatised as the victim. It made me have a lot more gratitude and respect for first responders and how difficult it is to live through feeling responsible for saving someone's life – literally having their life in your hands.

I talked a lot more to the people who were involved in my story and how they had coped and moved through that. A lot of them had not moved on. In fact, a lot of people get a lot of shit for being a responder and not being the real victim, and I've realised that's incredibly unfair because they can be just as traumatised, if not more, in some cases. When you're a responder, you see so much more than the actual person sees. For instance, I didn't see my own wound but all these other people did. They saw blood, flesh, everything. They saw the shark thrashing in the water. My memory is very different. I realise that's the same for everyone else that's been through a similar situation.

Trauma in general has all these different perspectives, and how they play a vital role in how we see the world and how we move through these feelings has really been eye opening.

I am so appreciative of Bite Club and having a place to meet people who can offer and receive support and talk about what to expect and what to do when things start getting obscured, because that's when life becomes so much harder than simply moving through physical pain and rehabilitation. Healing the mental scars is so much more challenging than the physical – at least it was for me – and I know that a lot of people have experienced a lot worse injuries than me. I cannot speak to those things but I can speak to the invisible wound, and that has been the most taboo thing to talk about and the most challenging thing to bring up with people because people dismiss it.

"Oh, just get over it … it's not a big deal … it's in the past … that's not who you are … it shouldn't be so hard to get back in the water … it shouldn't be so hard to drive a boat or to do your job or socialise or to live a normal life or to study."

You can't speak to someone else's experience and you can't guess or anticipate how it's going to be for people later down the track. Meeting Dave and the other people in the group has been unbelievably supportive and helpful.'

The power of Bite Club and the strength its members receive from and offer to the group has been perfectly illustrated with Anika's case, where her mental struggle seemed particularly acute because of the previous traumatic events she'd experienced.

'The flashbacks were most intense over a period of four to six months until March 2022. They stopped for a few months but I had another eyes-open hallucination of a shark swimming towards me, its mouth wide, while diving in Bali. It was my first dive since losing a dear friend to a diving accident. I was surfacing from a depth free-dive, with my trainer, Yoram Zekri, in front watching my dive for safety and training. I surfaced feeling so angry and wanted to pour out aggressive tears but held back because I didn't want to freak out the other students. I did dive again not long after but paused hard training. When the flashbacks were intense, I focused on meditation, psychology and yoga and stopped talking to a lot of friends and family who didn't get it and weren't supportive.

Bite Club people became closer than my family for a while – Dave in particular. Dave and my dad are very close. It's been really amazing. I even stayed with Dave and Deb [Debbie Minett, Dave's partner] for a while and met a few other Bite Club friends, and that really helped – like Garry, who is the lifesaving duty officer in Ballina, where there has been a spate of shark attacks over the years. He's been my main friend in Bite Club, who I've leaned on and vice versa. It's been so helpful to have people who just get it. Fellow shark bite survivor Rick Bettua from Mission Beach, in Queensland, has also been an amazing friend and support. He's someone who gets panic attacks in the water and the nightmares but continues to pursue a life in the ocean, continues to spearfish and dive, and works through the challenges. His support and guidance have made a huge difference to my journey.

I also sought out different therapy modules, not just psychology but things like hypnotism and float tank therapy, which is sensory deprivation therapy. That was really beneficial. I also did craniosacral therapy and Watsu, which is water massage. You are held in water, wearing floats, and someone tells you to hold your breath and then they pull you under the water. It's like a meditation practice combined with feeling safe in the water. It is really important for people like me that have not just had a trauma in the water, but water was also my place of healing and connection to myself and the world, so doing things in the water feels like rebuilding that trust. I found it really profound.

I also did a meditation retreat with Tom Cronin [a leading meditation master], which was one of the most intense experiences of healing and recalibration. It was incredible just to sit with your mind, with no external distractions, and sift through all the muck, clean it out and step back into the world with more confidence. The knowledge that this daily practice can provide such a powerful tool to reset the nervous system and clean out the build-up of negative thoughts brings so much peace.

I've had to borrow money from friends and family to pay for these different therapies. Bite Club also recommends different therapies. Of course, there are a lot of people who are sceptical about trying something different but I think it's worth being open-minded. A lot of these different therapy methods have really helped. I don't have flashbacks any more and haven't had a hallucination since January 2022.

I still get panic attacks and I still feel quite socially anxious. I had that when I was younger, but since working on the boat, I've been safety boat operator, I've been skipper, I've been a hiking guide and a dive teacher. You have to be a very outspoken, crowd-coordination person. I haven't felt shy for a long time but now I'm working through a teenage version of myself that is completely socially anxious. I don't want to meet new people; I don't want to have conversations with people. If someone asks me who I am and what I do, I burst into tears. It's getting easier but I think that was something I didn't expect and something that Bite Club has really helped with.

You have a kind of personality transplant after trauma sets in, and that's the hardest part – not knowing who you are any more. A lot of friends and family see me as a brave person and I don't feel like that person any more. But it's a work in progress and it's a lot better than it was. In January 2022, I couldn't leave my house, I couldn't drive my car. A few months later, I was in Bali doing a free-diving course, so I'm definitely making progress, it's just a lot slower. Bite Club really helped with that – relieving that pressure of having to meet certain goals at a certain time.

There is no time frame for working through living with PTSD. It's a mixture of you getting better but also you become more familiar with how to cope and how to handle panic attacks when they come along. There are a lot of different coping mechanisms that really help, like counting your breath and sensory focus – focusing on the sensation of touch and feeling your feet on the earth and counting all the different colours you see and what you can smell. There are other things too, like I have a tool kit in my bag: I have lavender oil, I have my teddy – a shark called Walter. I feel like a kid who has to have all these things, but I'm seeing other people doing the same thing and I've met quite a few people now with PTSD from various different things and they all have their coping mechanisms. Talking about that openly and shedding the shame makes a huge difference, as opposed to feeling like, "Oh my God, I'm broken. What kind of adult walks around with a teddy bear or has to sniff lavender or has to have a bracelet they can feel or something they can fiddle with?"

All these things can make you feel embarrassed, but I've seen so many people do the same thing and how it helps them. Getting rid of that shame is the first step to moving through it and not feeling broken. The most dangerous thing that comes from living with trauma is that you feel broken and you feel like that becomes an excuse for why you can't follow your dreams and live your life.

I definitely felt it before … giving up on the things you want to do and surrendering to not being able to live life at full capacity. I don't believe that any more. It's a lot more challenging but there are different ways of doing it and you just have to find a way to shed that shame and say, "I need that support."'

'I found out there was a fishing trawler boat washing fish blood into the water anchored just off the beach.'

'When I go on a plane, I ask the cabin crew to let me know when certain things are about to happen. I ask if I can be closer to the bathroom so I don't have to walk through people. All these little things. I don't like using the word "disabled". A friend said to me, instead of calling it a disability, she calls it a "diffability". You are different, you are not necessarily broken. Those language tools really help. A lot of people say they're broken but I think that's really self-defeating. For the same reason, I choose not to use the word "victim" in terms of trauma. I choose the word "survivor" because I think it has a more empowering resolution and takes more control of the narrative. I also try not to use the words "shark attack". I say "shark bite" because I feel like that's a lot more accurate description of what happened.

I feel like "shark attack" comes with a narrative of being singled out and purposefully hunted and, with me, that wasn't the case. I think in most cases it's not that way. It's an accident. It's a curiosity bite with an animal that is looking for prey and has made a mistake. In my case, especially, it was bite, release and swim away. It tasted me and it tasted my swimming fin and the plastic and it realised I wasn't what it wanted. It was confused, it was murky water, I had fish scales as a decal at the end of my fins. Those were the factors.

I also later found out there was a fishing trawler boat washing fish blood into the water anchored just off the beach, which is legal in that region, but it shouldn't be. I don't think it should be legal anywhere. When fishing boats wash the deck and cranes after a catch, it sends blood into the sea. As soon as the blood hits the water, the sharks will sense that. They get curious and go into hunting mode, which leads to a frenzy. There can be hundreds of interactions where sharks come in to check out people, but if they are not in a frenzy mode, it's not likely they will be out to hunt. If they can see you clearly in clear water, they are going to recognise you are not a seal or a turtle or a fish. But fish blood in the water changes the way they behave.

It's not safe for anyone; it's not safe for them either. That's not their intention; they're not singling you out as prey on purpose. They don't want to eat us; it's not what they prefer. If you look at the science around testing what sharks prefer, they always go for fish blood over human blood or fish blood over pig blood. There's been a lot of scientific research into what they prefer and they will always go for what their diet is. Sometimes they make mistakes, and different species of shark are gutsier than others. Tiger sharks are known to be a bit more of a garbage gut; they'll try and eat anything. They've been known to have licence plates in their stomach and things like that because they are more curious at test-biting things.

It's similar to dogs. There are a lot of different species of dog and not all of them are aggressive and not all of them are confident and hunt in different ways. It's the same with sharks: not all of them are aggressive, not all of them are out to kill; they are just trying to make their way in the world and work out what's food and what's not.

This is something I've been really passionate about – working on ocean conservation and changing legislation around marine park zones [protected areas of ocean and marine life, which in Australia cover four million square kilometres or 45 per cent of the country's oceans]. And they should be changed so fishing trawler boats are not allowed to enter anywhere near a swimming beach. Putting blood in the water anywhere near where people are swimming is going to change the behaviour of animals there, attracting not just sharks but other carnivorous fish that come in, splash around and attract other sharks.

All these things play a factor, and I think it's important that we have more education and change so that we can live in and around the ocean safely without interrupting the behaviour of animals that call the space their home, instead of saying we have to kill them because we want to enjoy it. We have to change how we live and how we interact with marine life.'

In analysing what happened with her shark encounter, Anika has reassessed what she wears when going into the ocean.

'The fins I was wearing at the time had a fish decal. I'd been told they were good for diving because for spearfishing, especially, you want the fish to think you are another fish. Now I realise, after speaking to a lot of shark scientists, that in clear water it wouldn't matter so much with a shark, but in murky water the shark is going to see the scales and think your foot is a fish. They think that could have been one of the factors why it went for my foot and not anywhere else on my body. That's one of the theories. They now encourage people to wear camouflage in the water.

Spearfishermen wear mirrored masks so the fish can't see their eyes. But I think it's better you have clear masks because if a shark sees you looking, it will determine you are a predator. Clear masks are not as beneficial if you're spearfishing but it's beneficial for your safety.

I now weigh that up. Are you more interested in fishing or being safe? I will always choose safety now so I wear clear camouflage, I wear shark deterrents. I have a Shark Shield, which is an electronic device that emits a signal that blinds the shark's electromagnetic receptors. A shark has dots, or pores, on its face called ampullae of Lorenzini that are used to detect electric fields; for instance, the movement of a struggling fish, splashing on the surface, or even a human heartbeat, and the Shark Shield blinds that sense. There are a few different versions of the Shark Shield. There is one that goes on the bottom of a surfboard and one that goes on your ankle. I have that one, because it means it's behind me when I am diving, but I also plan to get one for my surfboard.

It can't hurt to have these things. When I'm intentionally swimming with sharks, I don't use them, but if I'm spearfishing or feeling uncomfortable or panicked, I wear them and it helps. I also have Shark Eyes, which are stickers with big eyes that go on the back of your head, and I have stickers on my fins so it looks like eyes from behind. If a shark is behind me and it sees the eyes, it should recognise I am a predator and treat me differently. I can't say with 100 per cent certainty that it's going to change them from approaching but there is more of a likelihood of changing the way they approach, especially from behind.

I have done my own testing and I feel that it works. I just use as many different methods as possible and always swim with someone, never swim at dusk or dawn, don't swim in murky water, don't swim around where there's fish blood. All of these things make a difference and I encourage that for my friends and family as well.'

Just seven months before her shark trauma, Anika lost her home in bush fires that devastated an area of New South Wales in January 2020.

'I was living near Cobargo, in Verona, in the south-east of New South Wales. I had trained to be a firefighter the previous year. Two days earlier, I had left to go camping, and on New Year's Eve I got a text from my mum saying, "Have you seen the news?"
Fires had moved hundreds of kilometres in a day, and overnight they destroyed the entire valley. I found out too late. I packed up and went down there to see if I could help. It looked like a war zone. Nine hundred homes in the area were destroyed.'

That was why, when she was still coming to terms with what had happened, it wasn't helpful to have to defend herself against comments from a so-called expert. However, as she continues to rebuild her life, Anika bears no ill will against the professor whose comments unleashed a barrage of online abuse. Instead, she hopes for better understanding about all the issues involved when it comes to shark bites.

'Jamie Seymour is a marine biologist who has done a lot of fundraising for the Great Barrier Reef Foundation and has done a lot for tourism. I think what he's done is fantastic, but I think the job of a scientist is to work from facts and the fact he didn't talk to me about my situation and made rash comments that ended up having a severe effect on my mental health was really unfair and unprofessional. If it was someone working in tourism, I could be a little more forgiving and understanding. I still forgive him but I don't understand how a scientist can work without facts. He hadn't seen my leg, my injury, my fin or talked to anyone involved.

His comments had a spiral effect. He probably didn't anticipate it would have such a viral effect but it was followed by a series of stories that were very undermining and abusive towards me, which was not necessary. I want to have a sit-down interview with him but I'm not sure if he is open to that. He went on the radio not long after I spoke – and the tooth had been analysed – and he said that he was wrong and that it was identified to be a shark, but he never apologised and never reached out to me.

I asked if I could reach out to him and I don't think he was interested in talking to me in 2021. I don't want to attack him or retaliate but I would like to have an opportunity for him to understand that his actions do have consequences and unfortunately the consequences were quite severe, when I was already dealing with a lot of mental anguish. An unnecessary chain of events followed him commenting on something he didn't have the facts on.

I hope that can change in the future because I don't think anyone should experience cyber-bullying in any form, especially if you're already going through a lot of trauma and mental health challenges. It can be the difference between someone working through their problems and becoming suicidal. That's the truth I would prefer to be able to expose. I don't think enough weight is put on how these things can affect someone's progress, self-confidence and self-belief.

Having so many people say you are wrong, there was a point in my recovery where I felt, did I make up this story? I began to doubt myself and that's not fair. It's my story and no one else's experience so why should other people determine what did or did not happen? I wish there was more that could be done. The best way to move forward is to realise that scientists should work from science. Even if you're not a scientist, I don't think it's fair to comment on someone else's experience unless you've been through it yourself.

My perspective is very different from Emily's or Jacqui's or anyone else involved that day. It's affected them all in different ways and it's trauma to all of them, but I know a lot of people think it's not fair to call them victims of trauma because they didn't experience the bite, but they experienced just as much trauma. Something that came from Bite Club is that it made me profoundly aware that we all need to support each other.

No matter who is losing blood, everybody comes away with some scars and needs help and is worthy of seeking and receiving support through that journey. Emily went through it just as much as I did. It doesn't matter that she doesn't have a physical scar. She was in the water, fearing for her own life as well as mine. Her scars run just as deep. The actions of her trauma surfaced a lot sooner because she witnessed a lot more than I did. I was in the fight-or-flight mode a lot quicker. My body responded in an amazing way and flooded me with adrenalin, which protected me from panicking and not being able to function.

It's incredible that we have this amazing fight-or-flight response, and I'm really grateful for that, but I realise now – through free-dive training and meditation – that it becomes a problem later, when that same response switches on too often, invariably when it's not needed. It can be when you're in traffic or having a conversation with someone, and that's when it becomes a symptom instead of a survival mechanism. That's where therapy comes into play, to help you cope and calm down your nervous system.

You want that response when it's needed, not when there's no danger. You don't want to start panicking when you are sending a reply to a text. The body gets jumbled up and, because of the way we live these days, we are not challenging ourselves enough in experiencing a healthy way of responding to the hormones that flood our body. We are instead experiencing a lot of unhealthy hormonal responses – and not having coping mechanisms in place can be dangerous to mental and physical health. Our bodies can start shutting down, but if we have coping mechanisms in place – like meditation, yoga and eating and sleeping well and, for me, free-diving – we can help regulate the nervous system again and you can start to feel like a normal person once more.

It's about having the awareness to continue having a routine that benefits your wellbeing and having the awareness to admit when you're not coping. I did that for a while. I realise I was shutting people out. But I now see that the best response is just patience and kindness, and that's something I received a lot of through Bite Club and I really want to give it back.

I had been doing a course to teach diving because I want to be able to teach people to get back in the water and find a sense of peace. However, after that most recent hallucination in Bali, it was too stressful trying to finish a master and instructor course while I still needed be kind to myself. It was humbling to realise I had to slow things down a bit longer. Getting back into the water again – whether it's a swimming pool or freshwater pool or the ocean – requires lots of different coping mechanisms.

Not everyone has access to it. I'm one of the lucky ones that has, and I'd love to be able to impart that wisdom to other people at some point so they can benefit and work through their trauma and get back a sense of feeling safe and confident again.

I know a lot of people in Bite Club who are surfers, divers or marine biologists and they have never been able to get back into the water. That's heartbreaking because it's a place of profound healing and connection and community. That's what's amazing about Bite Club – to be able to support each other, whichever way we can. It's a really beautiful thing, it's an incredible family. I want to give back because they've given so much to me.

PTSD is like grief. Whether someone's died or they are lost from your life, it doesn't go away completely but you become more familiar with how to cope. Becoming more familiar with what makes you feel better and how to deal with those complicated feelings is best learnt, I think, in a community. That shared sense of grief, the shared sense of suffering – not necessarily to bond you but just to not feel as though you are alone and not feel weighed down by your experience – is everything.

It's not about getting together and saying how terrible this thing is, let's all feel broken together. It's about how we can get together and empower each other and realise we are all survivors of something and we are all grieving some loss, but we are able to find some joy in life and able to find things we are capable of doing ... whether it's swimming in a pool instead of the ocean and making our way back slowly and encouraging each other, instead of completely giving up and saying, "This happened and now I'm broken."

The danger of being alone through trauma and suffering is that you can push people out of your life and give up on the things you love doing, whereas with a group – whether it's friends or a support group – the benefit is that you can hold each other's hand and find ways to move through and set a goal for each other and encourage each other through it. I think that's the real power of community.

So, thank you, Bite Club!'

ACKNOWLEDGEMENTS

Listening to each and every person who has contributed to this book has been a privilege and I would like to thank them for their courage in sharing their stories with me. So, thank you, Mick, Amy, Laurel-Rose, Eric, Damon, Micki, Lauren, Wyatt, Cameron, Julene, Chad, Mike and Anika.

Special thanks to Dave Pearson, without whose help this book would not have been possible. I am hugely grateful for your help in introducing me to members of your group. What you have done in setting up Bite Club is truly remarkable and I hope this book captures, in some small way, the essence of what you – and everyone else who has helped Bite Club over the years – set out to achieve.

Many thanks to Della Commons, who doesn't just offer assistance to Bite Club members but also helped this author understand the nature of trauma around animal attacks and the importance of language when talking to survivors.

Thank you to Andrea Vance for your research help in New Zealand and to Nicola Stow for your support.

Thanks also to Leila Green for your help with the transcriptions.

I am grateful to the Global Shark Attack File at sharkattackfile.net, a hugely helpful and invaluable resource for anyone researching shark incidents worldwide.

I would also like to thank everyone at Ad Lib Publishers, particularly John Blake, whose original idea it was and for giving me the opportunity to write this book, and to Duncan Proudfoot for your help and support throughout.

Thank you to Lucian Randall for, once again, doing such a brilliant editing job.

Lastly, I'd like to thank Lorna Hill, who knows all about the importance of sharing stories, for your incredible support and wise words, and to Claudia and Grace for your constant encouragement (i.e. 'Have you not finished that yet?').